THROUGH INDIA AND BURMAH WITH PEN AND BRUSH

This edition published by Lector House in 2025

ISBN: 978-93-6138-341-0

Lector House LLP
Registered Office: H. No. 96, Block C, Tomar Colony,
Burari, Delhi – 110084, India
info@lectorhouse.com
www.lectorhouse.com

THROUGH INDIA AND BURMAH WITH PEN AND BRUSH

ALFRED HUGH FISHER

2025

LECTOR HOUSE LLP

The Moat, Fort Dufferin, Mandalay.

Reproduced by permission of the Visual Instruction Committee of the Colonial Office.

THROUGH INDIA AND BURMAH WITH PEN AND BRUSH

BY

A. HUGH FISHER

"The beauty of the world is simple like a looking-glass."

TO MY FRIENDS IN ENGLAND

PREFACE

The following series of "Travel Pictures" is an endeavour to embody some of my impressions and experiences in India and Burmah.

For kind permission to reproduce among the illustrations eight of the painted sketches I made for them, my thanks are due to the Visual Instruction Committee of the Colonial Office who sent me out to the East as their artist.

The two chapters "The Moharam Festival" and "Rakhykash" are included in this book by the courtesy of the Editor of *The Fortnightly Review*, in which publication they have already appeared.

A. HUGH FISHER.

CONTENTS

Chapter		Page
	Preface	vii
I.	Rangoon	1
II.	His Highness the Sawbwa of Hsipaw	16
III.	Up the Irrawaddy to Bhamo	24
IV.	The Dead Heart of a Kingdom	35
V.	Mandalay	44
VI.	Southern India, the Land of Hindoo Temples	51
VII.	Calcutta	63
VIII.	My First Sight of the Himalayas	77
IX.	Benares	82
X.	Lucknow	91
XI.	Cawnpore	96
XII.	The House of Dream	99
XIII.	Delhi	106
XIV.	Dehra Dun and Landour	113
XV.	An Evening of Gold	116
XVI.	"Guard your Shoes"	120
XVII.	"A Gate of Empire"	126
XVIII.	The Capital of the Punjab	132
XIX.	At the Court of His Highness the Rajah of Nabha	138

XX. In Sight of Afghanistan 144

XXI. Rajputana 149

XXII. Sir Pratap Singh 158

XXIII. The Moharam Festival 162

XXIV. Rakhykash 170

XXV. Political 175

Index 179

LIST OF ILLUSTRATIONS

Page

I. The Moat, Fort Dufferin, Mandalay.. iv

II. "They could not lie down without overlapping." 2

III. Mongolian Type of Mohammedan. 4

IV. Mutama, a Hindoo Baby. 6

V. Hindoo Girl, showing elaborate Jewellery. 8

VI. Altar Table at a Buddhist Society's Celebration. 11

VII. Boy Showing Tatooing customary with all Burmese Males. 15

VIII. In the Shan States: Guard and Policeman. 20

IX. Katha. 25

X. At a Burmese Pwe.. 28

XI. Burmese Actors at Bhamo. 29

XII. A Village on the Irrawaddy. 32

XIII. Burmese Murderers.. 33

XIV. Pagan.. 38

XV. Burmese Dwarf (3 ft. 5 in. high) Suffering from Cataract.. 40

XVI. Burmese Priest and his Betel Box. 45

XVII. Burmese Mother and Child. 48

XVIII. The Sacred Tank and the Rock, Trichinopoly. 53

XIX. The Main Bazaar, Trichinopoly. 54

XX. Karapanasami, the Black God. 56

XXI. Hindoo Mother and Child. 59
XXII. Bengal Government Offices, Calcutta.. 64
XXIII. Bengalee Actress, Miss Tin Corry Dass the younger. 71
XXIV. "A Charming Old Gentleman from Delhi." 74
XXV. Avenue of Oreodoxa Palms, Botanical Gardens, Calcutta. 76
XXVI. The Kutab Minar and the Iron Pillar, Fatehpur Sikri. 110
XXVII. The Fort of Ali Masjid, in the Khyber Pass. 127
XXVIII. His Highness the Rajah of Nabha. 139
XXIX. The Palace of the Maharajah of Udaipur. [Drypoint Etching.] 152
XXX. The Moharam Festival at Agra. 168

THROUGH INDIA AND BURMAH

CHAPTER I

RANGOON

Down came the rain, sudden, heavy and terrible, seeming to quell even the sea's rage and whelming those defenceless hundreds of dark-skinned voyagers in new and more dreadful misery.

Terrors were upon them, and in abject wretchedness and hopeless struggle men, women and children spread every strip of their belongings over their bodies and even used for shelter the very mats upon which they had been lying.

What trouble a Hindoo will take to keep his body from the rain! Extremely cleanly and fond of unlimited ablutions he yet detests nothing so much as a wetting from the sky, and now, wholly at the mercy of the elements, do what they would, no human ingenuity availed to keep these wretched people dry.

It was the season of the rice harvest, when South India coolies swarm over to Burmah much as the peasantry of Mayo and Connemara used to crowd to England every summer.

If anybody is really anxious to remember that there are paddy fields in Burmah he should cross the Bay of Bengal in December.

Somebody said that our ship was an unlucky one—that it ran down the *Mecca* on her last trip and killed her third officer; but we got through safely enough, though that crossing was one of the most disagreeable as well as the most weird I ever made—disagreeable because of the bad weather, and weird because of the passengers.

The deck and the lower deck were tanks of live humanity, and when it began to get rough, as it did the morning after we left Madras, catching the end of a strayed cyclone, it was worse than a Chinese puzzle to cross from the saloon to the spar deck, and ten chances to one that even if you did manage to avoid stepping on a body you slipped and shot into seven sick Hindoo ladies and a family of children.

There were six first-class passengers, all Europeans, and 1700 deck passengers, all Asiatics, and the latter paid twelve rupees each for the four days' passage, bringing with them their own food.

The first evening all six of the Europeans appeared at dinner—a Trichinopoly collector, a Madras tanning manager and his wife (who told me that half your American boots and shoes are made from buffalo skins shipped from Madras to the United States), a young lieutenant going to take charge of a mountain battery of Punjabis at Maimyo in Upper Burmah, and a young Armenian, son of a merchant at Rangoon, who had been to Europe about his eyes.

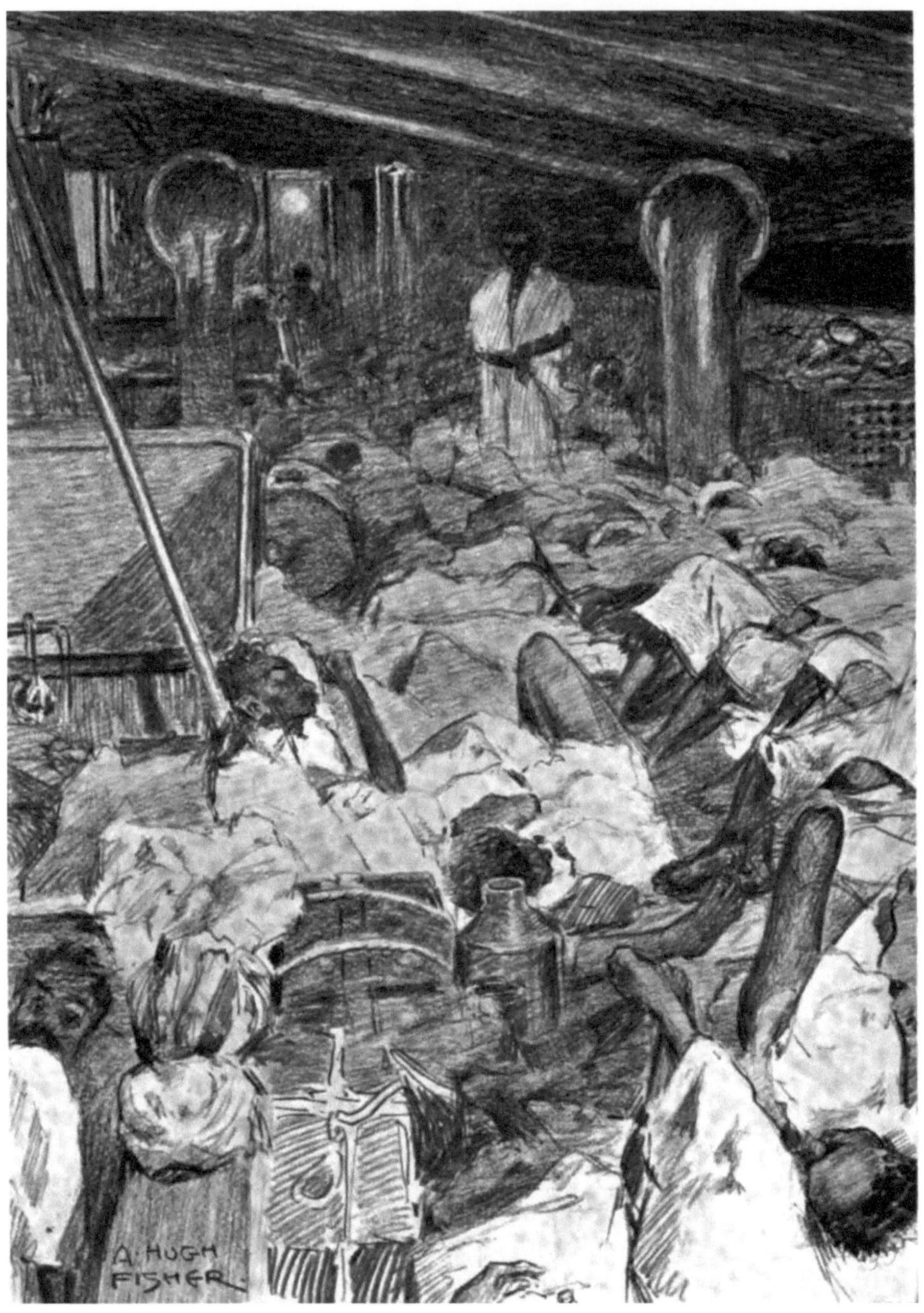

"They could not lie down without overlapping."

After coffee the man next to me suddenly leapt from his chair with a yell. He thought he had been bitten by a centipede. The centipede was there right enough, but as the pain passed off the next day we supposed the brute had only fastened his legs in and had not really bitten.

The nights were sultry and the ship rolled worse every watch. I think, however, that I never saw people try harder than those natives did to keep clean. They had all brought new palm-leaf mats to lie upon, but they could not lie down without overlapping. I asked the captain what he did about scrubbing decks, and he said it was always done at the end of the voyage! Next morning the downpour, already referred to, began and did the business with cruel effectiveness.

As we neared Burmah the sea grew calm again and the rain abated. The sun dried sick bodies and cheered despondent hearts. I spoke to a woman crouching by some sacks and tin cans, with an old yellow cloth round her head and shoulders, and another cloth swathing her loins. She had very dark brown eyes, and her fingernails were bright red and also the palms of her hands from the "maradelli" tied round the nails at night. She was the wife of a man the other side of fourteen people, some four yards away. I asked his name, not knowing that a Hindoo woman may not pronounce her husband's name. She called him "Veetkar," which means uncle or houseman: the man was of the Palla caste, which is just a little higher than the Pariah, and they had been married five years but had no children. This was the man's second marriage, his first wife having died of some liver complaint he said. Like most of the passengers they were going out for paddy-field work, but unlike so many others, they were "on their own" not being taken over by a labour contractor. The man said he should get work at Kisshoor village, about eight miles from Rangoon. Every year for seven years he had been over.

Altogether, this man had saved, according to his own statement, two hundred rupees in the seven years' work, and had invested this in bullocks and a little field near his village, which was named Verloocooli. He had left the son of his first wife to look after the house and the field.

Under a thin muslin an ayah was watching our talk. She said she was a Christian and came from Lazarus Church. Her husband ran away, leaving her with three children in Madras, so she works now as an ayah to an Eurasian lady, while her mother looks after the children in Madras.

About twenty people round one corner of the open hatch seemed to belong to one another. They came from the Soutakar district and were drinking rice-water—that is the water poured off when rice is boiled. A Mohammedan with two sons was going to sell things. The boys would watch the goods, he told me. He was returning to Upper Burmah, where he had lived twenty-four years, and he had only been over to Madras to visit his mother and father. He has "just a little shop" for the sale of such goods as dal, chili, salt, onions, coconut oil, sweet oil, tamarind, matches and candles.

Then there was the Mongolian type of Mohammedan. He was very fat and greasy, and had one of his dog teeth long like a tusk. He was a tin-worker and made large cans in his shop in Rangoon.

Mongolian Type of Mohammedan.

I went down between decks and never saw people packed so closely before except on Coronation Day. Even "marked" men discarded all clothing but a small loin cloth: most of them could not move hand or foot without their neighbours feeling the change of position; and as upon the deck above, they often lay partly over each other. Yet in spite of the general overcrowding, I noticed a woman of the Brahmin caste lying at her ease in a small open space marked out by boxes and tin trunks. There was a large lamp in a white reflector hanging by the companion-way, and some of those lying nearest to it held leaf fans over their faces to keep the light from their eyes.

The next day was brighter. There was a light wind and the whole sunlit crowd was a babel of excited talk. A little naked Hindoo baby, just able to walk, was playing mischievously with me. I had been nursing her for a while and now she was laughing, and with palms up-turned was moving her hands like a Nautch dancer as her eyes twinkled with merriment. She was called Mutama, and the poor mite's ears had had a big cut made in them and the lobes were already pulled out more than two inches by the bunches of metal rings fastened in for this purpose.

A purple shawl, tied up to dry, bellied out in the wind over the side of the ship in a patch of vivid colour. It had a border of gold thread and was of native make. Not that the gold thread itself is made in Madras. It is curious that English manufacturers have tried in vain to make these shawls so that their gold thread shall not tarnish, whereas the gold thread obtained from France does not do so.

On a box in the midst of hubbub, a Mohammedan was praying, bending his body up and down and looking toward the sun.

The following morning we reached very turbid water, thick and yellow, with blue reflections of the sky in the ripples. We could just see the coast of Burmah and about noon caught sight of the pilot brig, and entering the wide Rangoon river, passed a Chinese junk with all sails spread. Now the mats began to go overboard and gulls swooped round the ship. We had passed the obelisk at the mouth of the river when, above a green strip of coast on a little blue hill, the sun shone upon something golden.

"The Pagoda!" I cried, and a pagoda it was, but only one at Siriam where there is a garrison detachment. The Golden Pagoda—the Shwe Dagon—appeared at first grey and more to the north. The water was now as thick and muddy as the Thames at the Tower Bridge. It was full of undercurrents too, and there was a poor chance for anyone who fell in.

Over went the mats, scores and scores and scores of them!

There is a bar a little further on called the Hastings, and it was a question whether we'd get over it that afternoon. A line of yellow sand detached itself from the green, and then the water became like shot silk, showing a pale flood of cerulean slowly spreading over its turbid golden brown. On the low bank were green bushes and undergrowth, and beyond—flat levels of tawny-yellow and low treeclad rising ground that reminded me of the Thames above Godstow.

Beyond the green point of Siriam, just after the Pegu River branches off to the right, the Rangoon River sweeps round in a great curve, at the far end of which stretches the city. It was pale violet in the afternoon light, with smoke streaming from vessels in the harbour, and on the highest point the Shwe Dagon just showing on one edge that it was gold. Far to the right were some twenty tall chimney-stacks of the Burmah Oil Works, but their colour, instead of being sooty and unclean, was all blue and amethyst under a citron sky.

Mutama, a Hindoo Baby.

The Customs Officer came out in a long boat, pulled by four men in red turbans, and in his launch the medical officer of the port with a lady doctor. There is a constant but ineffectual struggle to keep plague out of Burmah, and every one of our 1700 deck passengers had to be thoroughly examined—stripped to the waist with arms up, while the doctor passed his hands down each side of the body.

The same night, on shore, I drove to the Shwe Dagon past the race-ground, where a military tattoo was going on by torchlight.

Two gigantic leogryphs of plaster-faced brick stand one on each side of the long series of steps which lead under carved teak roofs and between rows of pillars up to the open flagged space on which the Pagoda stands.

I left the "tikka gharry" on the roadway and went up the steps of the entrance alone. It was a weird experience, walking up those gloomy stairs at night. Alone? At first it seemed so—the stalls at the sides of each landing or wide level space between the flights of steps were deserted; but, as I walked on, a Pariah dog came snarling viciously towards me and another joined him, and then like jackals, their eyes glowing in the darkness, more and more of them came. I had no stick with me, and as I meant going on it was a relief to find that among the shadows of the pillars, to right and left, men were sleeping. One stirred himself to call off the dogs and I walked up another flight of steps, which gleamed a little beneath a hidden lamp.

Between great pillars, faced with plaster, red on the lower portion and white above, I walked on while more dogs came yelping and snarling angrily. I heard a low human wail which changed to a louder note and died away—someone praying perhaps. Then all was quite still except for the crickets. Now I was in a hall of larger columns and walked under a series of carved screens—arches of wood set between pairs of them. Half-way up these columns hung branches of strange temple offerings, things made in coloured papers with gold sticks hanging from them.

At last I came out upon the upper platform on which stands the Pagoda itself. Facing the top of the last flight of steps at the back of a large many-pillared porch, reeking with the odour of burnt wax, I saw a cavernous hollow, and set within it, behind lighted candles, dimly a golden Buddha in the dusk. Outside, a strip of matting was laid over the flagged pavement all round the platform, and in the stones little channels cut transversely for drainage in the time of the rains lay in wait to trip careless feet.

Some years ago when the great "Hti" was brought down from the summit of the Pagoda, after an earthquake, to be restored and further embellished, people of all classes brought offerings of money and jewellery through the turnstiles on to this platform. What a sight it must have been to see the lines of Burmese people crowding up through these two turnstiles, one for silver and one for gold—one woman giving two jewelled bracelets and the next a bangle; a receipt would be given to each donor and then bangle and bracelets thrown into the melting-pot after their jewels had been taken out for adding to the "Hti."

Hindoo Girl, showing elaborate Jewellery.

Glittering metal drops quivered from the edges of richly-decorated umbrellas; columns, covered as in a kind of mosaic with jewels and bright glass, shone and sparkled; colossal figures cast grim shadows, and over all the vast mass of the Shwe Dagon rose in its strange curved grandeur of worn and faded gold far up into the night sky with a compelling loveliness, and from the air above came floating down the sweet silvery tinkle of jewelled bells shaken by the breeze.

Night had driven unscourged the money-changers from the temple, and the magic light of the moon weaving silver threads through every garish tint of paint had changed crude colours to ideal harmonies. Not colour alone but form also was glorified. The grotesque had become dramatic, confusion had changed to dignity, all surrounding detraction was subdued and the great ascending curves of the Pagoda rose in simple, uncontested beauty. Nature adored, acknowledging conquest, and the sound of those far wind-caught bells was like that of the voices of angels and fairies singing about the cradle of a child.

I had seen no building of such emotional appeal nor any that seems so perfectly designed to wed the air and light that bathe it and caress it. But imagine the Shwe Dagon transplanted to the cold light of some gargantuan museum near the Cromwell Road; the nicest taste, the most steadfast determination, could not unlock its charm. Here, upon easy hinge, the door swings back at every raising of the eyes, and illumination is for all beholders.

The following afternoon I was again at the Shwe Dagon, and to watch its beauty under the glory of the setting sun was a further revelation. It seemed to show fresh and delicate charm at each part of the day, and after burning at sunset, like a man filled with impetuous passion, shone in the after-glow with the diviner loveliness of the woman who gives her heart.

The river front of Rangoon is a wide, busy and dusty thoroughfare, on to which wide streets open—Phayre Street, Bark Street and the rest, and great piles of office buildings face the water—buildings with Corinthian porticoes and columns with great drums like those of the Temple of Diana at Ephesus without their sculptures. A line of white stucco houses curves round the bend of the Sule Pagoda Street, wide and tree-bordered, like a road at Dorchester or a Paris boulevard, making a handsome vista with its Pagoda surmounting a flight of steps at the far end.

Building proceeds at such a rate that the big city seems to be growing while you look at it, but there are plenty of open spaces. Government House, in red brick and white stone, with an old bronze bell hung in front of the portico between two brass cannon, stands in a goodly park with fine trees and wide lawns and the Royal Lakes, across which there is a beautiful view of the Shwe Dagon, are surrounded by large grounds with trim, well-kept walks and drives. While I was painting by one of the lakes a water-snake every now and then lifted its head above the surface, sometimes a foot and a half out of the water like some long-necked bird.

I was driving back towards the hotel along the Calvert Road when I noticed a temporary wood-framed structure, covered with coloured papers and painted trellis-work. On inquiry I found it had been erected by a Buddhist Society of that quarter of the city, and that the same night upon a stage close to it in the open air a

"Pwe" would be given, to which I was bidden welcome about nine o'clock.

At my hotel two people had been poisoned by tinned food a few weeks earlier, but whatever the table lacked in quality it made up in pretentiousness. I quote that day's menu for comparison with the items of another repast the same evening:—

Canapes aux anchois.
Potage à la Livonienne,
Barfurt—sauce Ravigotte.
Inlets mignons à la Parisienne.
Civets de lièvre à la St Hubert.
Cannetons faits aux petits pois—salade.
Fanchonettes au confiture.
Glace—crême au chocolat.
Dessert.
Café.

It was after an early and somewhat abridged version of the above that I drove in the cheerless discomfort of a "tikka gharry" through Rangoon again in the moonlight. After twenty minutes I saw once more the paper temple. There were two long lines of lanterns high in the air in the shape of a horizontal V, and under them a great crowd of people. The trellised temple itself was also charmingly decorated with lanterns.

Inside I was effusively welcomed. A chair was placed for me on gay-coloured carpets at one side of a raised altar platform, at the back of which was a glass-fronted shrine containing an alabaster Buddha and strange lamps in front, with two large kneeling figures and a pair of bronze birds. The whole raised space before the shrine, some ten yards long by four yards deep, was covered with white cloths, on which was placed close together a multitude of dishes and plates of rich cakes, fruits and dainties. There were green coconuts, piles of oranges, melons with patterns cut upon them, leaving the outer green rind in curves and spirals, while the incised pattern was stained with red and green pigment, and a mighty pumpkin with a kind of "Christmas tree" planted in it, decked with packets of dried durian pickle pinched in at a little distance from each end so that they looked like Tom Smith's crackers. Now refreshment was brought to me in the shape of dried prawns and, upon a large plate in neat little separate heaps, the following delicacies:—

Green ginger, minced.
Sweet potatoes, shredded.
Fried coconut.
Sesamum seeds in oil.
Dried seed potatoes.
Tea leaves.
Fried ground nuts.

The president of this Buddhist Society, a stout Burman, with a rose-pink silk kerchief rolled loosely round his head, came and bowed to me, raising his hands and then sat upon another chair at my side, while a young Burman stood behind to interpret our mutual felicitations.

Altar Table at a Buddhist Society's Celebration.

Four silver dishes were now brought to me on a lacquered box, and these contained Burmah cheroots, betel leaves and areca nut, tobacco leaves and chunam (lime). Chilis were also brought, which made me long in vain for a cool drink.

Outside, beyond the walls of pale green trellis, glowed the lanterns, and faces peered at us between the strips of wood. Cloth of red and white stripes lined the roof, and countless flags, quite tiny ones, were fastened along the outer green railing.

In front of the Buddha had now been placed some beautiful gold chalices. The white alabaster figure of Gautama was half as high as a man, and a band covered with gems glittered across its breast.

The interpreter informed me that the whole gathering was a festival of the Buddha Kaitsa Wut Society, and he added:—"We are the people in Burmah always polite to everybody—do please whatever you like here." He spoke English with assurance, but to me his meaning was not always clear. Here are some of his actual words in answer to my request for further information:—"In time long past the monies of the members were according to the orders of the chief here, but they always used to pray every night with white dress, not any sort of fancy dress. Whenever we pray in order yearly we used to give charity to everybody."

About ten o'clock I moved outside, where another arm-chair had been placed for me, this time in the midst of a great crowd of people.

In front of me rose a staging of bamboo framework, with seven oil lamps hanging before it. Immediately below this staging a native orchestra played strange instruments by candle-light and upon the ground, which sloped conveniently, were ranged considerably over a thousand people. I counted thirty-six rows of over twenty-five each, and ever-increasing crowds thronged back and sides. Most of the seated audience were on mats or low bedsteads, and many were smoking the large light-coloured cheroots.

My interpreter had now gone to join some ladies, and I was left to make the best I could of this, my first, Burmese "Pwe."

Two characters were dancing on the stage when I took my seat. Perhaps they were a prince and princess—at any rate they were dressed in old Burmese court style, in very narrow skirts similar to the "hobble," and strange short jackets cut with curled bases like horned moons stretched and held in shape by bamboo frames. There was much swaying and posturing of the body, combined with quick, jerky movements, the arms were moved a great deal with bent elbows and the hands with fingers straight and the palms bent back sharply at the wrists. When these dancers left the stage two men entered in long white gowns, with broad white bands tied round the head in big bows. They turned their backs upon the audience at first, and then turning round squatted upon the floor. Two more similarly dressed came in in the same manner, and after they had squatted beside the others two quite astounding figures came on the scene with long bare swords.

The music all this while kept up an accompaniment of jingle and clapper and tum, tum, tum—jingle and clapper and tum, tum, tum, with a particularly squeaky wind instrument going ahead at the same time like a cork being drawn backward and forward over a pane of wet glass.

I discovered now that on turning their backs to the audience on first entering, the performers made obeisance to a draped bench at the back of the stage. Two more sword-bearing figures came in and two lance-bearers in very lovely bejewelled dresses of old gold. There was a long shrill speech now—then a loud bang, at which all the actors fell to the ground, and a figure entered bearing a short-pointed mace and sat at once on the draped bench.

It was the beginning of a long drama of old Burmese court-life which would go on all night long. The sword and lance-bearers went out, leaving the gentleman with the mace talking to the four white-gowned men (they were probably a king and his ministers), and he went on talking to them for a long half-hour, during which, at rare intervals, one of them sat up and made some remarks. At last a curtain came down, leaving two of the white-gowned ones outside it. These were joined by a manifestly "comic" character, a man with bare chest and a dark blue skirt, who kept the audience in continual merriment while he was on the scene.

Every now and then I turned my head to look up at the great V-shaped line of lanterns hanging high in the air overhead from tall bamboo poles, and the stars shining over all from the night sky. A number of the children were sleeping, though their elders made a good deal of noise, laughing heartily at the comic actor as the play went on and on and on. I should like to have stayed longer, but an appointment with some elephants at an early hour the next morning made me reluctantly leave the "Pwe" at midnight and hunt among the back rows of the audience for the driver of that "tikka gharry."

Everyone has heard of the Burmese elephants piling timber. The largest of the timber companies employing elephants is the Bombay Burmah Trading Corporation, Limited. The logs, floated down the river from forest-lands, eight hundred or a thousand miles upstream, are stranded at high rain-tides at Poozoondoung, a tract of lowland to which I drove in the early morning.

I reached there just after sunrise, before the dew of the night was yet evaporated, and the logs, on which one had to walk to avoid the mud, were very slippery and more difficult to negotiate with boots than without.

The work of the elephants is to push, drag or pile the teak logs, and on the morning of my visit there were three of the great quadrupeds at work:—Hpo Chem, aged fifty, a fine tusker who had been twenty years at the work, and two female elephants, Mee Gyan, seventy years of age, and Mee Poo, thirty. The male elephant has, of course, tremendous strength in his tusks and uses them for carrying, holding the log firmly with his trunk as he gravely walks up the pile of logs to place his burden on the top. Female elephants can only pile by a combined lift and drag, and do not raise the log entirely from the ground. Pushing with the head is called "ounging."

Most of the elephants in use in Burmah have been got by Kheddah operations, the Kheddah being a big stockade built under Government direction in a similar way to the Kraals of Ceylon. At the last Kheddah many elephants died suddenly of anthrax (some two hundred in about three days), and a number of the trained animals were lost as well as those newly captured.

The hours of elephant labour at Poozoondoung are strictly limited, being from six to nine in the morning and from three to six in the afternoon.

At Poozoondoung, not far from the timber-yards, the chief rice-mills are situated. They were idle now, but when I saw them again after the harvest their big chimneys were belching forth black smoke from the burning husk. The husk obtained from the milled grain is not only sufficient for all fuel requirements, but much has to be shot into the creek for waste.

The engine staffs are, as upon most of the flotilla steamers, Chittagonians, Burmese being employed chiefly as clerks.

Native boats called "Loungoes" brought such of the "paddy" from the country as did not come by rail.

"Hulling" the rice is the operation of breaking off the husk. There were rows of pairs of round flat stones, the under ones stationary, the upper ones revolving, not grinding but merely breaking off the husk. Both grain and husk fell from these stones together to the floor below, and were carried by bucket-elevators to a fanning-room, where the husk was blown off. After leaving the fans the grain had its remaining inner skin taken off in "cones"—cement-faced stones made to press the grain against an outer jacket of perforated wire. At the base of the cone a cloth hung round an opening in the floor, through which the rice dropped, while the white skin fell upon the floor outside to be called "bran," and shipped to Europe for use in the manufacture of cattle cakes.

In the process of "whitening" much of the grain is broken and sorted by graduated sieves, into four or five degrees of size. Finally the rice bags are shipped on to a cargo boat in the creek, for despatch by steamer to India or Europe.

When the rice-mills are in full work the smoke of their chimneys hangs above Rangoon, but overhead every evening the flying foxes pass as usual, and the beautiful Pagoda is far enough away to remain untarnished upon its little hill.

Boy Showing Tatooing customary with all Burmese Males.

CHAPTER II

HIS HIGHNESS THE SAWBWA OF HSIPAW

I left the Phayre Street station at Rangoon on a bright morning, which made me think of England and the perfect beginning of a warm summer day at home. The paddy-fields were like an ocean on each side of the railway line, and as yellow as ripe corn: some distant hills, the Eastern Yomans which divide Burmah from Siam, were faintly visible and became clearer after I had passed Pegu. There are no elephants in those hills, though they are yet in their thousands in the Western Yomans (one man I met had counted sixty in a single herd).

Railway journeys with unshuttered windows are like miscellaneous collections of snapshot photographs—now men in the paddy-fields wearing the huge low conical bamboo hats of the Shan States; then big anthills and snipe; a banyan tree—the gutta-percha banyan tree, Burmese Nynung, out of which the natives make their birdlime; grey squares of flat hard mud, the Burmese threshing floor; a crowd of brown hawks about a group of natives drying fish; a small eagle with four-foot spread of wings, sometimes called a peacock hawk, having blue eyes instead of the usual eagle yellow; an Eng tree, a taxed tree largely used for building purposes (a tree that comes up and is of no use is called here a Powk-pin); in a stream a man swinging a fishing-net hung on crossed arched hoops at the end of a pole—a net of just the same pattern I have seen on Arno shallows at Florence; a dull leaden-coloured layer of rotting fish on bamboo screens raised above the ground on poles—when rotted enough and full enough of insects, it will be pounded up to make a national dish called "Ngape."

In the distance on the other side of the line the Western Yomans now appeared: they are lower than the Eastern Yomans, and do not rise much above four thousand feet. The window pictures went on changing: little streams full of tree-climbing perch; small fisheries—everyone of them taxed to swell the revenue; bright coloured bee-eaters, the only insectivorous birds that build in the earth and not in trees; corrugated iron—oh! very much corrugated iron—even in the smallest villages, it is used for the hut roofs wherever the railway goes.

I was now passing through the home of the hamadryad, that serpent of temerity and unprovoked assaults, but soon came nearer to the foothills and the edge of the jungle. It was about five o'clock, the time when at this season of golden paddy-fields the jungle fowl come out to steal the rice—peacocks with tails longer than they grow in captivity, and even more numerous than those unnumbered I have seen in the grounds of Warwick Castle. About this time of year, when he has been feeding on rice for a few weeks, your peacock is considered very good eating and is not difficult to get on a moonlight night. He gives three calls before he settles to sleep, just to tell anyone who may be interested which tree he is in.

Pale and feathery the tall tufts of elephant grass quivered gently, and through them I could see a village stockaded against dacoits. A fellow-traveller told me that any man who owns ten houses has to fence the village, and remarked that two hundred dacoits were killed hereabouts during the previous year. My companion was a well marked man. He had a white scar on his chin where he had been clawed by a leopard, and a mark on one arm where he had been shot by boxers in China.

We were passing Kanutkwin, which means "the crooked place," and was the scene of great man-eating operations a few years back, when one tiger killed twenty-five people before he was accidentally shot! A man was out in the jungle after birds with a shotgun, and seeing something move near him, fired precipitately and with great luck ended the career of that four-footed dacoit.

The night was cold and the early morning colder still. I noticed that the third-class carriages were crowded with passengers—long compartments with a third row of people on a long bench down the middle. Rolled up in shawls or thick wadded and quilted coats, the natives kept their heads in woollen wrappers, hoods or "Balaclava helmets," while up on the racks and heaped at the open ends of the carriages were the huge bamboo hats, looking like savage shields or targes, which would be needed in the heat of the day. Some men also carried long swords, for here in the Shan States a man may go armed without question.

At Sedaw, a little after seven o'clock, I reached the beginning of the hills, and about three of that afternoon, with a live hen and some provisions obtained while the train waited at Maimyo (a station where there is a native Indian mountain battery), I got out at Gokteik—Gokteik of the famous bridge—Gokteik of the gorge and the cave and the highest graded railway in the world. But if you asked a Shan to take you to Gokteik, it is not here he would take you, but to a Shan village many miles away, surrounded as all Shan villages are by thick clumps of bamboos.

Along the steepest part of the railway track are laid a second pair of rails, which lie covered with sand between wooden side-slips, so that in case of brakes failing a runaway train could be switched on to these as retarders. At Gokteik Bridge I think the only purpose for a railway station is for the convenience of the engineer, who has occasionally to come up and examine the structure. I found a dak bungalow near the station, with clean rooms but without any cook, so that Tambusami, my servant, had an opportunity of showing his skill with the pots and pans placed there for the stranger's use.

I left him to attend to the kitchen and crossed the long trestle bridge of steel girders—it is 820 feet above the torrent at the bottom of the gorge; then, following the railway line through a couple of short tunnels, I climbed out on to a spur of the mountain from which I could look back at the gorge. The torrent below comes out through a vast stalactite cave or tunnel, the lower opening of which is like part of some great cathedral dome. The rock above crosses like a natural arch 500 feet high, and it is upon that arch that the stupendous, though spidery-looking structure of the viaduct has been raised by an American firm. Their tender was very much less than that of any English house, and although it is possible that American engineers have had more experience in this kind of work, it is suggested that the lowness of the tender was partly to ensure a big advertisement. Walking alone high in air across the 750 yards of that narrow bridge, which has no kind of railing, was certainly one of the "sensations" of my journey, and in a thick mist the experience must be weird in the extreme.

The present engineer of the line was, at the time of my visit, also staying at Gokteik (investigating a suspected change of curve through heat expansion), and he took me in the early hours of the morning through some of the dense jungle in the gorge above the feet of the bridge. The engineer carried a Winchester repeater, and I was armed with a good double-barrelled rifle, but our hopes of seeing certain stripes reported to be near were vain. We crept for a long time stealthily through dense jungle-growth, with a variety of prickles and spikes, and came upon fresh hoof-marks of wild boar, small deer, saumbur and buffalo but no sign of a tiger, and I could not remain for a second attempt.

My next stopping-place was Hsipaw, a town of some size, in which is the palace of Sawche, the Sawbwa of Hsipaw. I was sorry to find that this gentleman's English adviser, to whom the authorities had promised to write about my coming, was away on leave. There was no other English resident at Hsipaw except the keeper of the refreshment-room at the railway station, which included the usual accommodation of a dak bungalow. This was a man with a pronounced Cockney accent and a humorous twinkle in his eye, and in view of the approaching Christmas season he had laid in a large number of cured hams, which hung all round the room. At Hsipaw that evening there sat at table with me two other passengers who were changing trains; one, the medical officer for the Shan States, whom I had joined on leaving Gokteik, and the other, a mining engineer who had had black-water fever at Buluwayo and had come to Burmah for a change of air.

The doctor was on the look-out for plague cases, and where he had native assistants they waited at the railway stations to report to him as he passed through. Thus at Kyankine I had heard a native assistant tell the doctor that a Shan woman, who was selling bringalls in the market, had declared she had seen four or five people dying at an outlying village.

"Can you rely on her statement?" said the doctor.

"I can't exactly say."

"You should have sent for the poogi" (the "poogi" or "pudgy" is the village headman who collects the taxes and takes them to the "Nabang," the head of a circle of villages and responsible to the Government). "You should have sent for the poogi," said the doctor.

"I did, sir," the assistant answered, "but he said he had not heard anything about it."

"What about the Jaremai Nabang—isn't he here?"

"He is away from here, sir; he goes sometimes to Lashio—the woman said it was seven or eight days ago, but the poogi did not know anything about it."

"Well, keep your ears open and find out all you can. I'll run that poogi in—wire for Chatterjee for any bad case."

I was amused at the Cockney talk of the keeper of the refreshment-room as he brought in the dishes, when the mining engineer said to him as he came up to the table:—"I don't want to be offensive, but a man at Tongu told me you have committed bigamy."

"Let 'em prove it," said the Cockney, "let 'em prove it—that's what *I* say. I'm not a going to give myself away to you gentlemen nor to my own frens—what I say is, they've got to prove it. I'm not a-saying, mind yer, that there isn't nothin' I've been foolish about or no mistake as I 'aven't made in the past. They tried 'ard to arrest me yesterday—yes, they did, doctor, but they couldn't do it, not they."

"But the man at Tongu showed me a marriage certificate," said the mining engineer. Here the doctor applied the closure and we got on with our dinner.

When it was over I took a Shan boy as a guide to find the Sawbwa's house. Tambusami, my own Hindoo servant, was, of course, useless here as regards conversation. The Shan boy knew some English, being able to say "yes," "no," and "railway station." It was just after eight o'clock when we started, and after walking one and a half or two miles along a white road and turning twice, we crossed two small bridges over a stream or moat, and I saw in front of us some large buildings. When I asked at a guess if this were the house of the Sawbwa, the boy assented "Sawbwa."

Under a covered arcade two men were crouching in the cold over a fire of sticks, watching a giant kettle, which I think was copper and not brass. The arcade led into the hall of a large house whitewashed and with a coloured pattern running round the wall and across several doors. At one side was a staircase leading to the floor above, and at the bottom of the stairs eight or ten pairs of plush slippers were scattered about untidily near a large red-lacquered box and a cat, which was eating from a round dish.

Some kind of guard or policeman in a red turban and bearing a long sword outside his ample cloak came to have a look at me, and was soon joined by another in similar uniform. I talked to them and the men by the kettle and thought they understood that I wanted them to take my card to the Sawbwa, and that I wanted to see him. They all put their heads on one side with cheek on hand and shut their eyes, by which I supposed they meant he had gone to bed. It was not yet nine o'clock, however, and as I had been told that Sawche had been educated in England, I doubted such early hours and I persisted in pretending that I did not understand.

I walked up and down the covered way, and presently a little lady, with her face painted white, crept gingerly down the stairs and into the hall, furtively peeping at me. As soon as she knew that I could see her she scurried back like a frightened rabbit, and there was another long silence. Two big hounds, as tall as great Danes but with sharper noses, came strolling up and allowed me to pat them. It was bitterly cold, but at last I persuaded one of the men with swords to go into the house and presently he returned with the following message:—

"His Highness the Sawbwa has gone to sleep. If there is anything to be said please leave a chit to the policeman or come to-morrow again at about noon. Nothing is able to wake His Highness at present. This note is sent to explain what the policeman at the gate wanted to say."

In the Shan States: Guard and Policeman.

The next morning I was calling again at the house of the moat, when I beheld the Sawbwa approaching through the grounds carrying a black umbrella and followed by a dozen men, walking slowly behind him. He was rather thin and small-limbed, had dark eyes, not Mongolian in type, and a small moustache over a delicate mouth with a small narrow chin. On his head was a yellow turban, which added a little to his short stature, and he wore a dress or gown over-all of black silk with woven black pattern, fine black silk rolled round his neck for about five inches up to the chin. Thin white trouser-ends showed beneath the gown over dark socks and patent leather dancing-pumps with black ribbons. Of jewellery he wore little, his chief ornament being a fine ruby in a gold finger-ring.

The Sawbwa shook hands delicately and said, "How do you do?" and chatted in good English for a few minutes. He explained that he was extremely busy with an important case at the Court and asked me to join him there. He is a busy man, whose position is by no means a sinecure involving the direction of the three Shan States of Mihung, Hsunhai and Mintoung, and all the magisterial work of the district.

The Court-House was a two-storeyed wooden building, with a veranda and a balcony opposite the gate of the palace compound on the other side of a white dusty road. In the Court-Room the Sawbwa sat on a rotary chair upon a raised platform, and an arm-chair was placed for me beside him. Sawche had now discarded the yellow turban and wore a piece of rose-coloured silk round his head in the ordinary Burmese fashion. Behind us hung a portrait in black and white of Queen Victoria, and in front, on the top of a wooden railing, was a red narrow box, two feet long, tied in the centre with crossed tapes and containing some sacred writings for oath administration. On the platform beside the Sawbwa's chair, upon a low, round stool of red lacquer ornamented with a gold pattern, were china cups and teapots.

A man stood in one of two small docks or railed enclosures, and a number of people with documents in their hands squatted upon the floor outside.

I could not understand any of the speaking, and after he had been talking quite a long time to the man in the railed enclosure, the Sawbwa turned to me and proposed in his soft voice that he should send someone to show me round his compound. The moated house I had called at previously was far from here within the town.

Conducted by one man who spoke a few words of English and followed by another who did not, I crossed the road and entered the compound through red gates. It was surrounded by tall wooden palings, ten or eleven feet high, which were roughly whitewashed, and in the centre of the road-front, with small doors in the hoarding at each side, were these large wooden gates with a little rude carving about the top of them. Within, upon a rough cylinder of red brick in the middle of a level space of poor coarse grass, flying a little white fork-shaped flag, a tall flagstaff was set in front of the palace, which is built of wood upon a raised platform of cement and stucco-covered bricks, five or six feet from the ground. It is partly old and in the centre is surmounted by a series of gables, one above another, with well-carved barge boards. In the middle of the front, as well as at the two ends of the building, a flight of steps with low side walls leads to the top of the cement platform, and the centre flight is closed below by a small green railing with a wicket gate. Within, through the outer square-cut wooden pillars, you can see the red round stucco columns of the hall of audience. Outside, from the centre of the roof, a tall, very narrow spire shoots up above and behind the gables, and the top of this is richly ornamented and gilded like the "hti" of a pagoda.

The residence of the chief queen, the Maha Devi, a Shan woman, adjoins the palace immediately behind. A girl stood on the veranda bending forward and combing out her long black hair, which fell to the ground, and behind her between two of the posts of the veranda hung a large piece of tapestry with figures worked upon it in gold thread. Further back among trees are the houses of the second, third and fourth queens, and two for the twenty-six wives of minor importance. Here they live from one year's end to another, very rarely leaving the compound, and dwelling, though without its austerity, in the same seclusion as that of a nunnery.

Whatever influence it has had upon his ideals, an Oxford education has not led the Sawbwa to adopt Western practice in his matrimonial relations; yet it is doubtful if the Cockney keeper of the railway refreshment-room would have so far discounted his sense of superiority to an Asiatic as to have envied him even such privileges as these.

Soon after I returned to the Court-House the Sawbwa adjourned the sitting, and we were talking together upon the balcony when he went up to the railing and pointing to a figure upon the ground below said to me, "This is one of my gardeners."

I had noticed the man earlier; he was a thin tall Hindoo who had walked very slowly to the Court-House, and as if with much difficulty. He was dressed in a white robe and had squatted upon the ground, wrapping the drapery round him and over the top of his head. A fat man with a large buff turban had strolled after him and was walking up and down. It appeared that the latter was a doctor. The Hindoo gardener was suffering badly from dysentery, but was unwilling to go away to the hospital because he had a Shan wife and feared she would run away while he was shut up. "If he goes," said the Sawbwa, "I will keep his place for him and let him come back to work when he is cured." The man, however, was still unwilling and resisted all persuasion. "Then let him die," said the Sawbwa, and went on talking to me about England.

Although Sawche has so many wives he has only one son, a boy of twelve or thirteen, named Maung Nyo. I saw him coming through the central avenue of the bazaar, dressed in rich silks and with his face whitened like a woman's with ground sandalwood. He was being wheeled slowly along upon a smart plated bicycle by two men, while another pair of attendants carried a long-handled gold umbrella on each side of him. In a few days Maung Nyo was to enter upon his period of Hpoongi or priest-training, in accordance with orthodox Burmese custom.

The bazaar at Hsipaw was chiefly interesting on account of the Kachins who had come in from a distance. They carried gaily ornamented haversacks, and their women-folk, strong-looking and heavy-faced, wore about the waist and ankles large coils of bamboo as thin as fine string and black in colour.

The usual rows of bazaar shops were ranged under long arcades roofed with corrugated iron, and out in the roadway double and treble lines of sellers from outlying places had spread their market produce on plantain leaves. Of dried fish there was certainly an extraordinary variety—thirty kinds at the very least, but there was no profusion of strange fruits and no showy display of silks or finery, and the scene was animated without being gay.

The air was free and wholesome at Hsipaw, and the Shans had that healthy look which seems to be the common heritage of all people of the hills.

CHAPTER III

UP THE IRRAWADDY TO BHAMO

A group of white pagodas glowing in the sunlight: a flat shore rising to little hills further up the river—little hills with more pagodas on top of them, and beyond in the distance pale ghostly mountains almost lost in a faint haze. Perhaps there is no scene more typical of Burmah than this I looked upon from the deck of a steamer at Ferryshaw Siding, that meandered slowly across the wide water, just stirred by the least possible ripple.

A train waited on the far side above a stretch of loose grey sand. I was on my way to Katha to join there one of the Irrawaddy Flotilla Company's boats on its way up to Bhamo, and my dinner was eaten that Christmas evening in a small railway refreshment-room decorated with some prints after Landseer, and one of a sentimental girl's head called "The Soul's Awakening." Another man shared the same table in unbroken silence until, with some very bad coffee, the Hindoo "butler" brought the bills. "Excuse me," I said to the stranger, "but you are an Englishman, and this is our Christmas dinner—will you drink a glass of wine with me?"

So we drank toasts in port that was thick enough to have pleased Alfred Tennyson, and slept none the worse for it on the jolting lumbering train.

There was a dense mist at Katha when I left the railway for the river-boat, and progress was slow until the air cleared and long flat sandbanks became visible and a green tree-clad plain with blue mountains to the north-west. Teak rafts drifted past us downstream on their long journey to Poozoondoung Creek, and the old tusker Mpo Chem and his "lady helps." Many rafts of bamboos passed us also, supporting heavy teak logs below them, for teak is not easily rafted till it is three years dead, and recently-felled logs float reluctantly as if possessing still enough of life to tell their sorrow at leaving the upland forests.

It is not many decades since rafts freighted with human bodies, more nearly still in touch with life than the new teak logs, floated down this river. Our captain, whose name was Teeldrup, a Dane with Icelandic blood, ran boats for the Irrawaddy traffic some years before the final annexation, and described to me a passage on this very piece of the river when no less than thirty unfortunate Kachins came floating down the stream crucified upon bamboo frames. "A lot has been talked of the cruelties," said Captain Teeldrup, "but I think the poor devils were generally soon put out of their misery."

Katha.

Reproduced by permission of the Visual Instruction Committee of the Colonial Office.

Mora and Segaw we passed—villages on the banks—taking on a few native passengers from small boats that came out to us, and at eight o'clock in the evening we anchored in mid-stream. The deck was quite covered in with canvas, and canvas also covered all the cabin windows. Notwithstanding these precautions, however, the mist in the morning was so thick that when I came to dress all my clothes were thoroughly damp. At half-past seven the fog began to lessen somewhat, but there was no question of starting, although we were already many hours behind time. Lumps of brown spongy froth kept appearing to float past and out of sight again in the little space of thick muddy water visible round the boat.

Hours later we got away, and at length sighted Bhamo late in the afternoon. I could just make out the red building of Fort C and a white spot, which I was told was the "bell" pagoda. Of the two existing forts, A is for the military police and C for the regulars, B, the intermediate fort, having been done away with a few years ago.

The broad river with its innumerable eddies comes swirling down between its level sandbanks, and as the scenery was at Katha so it was at Bhamo—just a level plain of tall grasses and trees and beyond these, distant mountains now the colour of a ripe plum's bloom. Then suddenly slate-grey landing-flats appeared against the sand, and in a few minutes I was again on shore.

At Bhamo the agent of the Flotilla Company is a white-haired Frenchman, who once held an influential position in Burmah as minister to King Thebaw. He had gone to the East as a Bourbon exile and after years of unsuccessful schemes and vain intrigue, discredited and ruined by the failure of his own plans, Monsieur D'Avera, in a steamship office, now lavishes the distinguished courtesy of an old French family upon American tourists and such wayfarers as myself, and is said to have written an astounding book of memoirs for posthumous publication.

It is in trade that Bhamo's claim to attention lies, and in the street of Chinese offices and stores for the exchange of Manchester for Chinese goods. A Burman, to whom I had been talking on the boat, was related by marriage to the family of a Chinese merchant, and in the evening he took me to call at a house with the top of the gateway curved up at the ends in a way, he said, only affected by Chinamen of official position. The merchant was apparently some kind of consul, and over and above the details of his own business, watched on behalf of the Chinese Government the interest of his Bhamo compatriots.

The Chinese merchant himself was away, but his sons showed me over the warehouse and gave me tea in a living-room, where there was an aquarium of goldfish, and which was decorated with a few pieces of lacquer and long strings of Chinese New Year cards nearly a twelve-month old, which hung across the room near the ceiling.

Sitting there drinking tea I could see through the series of now dusky storerooms to the street entrance, and from little lattices at the sides of these rooms noted the glint of lamplight and saw that the clerks were busy over their books.

That night I went to another "Pwe," given this time under cover. A large bamboo structure upon the sandy shore of the river, which had been erected by Government for a recent durbar, had been rented by the "Pwe" impresario for use as a theatre, and as the affair was, in this case, entirely a business venture (a kind of Burmese touring company), a charge was made for admission, varying from four annas to one rupee.

The orchestra was very similar to the one I had seen at Rangoon, but being nearer to it I could see the performers better. It consisted first of a big drum slung in the air from a long horizontal dragon, whose fantastic head rose above the front of the stage; next, a circular wooden well frame or box, within which were placed a series of between twenty and thirty small drums, each about four to six inches across; then a lower circular enclosure with metal balls and cups in place of the drums. These three items were put in a line immediately in front of the stage, and inside the circle of small drums, with candles round him on the edge of the surrounding woodwork, sat the *chef d'orchestre,* who tuned up his drums, which he struck with his bare fingers, through all the intervals between the passages of music.

On one side of the chef sat a man at the big dragon drum and on the other one playing on the metal cups, while behind squatted several players of wind instruments and three or four men with split bamboo rods, four or five feet long, which made a loud clapping noise when suddenly closed. The playing of the tiny drums was extremely skilful, but the wind instruments were wheezy and screechy, though I thought the general effect of the whole orchestra was rather pleasing.

My Burmese acquaintance had come with me to the "Pwe"; and his knowledge of English, which he spoke with a peculiarly soft and gentle intonation, enabled me to understand the thread of the narrative. The entertainment was sophisticated enough to include some simple drop-scenes which, however, had no appropriateness nor any connection with the story, and a curtain which rarely descended as the divisions of the drama were of great length.

There was again a terpsichorean heroine, the daughter of a powerful nobleman, and after she had danced for half an hour there followed a very long scene between a king and his ministers. In dancing the hands and arms were moved more than the feet, and there was much jerky and angular movement of the body. The costumes were again of old Burmese court style, and a curious detail was that the hats worn by the four ministers were tall domes, which curved over at the top in the same manner as the head-gear of Venetian doges. The king, who wore on his head a veritable pagoda, was haranguing his ministers about revenue and the unsettled state of his frontiers, but my Burmese friend explained that he only instructed his ministers by suggestion and not with direct orders. The story was wrapped round the raids of a great dacoit who had been harassing border country and had carried away and married the ever-dancing heroine. There was a very amusing scene between the lady's father and her two servants, comic parts which were acted with such droll and humorous gusto that it was a delight to watch them, even without a key to their words. Indeed this scene had a motive worthy of Molière, and recalled to me at the same time the incident in Yeats' play—*Where there is nothing there is God,*—in which an English owner of land is tried for the uselessness of his life by Irish tinkers in a barn.

At a Burmese Pwe.

The foolish master agrees that one of the servants, who has explained that he is himself very wise and the master very foolish about all things, shall take the place of judge and bids him sit in the middle of the stage to conduct a mock trial in which he, the master, is the accused. The scheme breaks down, of course, and when the master finally goes for his servant and trounces him well, there is wild rough and tumble on the stage and riotous laughter from the audience.

No people in the world can give themselves more gladly and light-heartedly to enjoyment than the Burmese, and there was not a single member of the audience—man, woman or child—who looked as if there were such a thing as care.

Burmese Actors at Bhamo.

Another droll scene was in the house of a timorous villager. This was supposed to be at night and quite in the dark, though the lamps hanging along the top of the stage (there were no footlights) were not lowered at all, so that the acting of the dark was not obscured by any attempt at realistic effect. The dacoit and his followers were groping and feeling about the stage to find the villager, who quaked and shook as if paralysed with terror; then one of the searchers would come upon him and touching some part of his motionless body would describe it to the dacoit as something other than the part of a man, and go on groping round the room till he once more encountered the quaking villager.

Men, women and children shouted, shook and rolled in a very ecstasy of delight at this piece of pantomime. Really it should not be difficult to govern such people as these! Unfortunately, however, his natural love of pleasure is combined in this short dumpy man, Jack Burman, with an indolence fatal to business success. His mortgaged land falls into the hands of the chetty, and in commercial matters he is being quietly walked over.

Burmah, so rich in natural resources, in spite of the statements of school geographies, must look for the future to be exploited not for peaceful improvement of its own comparatively small native population, but for the speculators of Capel Court and Wall Street, and the hordes of Hindoos and Chinamen flocking through its doors. There is in all countries a clash of interests between practical success (which implies the largest possible aggregation of healthy, well-nourished bodies having freedom of action) and ideal success (of which I might dream indefinitely without continuing this book), and it is that eternal combat that makes at once the bitter and sweet of government.

I left the "Pwe" at last to go on unravelling its long story till dawn, and myself got some hours of sleep in readiness for a morning in the Chinese quarter of Bhamo.

This is a wide street with a gulley or gutter about 4 feet wide along the front of the shops, with four or five wooden planks laid across it close together as an approach to each. There were coolies under bamboo yokes or shoulder-poles bearing crates and baskets, Shan men on ponies bargaining green fodder, and Chinese women, with the traditionally contracted feet, making quilted woollen coats, while fat babies played securely in movable wooden pens. An Indian policeman, khaki-clad, with his legs in puttees, was trying to make himself understood by a party of Kachins—two men and an old and young woman. Three out of these four possessed large *goitres*, hanging wallets of flesh, which made them look dewlapped like bulls. La Naung was the name of the older man, and both the women were named Makaw. The girl was bare-headed and had her short hair cut in a thick fringe over the forehead, and had round her neck three large stiff rings. They carried the same gay-coloured haversacks I had seen at Hsipaw, and wore upon waists, arms and legs similar coils of thin black bamboo.

In the chief Chinese temple or joss-house two standing figures, about four times life-size—Shotsa and Quan Pin—were placed on either side of a central grille high up in the wall, through the meshes of which could be seen the long-bearded face of Quansa. The latter's expression might be described as benevolent; but that of the giant Shotsa, who held a mighty blade in the air with his left hand, was horrible enough to draw from an American lady, who came in while I was there, the remark:—"I guess if I stayed here that face'd just skeer me into religion." (Her companion replied:—"That's the only way you *would* get it!")

In a hall of this polytheistic temple beyond the one of Quansa, was a Buddha with small figures all round the walls, and in front of these as boxes for offerings an incongruous series of Huntley & Palmer's biscuit-tins, still decorated with their original paper coverings.

The Burmese houses at Bhamo are very different from the Chinese shops, being built on tall wooden piles with long flights of wooden steps up to them, and in sunset light a group of such houses is a pretty sight, especially if some silk cloths are spread to dry and some girls are looking out over the veranda.

Of course Bhamo has its pagoda too, and of more recent years its race-course and polo-ground, but I had only a peep at these before rejoining the river steamer.

On the return journey I had good views of the defile below Sinkan village, where the hills rise steeply from the edge of the water, and in some places sheer walls of bare rock rise precipitously several hundred feet—gaunt perpendicular cliffs more like some piece of scenery near Balholm or Dalen in Norway than any I had yet seen in the East, and doubly welcome after the comparative monotony of sandbanks. Most of the hillside was clothed with dense jungle, which made more effective contrast with the bare treeless places.

On the right bank, a little distance from the big rock of the defile, there is a village and this is where Lala was lost. Lala was a little black bear an engineer told me about. "It was one of those honeybears," he said—"had a white V-shaped mark on the chest." They kept chickens on board in a coop and one night Lala pulled a chicken out of this coop, practically skinning it between the bars; the Sakunny, the wheelman, declared that Lala took a piece of his bread and deliberately placed it in the chicken's trough outside the bars and waited till the bird put its head out. He was not the sort of man to make up such a story, but the engineer could hardly believe him and asked to be called the next time the Sakunny could see the bear was after the coop. Whether the engineer was in bed or not, Lala used to sleep not far from him on a mat by the engine-room door. One night the wheel-man called him up, and he actually saw the bear take along a piece of his bread and drop it into the trough. He was ready to cuff Lala if he touched a fowl, but the bear was too quick for him, and the very moment a hen put her head through the bars whipped it out clean through. The engineer never gave Lala meat, but somebody got feeding him on "bully beef," and that seemed to make him restive. He never really bit anybody, but the engineer felt it was safest to get rid of Lala. He got off one day at the village near the defile and took the bear a mile and a half away into the jungle and "lost" him.

Soon after the villagers petitioned the engineer to take the bear on board again. It seemed that Lala was haunting the village and stole chickens persistently. So there was nothing for it but to take him on to the steamer again. Then he gave him to the Rangoon Zoo.

It was months after that the engineer went to see Lala. He took with him a retriever, which had been a great chum and playfellow of the bear. When he asked about it at the gardens they said it had got very wild and would not take its food. I'll give the rest of the story in the engineer's own words.

A Village on the Irrawaddy.

"They were just going to give it rations, so I said, Give me the food and I'll go into the cage myself. I took the retriever in with me, and I'll never forget the way that bear looked at me as long as I live. The poor thing just stood up and put its forepaws on my chest and looked into my eyes as much as to say:—'Is this what you've done to me?' No, I'll never keep a wild animal again."

Below the defile the stream widened again and the banks were low sand-flats as before. The sun blazed on the water, but little pieces of tin tied to floating bamboo marks gleamed brighter than the water surface. In the evening a long wraith of white mist lay across the grey-blue of the mountains, and in the reflection of the afterglow bamboo stakes swung from side to side with the current, tied to the bottom by their sand-bags and shaken to and fro as a soul tethered to mortality quivers in the stream of circumstance.

Burmese Murderers.

On each side of the steamer a man was now trying the depths with a long pole, which he swung round in the air; like some monotonous prayer he chanted the depths of the water—*Sari ache balm—ache balm—ache hart*—chanted these words again and again.

The easy charm of the river-road gains a hold upon the traveller. There is none of the irksome noise and shaking of the railway, and even the huge cockroaches seem friendly. At every riverside village stopping-place there is a bright scene of talk and laughter. The people on shore get all their news and do all their shopping on the steamer's arrival, and friendliness is as pervasive as the sunshine.

One night on the Irrawaddy I slept on deck among a crowd of passengers, and my immediate neighbours were three chained criminals. Two of them had killed somebody and were handcuffed together, a chain from the handcuff being fastened to an iron stanchion. When brought on board they were roped as well, but the ropes were removed and they smoked cheroots comfortably enough. Two Punjabis and a couple of smart little Burmese policemen had charge of them, and the Punjabis slept, but all night the Burmese police took turn about to watch. Whether it was the influence of the river or of the tobacco I know not, but the murderers seemed no more ill at ease than the rest of us; only, whenever there was a little chink or jingle, the policeman's eyes brightened.

Slowly the mountains darkened and the mirrored magic of a little moon floated upon the ever-moving stream.

CHAPTER IV

THE DEAD HEART OF A KINGDOM

How the wheels of that bullock-cart did creak!

The reason they had never been greased was because the driver loved the sound. He believed that the Nats (who are supposed to throng the neighbourhood) dislike it, and that while the wheels creaked the Nats would keep away.

I had just come down the Irrawaddy by steamer from Mandalay, and very early on the second morning had reached Nyaungoo. At three o'clock Tambusami (my Hindoo servant) appeared at my cabin-door in a state of excitement. I looked out and saw the boat's searchlight playing about the shore, three or four brown bodies jumping into the water, and the usual Flotilla Company's landing-stage—then the steep sandbank and collection of stalls with their oil-lamps. The air was full of the shrill voices of women talking, shouting and laughing. I dressed hurriedly, while fellow-passengers lay peaceful in the ghostly seclusion of mosquito curtains. The electric fan whirled on with fitful spits. There was no mist and the stars were bright. Cocks crowed and dogs barked—the red ends of many cheroots glowed from the bank, where people squatted smoking and talking.

When the steamer moved slowly away I and my servant were left, a little before dawn, upon the steep sandy bank pitted with innumerable foot-treads.

Tambusami had laid in food supplies at Mandalay, and dividing ourselves and our belongings between two bullock-carts at the top of the bank, we jolted along the road through Nyaungoo. The higher clouds were just caught by the new daylight as we passed under the tamarind trees of the village. The walls of the houses were mere screens of plaited bamboo, though often there was also an outer fence of bamboo posts 6 feet high.

A wan amber light now began to bathe the tops of a grove of 50-foot toddy-palms.

After leaving the village I began to pass tall cactus hedges and then a dilapidated pagoda with old grinning leogryphs, pale lemon in colour, and a gilded dome. There were broken masses of crumbling red brick, and under the now dove-coloured sky the glass facets of tall bird-topped votive poles gleamed brilliantly. Then the road entered the district of a myriad ruins and long lines of broken gods. Purple and violet and fiery orange-red, a multitude of small clouds scattered across the pale steely-blue. Tall trees of cactus with small leaves on spreading branches, as well as the upright column cactus springing green from the sand, now bordered the road. Suddenly all the red of the clouds changed to gold, the purple to pale soft heliotrope, and in a burst of golden light the sun rose over a line of violet mountains. Past stray bushes of wild cotton, with their mauve blossoms and pale-bluish leaves, men were carrying loads of red lacquer bowls. These bowls, packed in column and swinging in nets from the shoulder crosspole, looked like bundles of giant red sausages.

Mile after mile we jolted and creaked and presently passed between two great piles of red brick with a Buddha in a porch on the exterior of either side—all that remained of the great gateway—or one of the great gateways—of the ancient city of Pagan.

The building of Mandalay was only commenced about fifty years ago; Pagan was founded before A.D. 200. In Mandalay there are now close upon 200,000 inhabitants; at Pagan there are eight miles of brick-strewn sand and a few poor villages. Mandalay, situated where the Irrawaddy is joined by its chief tributary, is likely to become a great railway centre; Pagan, in the dryest part of the dry zone, has had no practical importance since it was sacked by Kubla Khan in 1286. But in that wilderness of rubble and cactus the remains of 5000 pagodas and monasteries (it is said there were once 13,000) can still be traced, and among them are certain buildings in a good state of preservation, vast in size and of quite peculiar interest.

A few small black pigs and a number of very mangy dogs loitered about some huts. I was now in a land of ruins. Dismantled shrines, broken pagodas and dilapidated temples stretched in every direction, but here and there were vast structures of plaster-faced brickwork, either unharmed by time or restored in spite of the popular belief that there is no merit in mere reparation.

The Circuit House which I reached at last is a substantial building of iron and teak, and letting daylight and air into the empty rooms, which reeked with new varnish, I chose a suite upon the upper floor which has a wide covered balcony. Hitherto travellers who wanted to visit Pagan have had either to take camping equipment with them or else to sleep at Nyaungoo, five miles away. In preparation for a recent visit of the Viceroy, however, a large and comfortable circuit house was built near the riverside, in the very centre of the ruins, and for the future there need be no difficulty in obtaining "lodging for the night." The Viceroy, on the occasion of his visit, abode in his launch, and I was told I was the first stranger to sleep at the Circuit House. I had obtained the key of the cupboard, which harboured plate and kitchen utensils, and while I went off to look round, Tambusami prepared a welcome breakfast.

From the house you look over the wide river, which is not more than a quarter of a mile away, to a range of mountains beautiful at every hour of the day. I walked inland a little way to the Thatbyinnyu Pagoda (the Temple of Omniscience), the loftiest of the buildings at Pagan, 200 feet high and standing upon rising ground. It is square in plan but with a large projecting porch on one side. The middle portion is a huge quadrangular mass of brickwork supposed to be solid, but between this solid centre and the outside there are upon the lower three of the five storeys of the building external terraces and internal corridors with stairways connecting the floors, in the thickness of the walls. Dark and sombre within, it is easy on descending from the upper storeys to choose wrong stairways and to wander about as in a maze. Upon the third storey, on the side of the great projection, there is in a recess against the inner wall a colossal seated Buddha.

Again and again I found myself groping alone in the silence of dark passages, and after such an approach there is a strange solemnity about sudden intrusion on the presence of a mighty seated figure so grandly peaceful, so splendidly aloof and so serenely lasting.

Looking towards the river from the white terraces of this pagoda, another of somewhat similar design to the Thatbyinnyu, appears on the right among a number of smaller buildings mostly in ruins. This is the Gawdawpalin Pagoda, built as a thank-offering by Narapatisezoo, a king who reigned in Pagan through the last quarter of the twelfth century A.D. One day he boasted "I am the best of all kings who ever sat on the throne of Pagan," whereupon he was struck blind, nor could any doctor cure him; but when told what he had said, his ministers advised him to make images of the great kings he had insulted by such a boast of superiority and to do homage to them. Narapatisezoo did this and regained his sight, and then had the Gawdawpalin Pagoda erected in gratitude to Buddha.

I came again to these terraces in the late afternoon when the more mellow light of a low sun made everything glow with warm colour, as if it wanted to give back the heat of the day before night came. And standing then with my back to the river and looking inland I saw in front of me the great Ananda, the most beautiful as well as the most curious of the Pagan temples.

In the Ananda there is a large projecting porch on each of the four sides of the square, adding about 40 feet on each side and making thus a cruciform plan 280 feet across. The highest of its seven diminishing storeys is shaped like a tall pyramid with four sides curved vertically as in Hindoo temples.

An ingenious feature of the Ananda is the lighting of the four colossal figures of the Buddha which stand in niches of the central mass and face the four porches. They are all standing figures and are higher than the arches, the pointed arches of the entrance porches, and are lighted from above by hidden openings in the wall. Running round the central portion are two colonnades which cross the porch approaches to the four shrines. The gilded figures of the four Buddha dispensations, Gautama, Kathaba, Gawnagon and Kankkuthan, tower up gigantic, and in each case the mysterious illumination of the head and shoulders adds to their grandeur. Under tall white arches, as in some Gothic church, I walked slowly along the pavement, watching the upper portion of the statue appear as I advanced. In the west porch there is, about the middle of the transept, a raised circular slab with a pair of Buddha footprints cut in stone in conventional arrangement, and covered with engraved symbols. In the niche facing this porch the gilded figure is that of Gautama himself.

Pagan.

The horizontal circular slab is raised upon a four-sided white plinth to about the height of a man's waist. Looking across it the next tall archway is seen flanked on either side by 'guardian' figures, each with the arm towards the arch close to the body, except for the hand which is stiffly bent outwards and upwards. The other arms are bent sharply at the elbows and have the hands raised. To right and left of these figures the transverse colonnades cross parallel to the outer walls.

From the stone slab with the impress of the feet you cannot quite see the head of the great image in the distance, the top of the farthest arch still hiding the upper part of the face. The figure is gilded all over and stands upon a lotus. In front there is a low railing composed of thick glass balusters, and having two little doors in the centre. Approaching nearer you see at last in brilliant light the benign countenance.

Of the four of these colossal statues that called Kankkuthan on the north side is believed to be the original figure, though it has been frequently repaired. The hands are pressed together in front of the breast. The figure wears a garment with sleeves close-fitting from the elbow to the wrists, but from the elbows hanging straight down in a line with the upper arm to make a conventional shape, which stops at an angle and ends in a slightly curved border which meets the legs just above the ankle. The background of the niche is covered with very elaborate glass-work, and on the silvery face of some of this are patterns in a kind of gesso.

About the white walls of the corridors are numerous small niches in which in high relief, coloured in red and gold, are representations of scenes in Buddha's life. Parts of the corridors have tier above tier of similar niches right up to the top of the wall, almost as in some Roman columbarium.

In a similar niche on the right as you walk towards the centre through the western portico there is a small figure of the builder of the Pagoda, King Kyansittha, a remarkably intrepid warrior whose chief adventures happened before he came to the throne in the reign of his mightier predecessor, King Naurata.

Naurata was the greatest of all the kings of Pagan—it was under his rule that its territory increased till it stretched from Siam to Kachin and China, and from Chittagong to Tonquin, and it was Naurata who destroyed Thaton and brought 30,000 prisoners thence to Pagan, including artists and craftsmen, as well as a king and queen.

Kyansittha was in disgrace for some years before Naurata was killed by a white buffalo in the jungle. It was all about a certain present to Naurata from his vassal, the King of Pegu. The present was a princess in a golden palanquin, the King of Pegu's very beautiful daughter; and Kyansittha, who seems to have been able to resist everything except temptation, lifted the purdah, with the disastrous consequence of Naurata's jealous wrath. He only returned from banishment upon Naurata's death, and the building of this Ananda Pagoda was the chief event of a reign apparently much quieter than that of his stormy and zealous predecessor. Verily, great building is more lasting than the kingdoms of men!

On the outside of the Ananda Pagoda I saw a line of green glazed tiles upon the outer walls. All round the base a series of such tiles a foot square is let in just above a lower flange in the position of a dado. Each of them is a separate figure illustrating a Jataka story, and each has the title underneath it upon the tile in old Burmese characters. Many have been restored in an absurd way (which has led to their being wrongly described) and some have disappeared, but a great number remain, and careful drawings should be made of these spirited reliefs before it is too late.

Near the Ananda there is a small museum containing a number of stone slabs found at Pagan, covered with inscriptions in the old Burmese square lettering. Among the objects in the museum are some good small bronzes, wooden figures of Nats and some small votive bricks in the shape of a pointed arch, within which Buddhas have been stamped upon the clay. So little interest, however, are any English visitors expected to take in these objects that the labels are only in Burmese characters.

Burmese Dwarf (3 ft. 5 in. high) Suffering from Cataract.

On one of my days at Pagan, Tambusami drew my attention to someone riding towards us on a white horse. This was Mr Cooper, who had come over from Nyaungoo to call upon me. Tambusami and a Burman did the best they could to make a show with our diminished stores, and after dinner on the wide veranda we found that we both knew Haslemere and the old Portsmouth Road and Paris, and then Mr Cooper, who was a subdivisional magistrate, told me about the kind of cases that are brought before him in the Pagan district,—about an island for one thing. Now at Salay, just along the river, there is an island which has been steadily growing in size. Originally it was the property of one village on the mainland. It had been allotted to the villagers after it had first appeared, and then some time ago it increased suddenly in size a great deal more, coming up out of the river. Then the headman of another village, on the strength of saying that he had a verbal order from the Barman township magistrate, allotted plots to his own friends and relations. Naturally the people of the first village were objecting.

Most of the cultivated land here pays revenue at the rate of four annas an acre, and as assistant collector in revenue work, Mr Cooper had to put things right.

He went on to tell me about a question of property concerning two golden heads. There is a mountain called Popa (5000 feet high) standing right in the middle of the plain. We could see it from the back of the house. It is an extinct volcano and is the home of two of the most important Nats in all Burmah. They have lived on Popa ever since about 380 A.D. They were brother and sister, and used to have a festival held on this mountain every year in their honour.

About the middle of the eighteenth century one of the kings of Ava—Bodawpaya—presented to the Popa villagers two golden heads, intended to represent these Nats. At that time Popa village, for some reason, was a separate jurisdiction outside the jurisdiction of the Pagan governor. What happened was that these heads were kept in the Royal Treasury at Pagan for safety, and taken up to Popa every year for the festival and brought back again. Subsequently, Popa came under the jurisdiction of the Pagan governor. Then apparently the Pagan people began to think that these heads really belonged to them, and they were kept in Pagan until the annexation in 1886. After this, our Government, thinking they were very valuable relics which ought to be preserved, sent them down to the Bernard Free Library in Rangoon, where they have been lodged ever since.

Some time ago the Popa villagers sent in a petition that they might be allowed to have their heads back, as they wanted them for the festival. Investigations were started and about a month before my visit Mr Cooper had been up to Popa and there dictated a written guarantee, signed by the principal men of the village (the Lugyis, as they are called), that they would undertake the responsibility of looking after these heads if they were given back to them. Then Mr Cooper came to Pagan and had a meeting of the Pagan *Lugyis*, asking them to sign a written repudiation of claim, and that's where the matter rested.

I asked Mr Cooper to tell me the story of these famous Nats, in whose honour a coconut is hung up in houses in this part of Burmah just as regularly as we do for the tomtits at home, so that they can eat when they like, and here is the story in his own words as he told it to me at Pagan.

These Nats have a good many names, but their proper names are Natindaw and Shwemetyna, and they used to live in a place up the river called Tagaung, a thousand years ago. Natindaw, the man, was a blacksmith. He was very strong indeed—so strong that the King of Tagaung was afraid of him and gave orders that he should be arrested. The man (he had not become a Nat then) was afraid and ran away, but his sister remained and the king married her. After some time the king thought of Natindaw again and believed that although in exile he might be doing something to stir up rebellion. So the king offered Natindaw an appointment at the Court, and when Natindaw came he had him seized by guards and bound to a champak tree near the palace. Then the King had the tree set on fire, and Natindaw proceeded to burn up. Just at that moment the queen (Natindaw's sister) came out of the palace and saw her brother being burnt. She rushed into the fire and tried to save him, and failing, decided to share his fate.

The king then tried to pull her out by her back hair but was too late, and both the brother and sister were utterly consumed except their heads. That finished them as human beings, but they became Nats and lived up another champak tree at Tagaung, and there, because they had been so shockingly treated, they made up for it after death. They used to pounce on everyone who passed underneath—cattle and people. At last the king had the tree with the brother and sister on it cut down, and it floated down the river and eventually stranded at Pagan. Well, the King of Pagan, who was at that time Thurligyaung, had a dream the night before that something very wonderful would come to Pagan the next day by river. In the morning he went down to the bank and there he found the tree with the human heads of Natindaw and Shwemetyna sitting on it, and they told him who they were and how badly they had been treated. The king became very frightened and said he would build them a place to live in on Popa. So they thanked him and he built them Natsin, a little sort of hut on Popa, and there they have lived ever since.

Every year the kings of Pagan used to go in state and offer sacrifice to Natindaw and Shwemetyna of the flesh of white bullocks and white goats, and the Popa Nat story is still going on because of the latest development about the golden heads.

It is a Burmese saying that no one can point in any direction at Pagan in which there is not a pagoda, and on many of them in the mornings I saw vultures—great bare-necked creatures—thriving apparently on barrenness.

Lack of water is the great trouble to the villages. The average rainfall in this dry zone (which extends roughly from south of the Magwe district to north of Mandalay) is fifteen to twenty inches.

Tenacious of life, these Thaton villagers of Pagan and Nyaungoo, led into captivity by King Naurata, whose zeal as a religious reformer had been fired by one of their own priests, survived their conquerors. They became, nine hundred years ago, slaves attached to the pagodas, and under a ban of separation, if not of dishonour, they have kept unmixed the blood of their ancestors, are the only Burmese forming anything like a caste, and still include some direct descendants of their famous king.

In the villages there is some weaving and dyeing of cloth, and quite a large industry in the making of lacquer bowls and boxes.

It was not far to walk from the Circuit House to one of the villages,—across the dry baked, brick-strewn earth, past great groves of cactus and through the tall bamboo fence that surrounds the village itself. I passed a couple of carts with primitive solid wheels, and under some trees in the middle of the collection of thatched huts with their floors raised some feet above the ground, a huge cauldron was sending up clouds of steam. Some women were boiling dye for colouring cloth. This was Mukolo village. I called at the house of U Tha Shein, one of the chief lacquer makers, and he took me about to different huts to see the various stages of the work.

First, a "shell" is made of finely-plaited bamboo; this is covered with a black pigment and "softened" when dry by turning it on a primitive lathe and rubbing it with a piece of sand-stone. Then the red lacquer is put upon the black box with the fingers, which stroke and smear it round very carefully. In Burmese the red colour is called *Hinthabada,* from a stone I was told they buy in Mandalay. The bowls now red are set to dry in the sun, and next are placed in a hole in the ground for five days,—all as careful a process as that of making the wine of Cos described in Sturge Moore's *Vinedresser.*

When they are exhumed after hardening, a pattern is finally engraved or scratched on the lacquer with a steel point and a little gold inlaid on the more expensive bowls.

I was going from house to house to see the different stages of the work, when I heard a pitiful wailing and came upon the saddest sight I had yet seen on my journey. The front of a thatched hut was quite open. A mangy yellow pariah dog was skulking underneath, and some children were huddled silent upon the steps leading up to the platform floor. There lay a little boy dead, and his mother and grandmother were sorrowing for him. The grandmother seemed to be wrinkled all over. Her back was like a withered apple. She moaned and wailed, and tears poured from her eyes. "Oh! my grandson," she cried—"where shall I go and search for you again?"

She was squatting beside the little corpse and pinching its cheeks and moving its jaws up and down. "You have gone away to any place you like—you have left me alone without thinking of me—I cannot feel tired of crying for you."

And a Burman told me that the child had died of fever, and that the father had gone to buy something for the funeral. He added, "The young woman will never say anything—she will only weep for the children. It is the old woman only that will say something."

CHAPTER V

MANDALAY

Christmas morning at Mandalay was bright, crisp and cold, with just that bracing "snap" in the air that makes everyone feel glad to be in warm clothes. On such a day the traveller feels a sense of security about the people at home—they must be comfortable in London when it is so jolly at Mandalay!

I was drawn by some Chinese characters over a small archway in Merchant Street to turn up a narrow passage between high walls, which led me to a modern square brick joss-house. There were several Chinese about and I got to understand that the temple was especially for all people who were sick or ill, and I went through the very ancient method of obtaining diagnosis and prescription.

An English-speaking Chinaman told me that this temple was "the church of Doctor Wah Ho Sen Too," who lived, he added, more than a thousand years ago, and had apparently anticipated the advantages of Rontgen rays. The American who is watching in Ceylon the formation of pearls without opening of oysters, is yet far behind Doctor Wah Ho Sen Too, to whom all bodies are as glass. The stout Chinaman grew quite eloquent in praise of this great physician, explaining with graphic gestures how he had been able to see through every part of all of us, and follow the career of whatever entered our mouths.

In front of the round incense-bowl upon an altar, before large benevolent-looking figures, was a cylindrical box containing one hundred slips of bamboo of equal length (if any reader offers to show me all this at Rotherhithe or Wapping, I shall not dispute with him but gladly avail myself of his kindness). I was directed to shake the box and draw out at random one of the bamboo slips. This had upon it, in Chinese characters, a number and some words, and I was told that my number was fourteen. Upon the left-hand wall of the temple were serried rows of one hundred sets of small printed reddish-yellow papers. I was taken to number fourteen set and bidden to tear off the top one, and this was Doctor Wah Ho Sen Too's prescription.

I have not yet had that prescription made up; to the present day I prefer the ailment, but I asked the English-speaking Chinaman what the medicine was like, and he told me that it was white and that I could get it at Mandalay. When he was in South America Waterton slept with one foot out of his hammock to see what it was like to be sucked by a vampire, but I am of opinion there are some things in life we may safely reject on trust, declining taste of sample.

Burmese Priest and his Betel Box.

I went from the joss-house of Merchant Street to the Aindaw Pagoda, about the middle of the western edge of the city, a handsome mass, blazing with the brightness of recent gilding. From "hti" to base it was entirely gilt, except for the circle of coloured glass balls which sparkled like a carcanet of jewels near the summit. Outside the gate of the Aindaw Pagoda, where some Burmans were playing a gambling game, a notice in five languages—English, Burmese, Hindostani, Hindi and Chinese, announced, "Riding, shoe and umbrella-wearing disallowed."

The Queen's Golden Monastery at the south-west corner of the town is a finer specimen of gilded work, built in elaborately-carved teak, with a great number of small square panels about it of figure subjects as well as decorative shapes and patterns. Glass also has been largely introduced in elaborate surface decoration at the Golden Monastery, not in the tiny tessarae of Western mosaic but in larger facets, giving from the slight differences of angle in the setting, bright broken lights almost barbaric in their richness. No one seems to know where all the coloured and stained glass that is so skilfully used in Burmese temples came from—whether it was imported or made in the country.

The priests were returning to the monastery with bowls full of food from their daily morning rounds, but there were very few people about at all, and the place was almost given up that day to a batch of merry children, who came gambolling round me, some of them pretending to be paralysed beggars with quaking limbs.

It was very different at the Maha Myat Muni, the Arrakan Pagoda, which was thronged with people like a hive of bees. This pagoda includes a vast pile of buildings and enshrines one of the most revered images of Buddha, a colossal brass figure seated in a shrine both gorgeous and elaborate, with seven roofs overhead. Of shrines honoured to-day in Burmah the Arrakan Pagoda is more frequented than any except the Shwe Dagon at Rangoon, and is approached through a long series of colonnades gilded, frescoed, and decorated with rich carving and mosaic work. They are lined with stalls of metal-workers, sellers of incense, candles, violet lotus flowers, jewels, sandalwood mementoes, and souvenirs innumerable, among which the most fascinating to the stranger are grotesque toy figures, with fantastic movable limbs, which would make an easy fortune at a London toy-shop, and before long will doubtless be exported and gradually lose their exotic charm.

Passing through this Vanity Fair I at last reached the shrine, and in the dim interior light I climbed up behind the great figure and followed the custom of native pilgrims in seeking to "gain merit" by placing a gold-leaf upon it with my own fingers. At all hours of every day human thumbs and fingers are pressing gold-leaf upon that figure of Gautama. Outside in the sunlight white egrets strutted about the grounds, and close by was a tank where sacred turtles wallowed under a thick green scum. A swarm of rice-sellers besought me to buy food for the turtles, and their uncomfortable persistence was, of course, not lessened by patronage. The overfed animals declined to show their heads, leaving the kites and crows to batten on the tiny balls of cooked rice.

Now close to this turtle-tank and still within the precincts of the temple was a large structure, evidently very much older than the rest of the buildings—a vast cubical mass of red brick with an inner passage, square in plan, round a central core of apparently solid masonry. Against one side of this inner mountain of brickwork was the lower half of a colossal figure, also in red brick, and cut off at the same level as the general mass of the building. Whether the whole had ever been completed or whether at some time the upper half had been removed, I could not tell. It was as if the absence of head and shoulders cast a spell of death, which surrounded it with a silence no voice ventured to dissipate, and with the noise and hubbub outside nothing could have more strikingly contrasted than the impressive quiet of this deserted sanctuary.

That Christmas afternoon, as already told, I left Mandalay on my way to Bhamo, returning afterwards for a longer stay.

Far away, beyond Fort Dufferin on the other side of the city, rises Mandalay Hill which I climbed several times for the sake of the wonderful view. In the bright dazzle of a sunlight that made all things pale and fairylike, I passed along wide roads ending in tender peeps of pale amethyst mountains. I crossed the wide moat of Fort Dufferin, with its double border of lotus, by one of the five wooden bridges and, traversing the enclosure, came out again through the red-brick crenelated walls by a wide gateway, and re-crossed the moat to climb the steep path by huge smooth boulders in the afternoon heat. It was as if they had saved up all the warmth of noon to give it out again with radiating force. At first the way lies between low rough walls, on which at short intervals charred and blackened posts stand whispering, "We know what it is to be burned"—"We know what it is to be burned." They were fired at the same time as the temple at the top of the hill over twenty years ago; but the great standing wooden figure of Buddha, then knocked down, has been set up again, though still mutilated, for the huge hand that formerly pointed down to the city lies among bricks and rubble.

The Queen's Golden Monastery and the Arrakan Pagoda were hidden somewhere far away among the trees to the south of the city. Below, I could see the square enclosure of Fort Dufferin, with its mile-long sides, in which stands King Thebaw's palace and gardens, temples and pavilions, and I could see the parallel lines of the city roadways. Mandalay is laid out on the American plan, with wide, tree-shaded roads at right angles to each other. Nearer to the hill and somewhat to the left lay the celebrated Kuthodaw or four hundred and fifty pagodas, whereunder are housed Buddhist scriptures engraved upon four hundred slabs of stone. The white plaster takes at sunset a rosy hue, and in the distance the little plot resembles some trim flower-bed where the blossoms have gone to sleep.

One of the loveliest things about Mandalay is the moat of Fort Dufferin. In the evening afterglow I stopped at the south-west corner, where a boy was throwing stones at a grey snake, and watched the silhouette of walls and watch-towers against a vivid sky of red and amber and the reflections in the water among the lotus leaves. Each side of the Fort is a straight mile long, and the moat, which is a hundred yards across, has a wide space all along the middle of the waterway quite clear of lotus. But moat and walls are both most beautiful of all at sunrise. The red bricks then glow softly with warm colour, and against their reflection the flat lotus leaves appear as pale hyaline dashes.

Within, upon the level greensward, you may find to-day a wooden horse—not such a large one as Minerva helped the Greeks to build before the walls of Troy, nor yet that more realistic modern one I have seen in the great hall, the old "Salone" of Verona—but a horse for gymnastic exercises of Indian native regiments of Sikhs and Punjabis. Strange barracks those soldiers have, for they sleep in what were formerly monasteries with halls of carved and painted pillars.

Burmese Mother and Child.

I was asking the whereabouts of the only Burmese native regiment and found it just outside Fort Dufferin, in "lines" specially built. It is a regiment of sappers and miners. On New Year's Day Captain Forster, their commanding officer, put a company of these Burmans through their paces for me. In appearance they are not unlike Gourkhas, sturdy and about the same height, and like the Gourkha they carry a knife of special shape, a square-ended weapon good for jungle work.

King Thebaw's palace stands, of course, within the "Fort," which was built to protect it. It is neither very old nor very interesting, and the most impressive part is the large audience hall. The columns towards the entrance are gilded, but on each side the two nearest the throne are, like the walls, blood-red in colour, and the daylight filtering through casts blue gleams upon them. It was not here, however, that the king was taken prisoner, but in a garden pavilion a little distance from it with a veranda, and according to a brass plate let into the wall below:—

> "King Thebaw sat at this opening with his two queens and the queen mother when he gave himself up to General Prendergast on the 30th November, 1885."

I was talking one day with an army officer in a Calcutta hotel about Burmah, and he told me how he himself had carried the British flag into Mandalay with General Prendergast, and that it had been his lot to conduct the Queen Sepaya (whom he declared does not deserve all that has been said against her) to Rangoon, and he gave her the last present she received in Burmah. She was smoking one of the giant cheroots of the country and he gave her a box of matches.

I had never quite understood the annexation and that officer explained it as follows:—"We knew the French were intriguing—that Monsieur Hass, the French Ambassador at Rangoon, was working at the Court—and we got at his papers and found he was just about to conclude a treaty with Thebaw. The chance we seized was this—a difference between Thebaw and the Bombay Burmah Trading Company. For their rights in forest-land in Upper Burmah they paid a royalty on every log floated down. Now other people were also floating logs down, and Thebaw claimed several lakhs of rupees from the Bombay Burmah Company for royalties not paid. The Company contended they had paid all royalties on their own logs, and that the unpaid monies were due on other people's timber, and we seized the excuse and took Mandalay in the nick of time, defeating the French plans."

The most noticeable feature of the Mandalay Bazaar is the supremacy of the Burmese woman as shopkeeper. The vast block of the markets is newly built and looks fresh and spick and span, though without anything about its structure either beautiful or picturesque. It is like Smithfield and Covent Garden rolled into one, and given over entirely to petticoat government. I am told there are close upon 200,000 people in Mandalay, and those long avenues of the great bazaar looked fully able to cope with their demands. There is the meat-market, with smiling ladies cutting up masses of flesh; the vegetable-market, with eager ladies weighing out beans and tamarinds; the flour and seed-market, with loquacious ladies measuring out dal and rice-flour and red chili and saffron powder; the plantain-market, with laughing ladies like animated flowers decorating a whole street of bananas; the silk-market, with dainty ladies with powdered faces enticing custom with deft and abundant display of tissues and mercery,—and yet this does not tell one half of the Mandalay Bazaar. I have not even mentioned the flower-market, with piquant ladies—fully alive to the challenging beauty of their goods—selling roses or lotus, with faces that express confident assurance of their own superior charms.

Perhaps it is not hardness—perhaps it is merely some lack of appreciation in me—but in spite of all that has been said or written in their praise, I could not find those Burmese women as charming as the shop-girls of London. I admit that they have a very smart way of twisting a little pink flower into the right side of their hair, and although I have seen a great many sleeping upon the decks of river steamers, I never heard one snore. Many men find wives, I was told, in the Mandalay Bazaar, and they are said to make excellent housekeepers. One perfectly charming little woman I did see, the wife of an Eurasian engineer (or is not "Anglo-Indian" now the prescribed word?), but she looked too much like a doll; and while a real doll who was a bad housekeeper would be unsatisfactory enough, a good housekeeper who looked like a doll would surely be intolerable.

Thinking of dolls brings me to the marionettes which still delight the Burmese people. They have long since gone out of fashion in England, "Punch and Judy" shows fighting hard to keep up old tradition; in Paris, the "Guignol" of the side alleys of the Champs Elysées are nowadays chiefly patronized by children, and you must go further East to find an adult audience enjoying the antics of dolls. Marionettes had a vogue in ancient Greece, and in Italy survived the fall of Rome. Even in Venice the last time I went to the dolls' theatre I found the doors closed, but in Naples they flourish still, and at the Teatro Petrilla in the sailors' quarter I have seen Rinaldo and Orlando and all the swash-buckling courage of mediæval chivalry in animated wood.

At Mandalay there is the same popular delight in doll drama, and one evening I watched a mimic "pwe" for an hour. The story was another version of that which I had already seen acted by living people. The showman had set up his staging in a suitable position, with a wide and sloping open space before it, and there was the same great gathering of young and old in the open air, lying on low four-post bedsteads or squatting on mats, while outside the limits of the audience stalls drove a thriving trade in cheroots and edible dainties. How the people laughed and cackled with delight at the antics of the dolls! These were manipulated with a marvellous dexterity, and seemed none the less real because the showman's hands were often visible as he jerked the strings. I walked up to the stage and stood at one end of it to get the most grotesque view of the scene. A long, low partition screen ran along the middle of the platform. Behind this, limp figures were hanging ready for the "cues," and the big fat Burmese showman walked sideways up and down, leaning over as he worked the dancing figures upon the stage. The movements were a comic exaggeration of the formal and jerky actions of the dance, but the clever manipulation of a prancing steed, a horse of mettle with four most practical flamboyant legs, was even more amusing.

The parts of the dramatis personæ were spoken by several different voices, and the absence of any attempt to hide the arms and hands of the showman did not diminish the illusion, while it increased the general bizarre character of the scene rather than otherwise, and was an excellent instance of the fallacy of the saying—*Summa ars est celare artem.*

Blessed be the convention of strings! The success of a marionette show, as of a government, is no more attained by a denial of the wire-puller's existence than the beauty of a marble statue is enhanced by realistic colouring.

CHAPTER VI

SOUTHERN INDIA, THE LAND OF HINDOO TEMPLES

A long line of rocks and a white lighthouse in the midst of them—this is the first sight of India as the traveller approaches Tuticorin, after the sea journey from Colombo. He sees the sun glinting from windows of modern buildings, the tall chimney of a factory and trailing pennons of "industrial" smoke. Far to the left, hills faintly visible beyond the shore appear a little darker than the long, low cloud above them. Then what had seemed to be dark rocks become irregular masses of green trees. Colour follows form—the buildings grow red and pink and white, and the pale shore-line a thread of greenish-yellow. The sea near Tuticorin is very shallow, and the steamer anchors at least four miles out, a launch crossing the thick yellow turbid water to take passengers ashore. On nearer view the lighthouse proves to be on a tree-clad spit or island, and to the left instead of the right of the harbour. Near the jetty I saw large cotton-mills, and passed great crowds of ducks (waiting to be shipped to Ceylon), which dappled the roadside as I made my way to the terminus of the South Indian Railway. At first the train passes through a flat sandy country with little grass, but covered with yellow flowering cactus, low prickly shrubs and tall palmyra palms. The shiny cactus and sharp-pointed aloe leaves seemed to reflect the bright blue of the sky, and by contrast a long procession of small yellow-brown sheep looked very dark.

Presently the ground changed to red earth and tillage. Then we passed more aloes and bare sand and a few cotton-fields. A thin stream meandered along the middle of a wide sandy bed, and a line of distant mountains, seen faintly through the shimmery haze of heat, seemed all the while to grow more lovely. Taking more colour as the day advanced they stretched along the horizon like the flat drop-scene of a theatre, abruptly separate from the plain. After passing several lakes like blue eyes in the desert some red sloping hills appeared to make a link in the perspective, and I reached my first stopping-place, the famous Madura.

First I drove to that part of the great temple dedicated to Minachi, Siva's wife, and then to the Sundareswara Temple dedicated to Siva himself under that name.

The typical Dravidian temple, the Southern form of the Hindoo style of architecture, consists of a pyramidal building on a square base divided externally into stories, and containing image, relic or emblem in a central shrine. This Vimana is surrounded at some distance by a wall with great entrance gateways or Gopuras, similar in general design to the central building but rectangular instead of square in plan, and often larger and more richly decorated outside than the Vimana itself.

Then there is also the porch of the temple or Mantapam, the tank or Tappakulam, the Choultry or hall of pillars and independent columns or Stambhams, bearing lamps or images.

It was a vast double door some distance in front of me, beyond a series of wide passages and courts, a colossal door larger than those two of wood and iron at the entrance to the Vatican, where the Swiss guards stand in their yellow-slashed uniforms with the halberds of earlier days, doors with no carving save that of worms and weather, but, like the one before me, more impressive by tremendous size and appearance of strength than the bronze gates of Ghiberti. It was a portal for gods over whose unseen toes I, a pygmy, might crane my neck. The vast perspective in front, the sense of possible inclusion of unknown marvels commensurate with such an entrance, a mystery of shadow towards the mighty roof,—all made me stand and wonder, admiring and amazed. Porch succeeded porch, with statues of the gods, sometimes black with the oil of countless libations, sometimes bright and staring with fresh paint. Dirt mingled with magnificence and modern mechanical invention with the beauty of ancient art. Live men moved everywhere among the old, old gods.

Walking along a corridor, astounded at its large grotesque sculptures, I noticed at my elbow two squatting tailors with Singer sewing-machines, buzzing as with the concentrated industry of a hive of bees. I wished that a prick of the finger would send them all to sleep, tailors, priests, mendicants and the quivering petitions of importunate maimed limbs.

Neither Darius nor Alexander, had they been able to march so far, could have seen Madura, for, after all, these temples are not yet so very old, but Buonaparte—Ah! he of all men should have seen it! I think of him on his white horse, gazing with saturnine inscrutability at the cold waves of carved theogonies surging, tier on tier, up the vast pyramids of the immense gopuras, till the golden roofs of inner gleaming shrines drew him beyond.

Brief—oh how much too brief—was the time permitted me to spend at Madura, for the same night I was to reach Trichinopoly.

I dressed by lamplight and was on the road just at dawn, driving through the poorer quarter of the town. By a white gateway of Moorish design, erected on the occasion of the last royal visit, and still bearing the legend—"Glorious welcome to our future Emperor"—I entered the wide street of the main bazaar at the far end of which the "rock" appeared.

Trichinopoly, inside this gate, is entirely a city of "marked" men, the lower castes, together with the Eurasians and the few European officials living outside its boundaries.

The great bare mass which rises out of the plain to a height of 273 feet above the level of the streets below, was first properly fortified in the sixteenth century, under the great Nayakka dynasty of Madura, by which it was received from the King of Tanjore in exchange for a place called Vallam; and after being the centre of much fighting between native powers and French and English, it passed quietly into the hands of the latter by treaty in 1801.

The Sacred Tank and the Rock, Trichinopoly.

Reproduced by permission of the Visual Instruction Committee of the Colonial Office.

The Main Bazaar, Trichinopoly.

From a painting by permission of the Visual Instruction Committee, the Colonial Office.

From the roadway at the foot a series of stone stairways leads to the upper street, which encircles the rock and contains a hall from which other stairways lead up to a landing with a hundred-pillared porch on each side of it. In one of these lay in a corner with their legs in air a number of bamboo horses, life-size dummies, covered with coloured cloths and papers for use in the processions. On a still higher landing I reached the great temple (whither the image of Siva was removed from its former place in a rock-temple at the base of the precipice), which Europeans are forbidden to enter.

By engaging a man in a long argument with Tambusami as interpreter, about certain images visible as far within as I was able to see from the landing, I managed to rouse a desire to explain rightly, so that he made the expected suggestion and took me twenty yards within the forbidden doorway. Deafening noise of "temple music" filled the air, the most strident being emitted from short and narrow metal trumpets.

Twenty yards within that stone doorway guarded by the authority of Government embodied in official placards fastened on the wall! Shall I divulge the mysteries within? Indeed it would fill too many of these pages to spin from threads of temple twilight a wonder great enough to warrant such exclusion of the uninitiated.

Yet another flight of steps leads up round the outside to a final series roughly cut in the rock itself, rising to the topmost temple of them all, a Ganesh shrine, whence there is a grand view over the town and far surrounding plain.

Among the smaller shrines in the streets the one which seemed to me the most curious—was that of the "Black God, Karapanasami," a wooden club or baluster similar in design to those carved in the hands of stone watchmen at temple gates. Wreathed with flower garlands it leaned against the wall on a stone plinth and was dripping with libation oil. I was told that Karapanasami may be present in anything—a brick, or a bit of stone, or any shapeless piece of wood.

Among the native people, quite apart from the would-be guides who haunt the temples, those who speak a little English seem proud to display their knowledge and ready to volunteer information. Before a statue of Kali in a wayside shrine a boy ventured to say he hoped I would not irritate the goddess, adding, "This god becomes quickly peevish; it is necessary to give her sheep to quiet her."

That afternoon I painted the "Tappakulam" or tank at the base of the great rock with the dainty "Mantapam" or stone porch-temple in the middle of it, working from the box seat of a gharry to be out of the crowd, but their curiosity seemed to be whetted the more, and Tambusami was kept busy in efforts, not always successful, to stop the inquisitive from clambering the sides of the vehicle, which lurched and quivered as each new bare foot tried for purchase on the hub of a wheel.

The dazzling brilliancy of the scene was difficult to realize on canvas, for beyond all other elements of brightness a flock of green parrots flying about the roof sparkled like sun-caught jewels impossible to paint.

The next morning I dressed by lamplight, and it was not yet dawn when Tambusami put up the heavy bars across back and front doorways of my room at the dak bungalow for the safety of our belongings during a day's absence. Old Ratamullah, the very large fat "butler," watched us from his own house a little further back in the enclosure, as in the grey light we started to drive to Srirangam, and before the least ray of colour caught even the top of the Rock we saw a group of women in purple and red robes getting water at a fountain. The large, narrow-necked brass jars gleamed like pale flames, the colour of the words John Milton that shine from the west side of Bow Church in Cheapside.

Karapanasami, the Black God.

Outside the houses of prosperous Hindoos I noticed, down upon the red earth, patterns and designs that recalled the "doorstep art" practised by the peasants in many parts of Scotland. The dust of the day's traffic soon obscures the patterns, but at that early hour they had not yet been trodden upon. Brass lamps glimmered in the poorer huts, but we were soon away from Trichinopoly and crossing the long stone bridge over the Cauvery. The river was very wide but by no means full, and scattered with large spaces of bare sand. Over the water little mists like the pale ghosts of a crowd of white snakes curled and twisted in a strange slow dance.

When we had crossed the thirty-two arches of this bridge we were upon the island of Srirangam, on which there is that vast and, it is said, wealthy temple to Vishnu, about which one is always told that its design ought to have been turned inside out, as it becomes less imposing the farther one penetrates within. To me it was one long succession of delights and wonders, and in the freshness of the early morning I found an enjoyment in the crude designs of gods and heroes, freshly painted in strong outline of burnt sienna colour on whitewashed walls, as well as in the older elaborate and sometimes beautiful carvings of pillar and panel, niche and architrave.

Adjoining the so-called hall of a thousand columns a great bamboo scaffolding was being put up for the erection of an annexe roof, to be supported by sixty temporary pillars to make the full complement for the December festival. It was from here that I painted a sketch looking through the great passage, festooned with dry and withered mano leaves, under the White Tower, with a Gopura beyond, mauve in the early morning light. The Ana on one of the temple elephants was very pertinacious in his demands for backsheesh, and his very obedient servant caused me some inconvenience by the way in which the end of his trunk kept appearing between my brushes and palette.

Before driving back to Trichinopoly I stopped to have a good look at the great outer gateway of the temple, a magnificent granite structure of a different style to the rest of the buildings. It gives the appearance of breaking off suddenly at a lower height than its completion would have attained, but its splendid symmetry, its severe contours and its fine proportions stamp it forever as a grand piece of architecture and confute those who speak of the Dravidian style as careless or haphazard in planning.

All that it was possible for me to do in this part of Southern India was to visit a few of the most important temples, and as they are well known and oft described I will not devote much space to them here.

The chief in the Dravidian style after Madura and Trichinopoly is, of course, Tanjore—much earlier in date, being of the fourteenth century, if not much earlier still—with a pyramidal sikra of thirteen storeys high (it is surmounted by a spiked ornament, which gives its name to the construction), and a stone *Mantapam* covering the famous Nandi, the colossal stone bull of Siva, which is over 12 feet high and blackened with centuries of oil anointings.

The temple is partly surrounded by the great walls and bastions of the old fort of Tanjore and a wide moat, over which a bridge leads to the gateway. All along the west and north sides of the great open space within the walls runs a colonnade in which are placed, as in a long series of side-chapels, 108 lingams. The walls of these cloister-like recesses are covered with pictures of gods and miracles in sienna red, and on another side of the enclosure is the superbly graceful later shrine, called Subramanya, to the warrior son of Siva. The whole temple is attached to Tanjore Palace and under the control of the Senior Ranee, Her Highness Matosree Jijayeeamba Boyee Sahib.

The huge apartments of the five-storeyed palace are still inhabited by this lady and her sister, also a widow, and a host of dependants. In the courtyard stands a tower which served for many years as an armoury, and still contains the wooden stands and racks used for storing guns. It is a characterless stucco building, and its upper part has been for some time in a dangerous condition; but I was well repaid for the long clamber up its dark narrow stairway by the wide view from the top. In the palace there were durbar halls to see and indifferent oil-paintings of the rajahs and their ministers; but far more interesting than these is the old library, a famous collection including many valuable manuscripts, of which a great number are written on palm leaves. It was here I found, to my delight, the *Elephant Book*. The words are older than the illustrations, and are the writings of a certain rishi about all elephants. When the Hindoo librarian brought out this treasure the daylight was rapidly going, and as I did not wish to see the pictures by lamp-light, he had it carried outside for me and I turned the pages to the sound of music, which was being played under a tree in a corner of the courtyard. In the time of the rishi, elephants had wings, but the sound of their flapping disturbed him when he wanted to rest, and that is why elephants have no wings at all nowadays. In the pages of this book there were painted elephants of every colour imaginable, and a large simple treatment characterised the designs throughout. Some of the pictures made me think of Blake, though they rarely contained human figures, and one of a tree covered with little winged elephants reminded me of Blake's first vision as a child when he saw a fruit tree full of winged cherubs.

Madras I would call the dusty town of interminable distances. Everywhere seems to be miles away from everywhere else, and more liberal space about public buildings was surely never seen. The great desideratum is some kind of gliding shoe which will carry you back and forth at will, without any demands upon the muscles of the leg.

About the middle of the great front is Fort St George, with its three and four-storeyed barracks and officers' bungalows. It is of no strategic importance, but there are very rightly stringent regulations against sketching within its precincts. Thanks to the courtesy of the officers in charge I obtained permission with regard to St Mary's Church where Clive was married, and which claims to be not only the oldest English church in India, but the oldest English building in India of any kind, dating from 25th March 1678, when the first sod was turned for its erection.

I had received a verbal permission from the commanding officer, but had no sooner taken up my position than I was stopped by a sergeant. He insisted on the need for a written permit. Now this involved a second walk of some distance to the commanding officer's house, but I was sufficiently far from any feeling of annoyance to smile at that sergeant, saying I would comply with pleasure, and complimenting him on his zeal. His severe rejoinder was a delicious contrast to the fluent suavity of Eastern politeness. Looking at me sternly with flashing eyes, my compatriot exclaimed:—"Now look 'ere, don't you give me none of your sarcasm neither!"

Hindoo Mother and Child.

Most of the public buildings in Madras, such as the Railway Station, the Government Offices and the Law Courts, are of red brick, and their architecture an ingenious mixture of East and West.

Maimed and deformed beggars seem to abound. They come up to you shaking their quivering limbs, showing you sores or touching your arm softly with uncanny hands to draw your eyes to see some monstrous horror of a leg.

I wanted, before leaving the South, to see the Nilgiris, and with this end took train inland to Mettapalaiyam, where I changed on to the narrow gauge railway which climbs one in twelve, a central rack-rail making such an angle possible. As the engine was at the lower end I was able to sit on the extreme front of the train and watch the scenery to advantage. A look-out man by my side stopped the train in one deep cutting as we caught sight of a piece of rock which had fallen from above and lay across the metals in front of us. There were some coolies near at hand, and the obstacle was quickly removed, but it dramatically suggested one of the dangers of mountain railways.

The vegetation was very like that on the journey to Newara Eliya in Ceylon; bamboos, areca-nut palms, plantains and the same little orange-flowered shrub everywhere. Here and there the red earth showed but only rarely for where there were no trees the ground was generally bare grey rock. Hanging in gum trees or eucalyptus I noticed many paper nests of wasps. At Runnymede Station, 4500 feet above sea-level, we were turned into a siding for a down-coming train to pass. This was full of children shouting and cheering loudly, coming away for Christmas holidays from the Lawrence Asylum School at Ootacamund.

As we crossed small bridges over clefts and gorges I could see torrents under my feet between the sleepers; and then, rugged and precipitous, the hillside dropped below on one side and reared up on the other far above our heads, as we crept along some narrow ledge.

At Coonoor, which was, at the time of my visit, still the end of the railway, I shared a two-horse "tonga" with an engineer. He had been for many years making railways in Assam, had been down with dysentery and about to go home on leave when he was asked at Calcutta to get the "Ooty" railway finished, and change of air and a "soft" job had decided him to take the work.

A good linguist, he was fond of the natives generally and especially of the Hindoos. Living for long periods sixty or seventy miles from any white face, he had grown to dislike "society" and hated calling at the private houses of officials. "They don't understand me," he said, "and they never know the native as I know him. At the 'Holi' festival I make holiday with my people. Early in the morning I go into their quarters, right into their houses and throw the red water at their women, and then I have them all up to my camp in parties and they dance to me and all have a royal time. Sometimes it costs me three or four hundred rupees but I enjoy it, and they have few pleasures in their lives. Put a lighted cracker in a Hindoo girl's hand and tell her just when to throw it away, and the delight of it will last her for months. Of course they buy a few fireworks themselves, but they can't afford the big pieces and their joy well repays me. As to the talk of unrest, it's all bunkum,—except among the baboos and a few mischievous priests in their pay. What does the average native know about the partition of Bengal? He knows nothing, as a rule, about political divisions at all, and as for wanting to be ruled by his own people, the last thing in the world he wants is a native judge. He knows well enough what that means—judgment for the side that pays most. No—they get some Western learning, but they don't get made straight. That's one of the reasons why it's impossible to give a native engineer a top post anywhere. He can't resist bribery, and his sense of 'izzat' makes him diddle his employers twice over. After all it is a point of honour with your native not to take a bribe from an Englishman; he regards it as entirely different from taking bribes from his own people. That is his sense of 'izzat,' and to compensate for his loss of personal honour he must make double out of the deal. The other reason is that a native always loses his head in a crisis."

I do not think there was one thing this engineer said, except the last, about which I had not heard the direct opposite from other Englishmen; but he spoke from his own experience as they did, and the various views must be weighed against each other.

"Ooty" was deserted. There were no happy holiday bachelors under canvas tents on the club links, no one at all in the hotels. The place is not unlike Newara Eliya from the scenic point of view as well as the social. There were the same arum lilies growing near the lake.

Living in small huts on the hillside I saw a few Todas, some of the few remaining of those early inhabitants of India allied to the Dravidians, but of Scythian or Mongolian origin. Driven out by the Aryans, in their assumed invasion from Central Asia, the Dravidians and their Mongolian cousins were forced down to Southern India and Ceylon, remaining here and there among the hills. The Todas number only a little over a thousand and are said to be steadily decreasing in numbers. As they are polyandrous, it is indeed surprising that any are left at all. Other tribes surviving from these early peoples are the Bhils, Kols, Ghonds, Santals and Nagas.

"Ooty" is 2000 feet higher than Coonoor, but the finest mountain views are from the latter neighbourhood. I drove back by night and all along the road bullock-carts, with lanterns swinging underneath them, were slowly plodding down with loads of coffee and tea. On the rack-railway there is only passenger traffic, so they have to go all the way to Mettapalaiyam. The drivers were all sound asleep and my "sayce" was on the road pretty often, turning the cattle aside to let us pass. On one side the rocks rose precipitously, and on the other stretched out a vast panorama of hills, clothed in a dress more mystic than white samite, the soft pale clarity of moon-lit mountain air.

It was very late when I reached the railway station, and finding all locked up I slept on the pavement rolled in rug and ulster.

When I awoke at sunrise the Eastern sky was all rose and amber, and in the sharp crisp morning air the bells of the horses jingled gaily as I drove up through the woods above Coonoor, past snug villas now nearly all "to let," for the season does not begin till February. A zigzag road it was, with roses and wild heliotrope along its stone-built sides. The eucalyptus were 50 feet high, rhododendrons with profusion of crimson blossoms grew to large trees, and the graceful star-topped tree-ferns were very tall.

Suddenly rounding a corner of the road a majestic landscape broke upon my sight, rising sheer out of plains which seemed to stretch away to a misty infinity. There was a waterfall above the road, and the horses splashed through a torrent under creepers hanging from bending tree-tops. Then the road crept along a narrow ledge with four or five hundred feet of sheer drop below. I left the carriage to climb to the view-point I wanted, near what is called Lady Canning's Seat, and thence painted the Droog, the hill from the steep summit of which Tippoo Sultan is said to have thrown his prisoners of war. I have seen since other "blue mountains," and it was interesting to compare the rich intensity of the colouring in the Nilgiris with the more violet "bloom" of the gum-clad mountains of Australia, and especially this view of the Droog with Govett's Leap, a scene in New South Wales of similar configuration.

CHAPTER VII

CALCUTTA

In a heavy storm of rain, thunder and lightning early one Sunday morning the British India Company's steamship *Bengala,* on which I had travelled from Rangoon, began making her way up the Hooghly. Grey mud-banks appeared vaguely in the stinging drift. There were toddy-palms here and there and villages of thatched huts with plantains about them, the broad green leaves standing out against the darker background. Leaves, blown on the wind, whirled aimlessly across the dirty sea.

The few passengers on the *Bengala* were all eager to see "James and Mary"; and beyond another village on a spit of sand with a crowd of small fishing-boats at anchor, we passed the now celebrated spot where a couple of masts still protruded above the water. All hands had been called to be ready before we reached this fatal place, but no siren voices sounded from the tragic sands.

At Budge Bridge, about 14 miles from Calcutta, where there are large oil storage tanks, we began to pass jute-mills on the opposite bank and many brick-making places. At Garden Reach we dropped the pilot and picked up the Harbour Master just as a Natal coolie emigrant ship, the *Umfuli,* passed us on her way out.

Then—a crowd of shipping—the usual slow scramble of disembarking—and I stood in the capital city of all India.

In a large park called the Maidan, a tall white-fluted column rises from an Egyptian base. This is the Auchterlony Monument, and from the top of it a splendid view is obtained of the general plan of the town. At one end of the Maidan you can see Government House, and at the other the race-course and polo-ground beyond the skating rink, boxing-booths and circus tents. Fort William lies on the riverside and opposite to it, looking on to the Maidan as Piccadilly does on to the Green Park, lies Chowringhee, with the Grand Hotel, clubs, stores, museums and English residences.

And beyond Chowringhee, north of all this, is an immense city of native streets, bazaars, squares, temples and theatres; while at Howrah, on the south side of the river, extends a long series of mighty factories, jute-mills and engineering works. It is on this side that is situated the great Howrah Railway Station, the terminus of the Eastern Bengal State Railway, and there is as yet only one bridge to carry the heavy traffic across the river. This is in appearance a kind of glorified pontoon, but its series of projecting barge ends recalls a little the long line of buttresses on old London Bridge, seen in Van Wyngaerde's drawing. At every hour of the day this great artery of pulsing life is a close-packed moving mass of men and traffic (at night for a couple of hours it is sometimes closed to vehicles).

Bengal Government Offices, Calcutta.

Reproduced by permission of the Visual Instruction Committee of the Colonial Office.

The English stranger, anxious for his mail, will probably soon find his way to the white marble steps of the General Post Office. At the top of the steps seven tall columns support the great dome, and the round-arched entries between them are closed as to the upper part by wooden screens with cross shutter-bars. At first as you walk into the shadow out of the blazing sunlight all seems dark as Erebus, and then gradually you make out between columns the various bureaux with their little brown-framed peep-holes like railway station booking-offices.

Inside the poste restante division a native gentleman, in gold-rimmed spectacles and a shawl of a reddish-yellow plaid over his shoulders, is looking through the letters of a mail just arrived, and some empty chairs at a neighbouring writing-table covered with blue cloth offer comfort for immediate perusal. In the roof yellow light comes faintly through the covered windows which circle it just below the dome—that vast white dome which dominates the city more than do the towers of the High Court, even as news is more clamorous than justice.

Chuprassees and servants come and go and presently you thread your way among them and emerge again, as I did, into the glare of daylight in Dalhousie Square, where the Bengal Government Offices are reflected in the blue water of a large "tank."

I crossed Koda Ghat Street, among bullock-carts and gharries, and turned to look back at the Post Office clock with its black hands pointing to black figures. At the gate into the square a policeman was buying betel, and close by, with sage-green railings round it, I saw the white marble statue of Dharbanga sitting cross-legged, with sword in one hand held across his knees and the other resting on a small shield target,—a fine piece by Onslow Ford. This is a stopping-place for electric trams, and great blocks of office buildings face the road on this side of the square, such as those of the Hong Kong and Shanghai Banking Corporation, the Standard Life Assurance Company, and, in slate-coloured plaster and red brick, the Central Telegraph Office. Opposite to them on the edge of the square the Doric columns of the Dalhousie Institute shield a statue of the Marquis of Hastings.

A young man was carrying an old one upon his shoulders, as Aeneas carried his father Anchises: beggars importuned: and as I turned up Old Courthouse Street a child, weighed down by a heavy baby, touched my arm appealingly. I hurried on past great shops, Cook's Offices and a jeweller's shining in white and gold, big chemists and diamond merchants. Four nearly naked coolies carrying a black palanquin knocked against me at the end of Government Place.

Crossing the West Entrance to Government House you notice how the lawns in front are covered with great marquee offices on either side of the dragon-borne gun on the red ground-space in front of the main building. I was now on the Maidan, and walking past a group of Chinamen across the grass to cut off the corner, soon reached Chowringhee and my rooms in the Grand Hotel, that huge straggling caravanserai, otherwise known as "Mrs Monks!" They were in a part of the building dubbed by Calcutta youth "The Monastery," from its proximity to the stage-door of a Vaudeville Opera House. The windows of the auditorium, always open, were only separated by a few yards from my rooms.

A Door must be Open or Shut is the title of one of De Musset's plays, but I had already learned that in India a door locked is by no means shut. It is often a mere skeleton of wood provided with cross slats; and although an inner curtain ensures privacy, no external sound escapes the inmate. During my stay in Calcutta, until after each midnight, *The Merry Widow,* alternated with other musical comedies and like Coleridge's *Wedding Guest*—"I could not choose but hear."

The other inmates of the hotel consisted partly of tourists, partly of residents, partly of men "on short leave" with nothing to do, and partly of officials whose patronage they desired. My immediate neighbour, who borrowed a new shirt from me, which he did not return, was by no means a typical member of the service. He would have afforded copy to an anti-English agitator, but to me appeared merely an instance of a man whose character was unsuited to the mixture of freedom and isolation which life in India involves.

A very different type of man was D. who had just come up from the Malabar Coast. In that part of the country long settled, or rather long unsettled, there are a number of people of Arab descent. A riotous and lawless crew, they gave such constant trouble that a law was finally passed called the Mopla Law, under which any Mopla, as these people are called, could be instantly deported "on suspicion of being a suspect." Still they were rampageous, and not infrequently a party of pillaging scoundrels would only be overcome by military aid.

Now, shortly after my acquaintance was moved to that part of the Madras Presidency a party of Moplas, after generally running riot, entrenched themselves in a strong position on a rocky hilltop. D. was called over to the place in a hurry, and a captain in command of some British troops at hand was eager for action. "Just give me the word," said he, "and we'll soon have them out of that." He could not, of course, move without the civil authority giving permission.

"No," D. replied; "if I gave you the word, you would shoot or take these Moplas, but in doing it you would certainly lose some of your own men. Every soldier killed means incalculable harm, and I don't intend one single life to be lost over this affair." He insisted on their merely sitting round the hill to prevent escape, and in a few days' time down came the Moplas to treat. D. talked to them, deported nobody, and for many many years there has, he told me, not been one serious case of Mopla trouble on the Malabar Coast. Well, there's nothing in that story warranting any general statement. It only shows one of the countless situations with which the Indian civil servant has to deal. The English officer was ready to risk his own and his men's lives in a moment, as he should be, and the English magistrate knew when to hold him back. Both were needed and both were there.

On my first evening in Calcutta, wishing to see the largest number of Europeans together that I could, I went to the evening service at St Paul's Cathedral. The church consists of an unusually wide nave, with a green barrelled roof studded with Tudor roses—side aisles and a tall spire at the western end. The rain had stopped and the roads were drying a little, but it was cold and raw, and many ladies were actually wearing furs! Choir-boys in violet gowns and white surplices began to congregate near the large organ at the north-east corner. Gradually the church filled. There was just a small sprinkling of Eurasians and here and there a native face, but the congregation was almost entirely European.

Hanging from the ceiling were candelabras of electric lights, but a brighter galaxy of ecclesiastical stars was shortly to appear. A Synod had been held during the previous week, and ten out of its eleven bishops took part in this service. The procession, with so many pastoral staffs, was quite an imposing one, and it was most interesting to compare the genuflexions of these people, the rich vestments, gilded staffs and various emblems of worship and authority with those of the native religions. The sermon, which was preached by the then Bishop of Calcutta, dealt largely with the allegory of the Church as the Bride of Christ, and the duties of bishops in her preparation for Marriage. It was rambling and tedious, but the choir sang well and the playing of the fine organ was admirable.

The 12th of January was the ninth day of the ten days' Hindoo festival of the Sankarati Puja. I went over to the Howrah Bridge to see the bathing. On the stone building on the right, as I looked over the bridge railing at the top of the great flight of steps, a slab is let into the wall inscribed in English:—

> "This stone is dedicated by a few Englishwomen to the memory of those pilgrims, mostly women, who perished with the 'Sir John Lawrence' in the cyclone of the 25th May, 1887."

A golden-brown butterfly was settled near the stone on the grey stucco wall. The river, dirty everywhere, was here thickly strewn with floating rubbish. The whole of the steps and the edge of the river were crowded with bathers and people ministering to them—some grave and deliberate, others lively and splashing, washing their bright-coloured draperies and clothes and rubbing their own brown bodies with the sacred water.

They were Mahrattas, these people, and about the steps squatted men ready to paint the caste mark afresh upon their foreheads for a few pice. They trimmed and twisted and smoothed their hair, gazing in little looking-glasses for the final touches, and passing through the stone shelter building above the steps, put pice into a brass tray in the street, where a trunk of sandalwood was set up in plaster and four lingams, two white and two black, were heaped with marigolds and other flower garlands in an altar shaped like a well-head.

All this was, of course, going on cheek by jowl with the traffic of the town. The stream of laden bullock-carts, gharries and palkis flowed over the bridge as swiftly as the water beneath it. On the opposite, the Howrah side, are many works and factories, including the chief jute-mills. From there to Ulabaria, far down the river, there are on the Hooghly banks seventy-eight jute- and cotton-mills and presses. They have doubled during the past eight or ten years, and in the works I visited of one company some distance south of the great Howrah Railway Station, from 110 to 120 tons of sacks called gunnies and Hessian cloth are turned out daily. That company alone employs 8000 hands. I saw the great piles of raw jute in coarse strands as it comes up from the country, and the carding machines and weaving machines. For the weaving and finishing, most of the machinery comes from Dundee, and for the spinning from Leeds. Amid the ceaseless whirr, buzz and bustle of the workshops, I watched the dexterous children using their feet with almost equal skill as their hands, catching bobbins between their toes while twisting up broken threads with their fingers. I saw the main driving engines—from Hargreaves, Bolton—of 2020 horse-power, and outside in a narrow and squalid alley I saw a shrine of Juggernaut, grotesque and hideous!

I visited the great Iron Foundry of Burn & Co., who have also, 100 miles away on the East India Railway, great pottery works, whence 30-inch drain-pipes and stoneware and tesselated pavements are sent all over India. At the engineering works they employ 5000 natives and as many as sixty Europeans. Here was a batch of plate girders just finished, each 10 feet deep, the largest yet made in India. In one of the vast and deafening workshops three 10-ton overhead electric trains were moving up and down. Here were electrically-driven machines for heavy punching and shearing, and I asked the young English clerk, who was taking me round, how he liked the native people. He said:—"I like 'em well enough, but you know—the fact is—they're chronic"; and at one side of a noisy yard, on a small square landing at the top of some steps, I saw a Mohammedan at prayer.

In the afternoon of the same day I went out by tram to Kalighat. Near one side of the road where I left the tram was a pond—an old-established washing- and drying-ground—where, from early days, the clothes of Calcutta have been severely banged. I walked under some linen flapping from clothes-lines to watch a dhobie at the water-edge beating clothes upon a ridged wooden board. He punctuated the action with such ejaculations as "Oo-er! oo-er! oo-er! oo-er! om! om! om!" and "e-ay! e-ay! ee-ay!"

These men are all independent dhobies who pay to the Government one rupee per annum for the right to wash here and to use the drying-ground.

I turned up a side road for the famous Kali Temple past a building labelled "Dispensary," with plaster falling away from its brickwork and several rows of dung-cakes patted on to the wall to dry for fuel. There were a number of loiterers hereabouts, and a man soon tacked himself on to me as "guide." I came to a temple of Siva (husband of the blood-loving Kali), where there was a well-shaped depression under a stone octagonal-pillared canopy or cupola. I went up some brick steps outside at the back, whence looking down from above I could see in the centre of the shallow well the flower-adorned lingam of the god who is worshipped here with garlands and Ganges water. At each side of the narrow road were now small shops filled with large crude hand-paintings and coloured plaster figures of the terrible goddess.

Here, another would-be guide assailed me with these words:—"I will explain myself to you: follow me, please; no need to listen to other people"—and another:—

"I am an old priest here—talk with me"—and another:—

"Listen to me and I will explain all things here."

Then the third, pushing one of the others aside:—"Let him listen to me, an old priest."

I passed another Siva shrine with a copper cobra attached to a lingam. On the left of the road here was an old tank, a filthy-looking pond covered with green scum, with some coconut palms hanging over it. "Barren women bathe here and then they get children," said one of the would-be guides.

The other men now tried to get my recognition. "What is the necessity of so many to explain—I am the priest."

"*You* the priest—ah! *who* are you—you are the *broker*!"

They were beginning to quarrel, and I settled the matter by declaring I would have for guide the oldest among them.

I had now reached the precincts of the Temple of Kali and passed under an arch into a quad where three small cows were eating accumulated leaf and flower refuse, trodden marigold garlands and scattered leaves.

The temple, which had very little beauty, was in the centre of this quad. At one corner was a Munshi tree. "If any man will be bite of a snake," said the old priest, "and come here, he will be cured from the bite; and the barren women who get no sons, they will tie stones like this"—upon the branches many small pieces of stone hung by short strings. The trunk of this tree was patched and smutched with dabs of red colour put on by pilgrims.

"And this," pointing to the building in the centre, "is Mother Kali's Temple, and the image of Mother Kali is in the inside of this temple."

The worshippers of Siva's wives, of whom Kali is the most popular, make one of three divisions of modern Hinduism, the other two being that of the Siva worshippers and that of the Vaishnavas or worshippers of Vishnu.

As I walked round to the other side I saw some women upon the ground with bleeding heads of kids and goats. These women are the servants of the temple. They and "the poor" have the heads as perquisites; the bodies of the victims are taken away by those pilgrims who brought them for sacrifice, and are either cooked and eaten upon the Ganges bank or at home.

Two forked posts, one very much larger than the other, stood upright in the ground. The creatures to be killed have their heads forced down between the forks of wood—to be cut off by one blow of a sword. The larger post is for buffaloes, slaughtered one day a week; and the smaller for goats and kids, many of which are killed every day. A stream of blood trickled away from this smaller post, and a number of crows were hopping about the ground. "If you will kindly come a little earlier at time of sacrifice, that is very nice," said the priest; but I had no eagerness for that sight. It was far from the sides of Latmos—here was no sacred sward, and the poor flowers crushed into a sodden mass had long forgot the dew. Paris' voice was silent here. The deeper feelings of these people were of dread rather than veneration, the scene lacked all dignity and squalor reigned.

The man who kills is a blacksmith—a low caste man, and two pice are paid to him by the pilgrims for every goat killed. There were many naked and half-naked children about and a few mangy and diseased dogs. To most English people flesh is, of course, not the rare luxury it is to these Hindoos, and the English avoid the sight of its preparation for the table, although some still invoke the blessing of God upon its consumption. The scene was disagreeable, but so also is that of the more protracted family pig-killing outside a Wiltshire labourer's cottage!

In another corner of the quad I looked at a shrine to Vishnu—the creator, and his favourite lady, Radha—and then turned down the narrow street between the temple and the river, lined with shops containing articles for the pilgrims. Some were filled with little sets at three pice each of the following articles: a small purple mat which, if wetted, will give blood-colour to water, three thin bracelets, two red and one black, and a tiny box of red powder.

Near was another shrine—a red Ganesh—Mother Kali's son—and more Siva lingams garlanded with marigolds. There were men with faces painted red near some pilgrim's restrooms, and stalls of Bengali toys such as pilgrims take home to their children. There were also on sale here English tin-made abominations with the familiar poisonous colouring, trumpets and hansom cabs—perhaps more appropriate in the vicinity of the death-delighting goddess than in Ealing or Bermondsey. The whole of this narrow street, which is long and leads all the way to the river, had been paved with flagstones by one, Gobordhour Dass, as an offering to Kali.

Juggernaut, Hanuman, and in addition to these Hindoo deities—Buddha—I saw together in one shrine. On the bank of the river are some large houses for pilgrims, painted all over with various subjects. Kali, holding her head in two of her four hands, spouts blood in tall fountains: Hanuman, the monkey god, fights with the eagle god, and the wife of Vishnu plays peacefully with her husband's legs.

Near by were five trees (not pictured but actual) growing together as one, with their roots intertwined—Peepul, Bodh, Banyan, Neem and Oshhuck, their many-shaped leaves trembling in the air in an arboreal *pas de cinq*, with lingams round the base of the joined trunks. Four men passed me here carrying a dead body.

I had to walk back the same way that I had come; and as I crossed the courtyard of the Kali temple a strange figure in rags stood blowing upon a large white conch-shell a long, long strange note. A white conch-shell on the wrist marks a pilgrimage to the great seaside Siva Temple of Rameswaram in the South, but the conch-shell is also one of the marks of the Vaishnavas. "He is a mad one," said the priest; "he eats the mouse and snakes."

While I was in Calcutta I wanted to go to one of the native theatres, but the only one the hotel people knew about was a Parsee theatre in Durumtolla Street. I saw there *Kismatka Sitara*, a serious version of *Ali Baba and the Forty Thieves*; but I was determined to see a Bengali company, in spite of the remonstrances of my table companions at the Grand Hotel, who were perfectly satisfied with the Merry Widow touring company, and declared it was not reasonable for an Englishman to visit native theatres at all.

It was a Sunday evening when I drove along Bentinck Street and approached the neighbourhood of Beadon Square. The performances at the Bengali theatres begin very early, so it was not yet dark and a soft after-sunset light irradiated the thousands of tiny shops with all the myriad kinds of work going on in them.

There were large three-storeyed houses on each side of the road, now with balconies full of women; then I passed a vast building with tall Ionic columns and two great porticoes—a Nawab's palace; then hundreds more little houses, and at last Beadon Square with its palm trees and white statue. And the warm glow fell upon the ample robes of many people walking up and down after the heat and turmoil of the day and upon many white oxen, and against the sky, rows of seated figures watched from the tops of walls and from the edges of roofs; while all the time, interwoven with humanity like the warp and woof of Indian city life, here, there and everywhere skipped and walked and flapped and scrimmaged the squawking black innumerable crows.

Bengalee Actress, Miss Tin Corry Dass the younger.

After I had been in to the box-office in front of the theatre and purchased my ticket—an orchestra stall for three rupees—I waited in a rectangular court at one side of the building. Over the row of doors giving entrance to various parts of the house, there was a veranda, and facing this, some seats by an oval-railed enclosure containing ornamental plants. On the other side of this gambolled fifteen or twenty white rabbits behind wire-netting. One star was just showing in the sky, which was now a pale rose colour, and against it I could see the top of a coconut-palm.

Most of the baboos waiting outside the two rupee places wore socks and leather shoes and white muslin drapery over which they had a short coat and then the toga-like outer coloured robe. I was thinking of the first scene in *Cyrano de Bergerac* when I saw someone setting up a stall of mineral waters, but was still more reminded of it when I was admitted before the other doors were opened, and watched a man lighting the lamps in the vast empty theatre.

The interior was arranged very much like most of the London theatres, with a few special differences. There was one row of orchestra stalls, then rows of seats at two rupees, and behind, the "pit" of one rupee places. When their door was opened, the pit crowd came in, laughing and scampering over the benches. I caught sight of my servant, Tambusami, among them. He had bought a grand orange-red scarf with silk flowers on it for this occasion, and with his long black hair tied up behind, had a droll air of vanity mingled with restrained and decorous enjoyment.

Over the pit hung the oil-lamps, but now electric lights flashed out from the ceiling. I had thought at first there was only one floor above the ground level, a tier of loges or boxes (some of which were arranged so that their occupants could lie or sit upon cushions), with a large one in the centre facing the stage. Suddenly I realized that what I had taken to be dark hangings over the lofty wall-space above this tier of boxes was net blind, and a momentary effect of light showed me that behind it zenana ladies, safe in its reticulated seclusion from roving eyes, were examining the house with more eager curiosity than was shown by the male audience.

Behind me a boy brought two baboos some betel (green betel leaves wrapping the crushed areca nut and lime). The orchestra in this theatre was under the boxes to the left of the stalls, and the musicians in white robes were now moving to their places.

The name of the play was *Sarola,* a serious drama of modern Indian life, and fearfully pathetic—Richepin rather than Balzac—and yet a study of manners. The hero, Shoshifuzu, who has hitherto lived on the bounty of a more prosperous brother, is brought by the meanness and intolerance of that brother's wife to leave his own wife Sarola and their child at home, while he journeys on foot to the distant capital to seek for remunerative employment. The journey itself is full of picturesque incident, but the greatest interest centres in the home of Shoshifuzu, where an ingenious scoundrel, Godadhar, played with great drollery and inimitable skill by Kasi Nath Chatterjee, intercepts all the supplies forwarded by the absent husband. Godadhar has far more real villainy about him than either Jingle or old Eccles, but is yet a low comedy character and is played by Chatterjee with an unction and humour that none but the elder Coquelin could have surpassed.

The day when no woman acted at the native theatres is evidently as much forgotten as it is with us; and Miss Tara Dasse, who played the intensely pathetic part of Sarola with a most tender voice, recalled to a Western mind in a protracted end some of the most appealing deaths of Sarah Bernhardt.

Another evening I went to the Minerva, also a Bengali theatre close to Beadon Square, and saw *Dolita Fronini*. A gentleman, who introduced himself to me as the stage-manager, came and sat by me for some time, kindly telling me the story of the piece, and for the sake of his new interpretation of "melodrama," as well as for the light thrown on the life of any people by a study of its amusements, I made the following note of his actual words:—

"It is an opera," said the stage-manager, "like full of music and dramatic of course—there are a good many melodies, so you can call it a melodrama. Dolita Fronini is a name according only to the circumstances of the heroine, so that she is not liked by the lover and therefore she is as if a smashed snake. That snake bites very ferociously, and that snake is her. A Bengali baboo went to Bombay to see: and he waited to a friend of his who is a Mahratta, and he has been very carefully taken in to the family and is allowed to wait till he fully sees the Bombay city. And that Dolita Fronini was not named that, but her name was Bilas Bottee. She was a Bengali lady too, long living in Bombay with that Mahratta gentleman and his wife. When the Bengali gentleman was first introduced into the family, he was unaware about the family custom of the Bombay Mahrattas. There is no zenana system with them—their ladies are open to all. This baboo looked at their behaviours with a strange look, because the Bengali family system is the zenana; but that Bilas Bottee, who was an inmate long in the Mahratta house, was a Bram-maker, a follower of Brahma, and she had no zenana system also. This lady Bilas Bottee loved the gentleman, that Bengali baboo, but the baboo loved the Mahratta lady. The Mahratta lady, according to their customs, behaved with the baboo freely. The baboo thought that she loved him, but she did not—she behaved freely, only not with any viciousness. The Mahratta lady explained to the baboo that her husband was examining him about the firmness of his character. When the mystery is all out and the baboo came to understand, Bilas Bottee went away as a mendicant,—Dolita Fronini!"

But the gun, which is the curtain signal at the Minerva, had sounded before this—the opera had begun and a chorus was singing. "They are singing," said the stage-manager, "that you will never see such a city in the world as Bombay. The climate is temperate here, not very bitter wind too, and there is no cold. You ought to come to walk in the morning and the evening in Bombay, and you would forget all about the world. Wine is very cheap here, and if you drink a little you will be jolly all about."

Between the acts an old gentleman was introduced to me as a very famous actor—he was a Mr A. Mustaphi, and his greatest role is that of Mirzapha in the historical play, *Siraj ud Doulah*.

After another act I was entertained behind the scenes by the actor who was playing the part of the Bengali baboo. He received me in a pale-blue quilted dressing-gown, and wanted me to sketch every member of the company in my notebook. His crowning attention was to send for the scene-painter of the theatre to sit on one side of me for the rest of the evening!

At these theatres I met with extreme courtesy from first to last, and shall long cherish the kind attention of a charming old gentleman from Delhi (to judge by his head-dress) who, speaking little English, showed me the miniatures of his children upon his watch-chain and went out, between the acts, to buy me a little buttonhole of roses.

"A Charming Old Gentleman from Delhi."

The mention of roses reminds me to say a few words of the Calcutta Gardens. At one end of the Maidan, beyond the race-course, are the Zoological Gardens laid out, I know not by whom, with very good taste—worthy of Milner or Sir Joseph Paxton. The houses are handsome and commodious, the open air enclosures are both wide and spacious, and there are good collections to fill them. I especially enjoyed watching here a native of the Nepaul Terai, a big one-horned rhinoceros. On the evening of my visit he was energetic and lively after a splash in his tank. There was an irresistible comicality about the great unwieldy brute—a very Falstaff of quadrupeds—trotting at express speed.

But more beautiful is the Kampani Bagan, the botanical garden on the other side of the Hooghly. In that garden there is no traffic and no dust—only a few delicate little Anglo-Indian children taking tea under the giant banyan.

March is the time to see the orchids, of which these gardens have a large variety, but few plants were in flower at the time I was there. The houses are curiously different from such as we know at Kew. They are simply wire frames covered with creepers to keep off greatest heat and heaviest rain—creepers such as the *Tinas pora crispa* from Java, with its hanging roots. Sometimes the roof is covered with dry palm-leaves (*Phoenix sylvestris*).

There is one tree in the garden which I think quite as interesting as the world-famous great Banyan—a large handsome tree fifty or sixty feet high, with big leaves. Dr Gage, the Director of the Gardens, told me it is the only specimen of its kind known in the world, and that every leaf shown in European herbaria has come from Kampani Bagan. Unfortunately, the trunk is being honeycombed by big black boring bees (it is dangerous to go up into the tree because of them). This solitary giant is called *Anthocephalus macrophyllus*. It came many years ago from Abornia, a small island in the Malay Archipelago, and has a flower like a miniature drumstick.

In the palm-house in "Griffith Avenue" I saw some double coconuts (coco de mer) from the Seychelles.

Along the waterside is a handsome row of the country almond-tree, which grows in the moister regions of Bengal and Siam. This is the *Terminalia catappa* with large leaves and is not in the least like the almond proper.

The avenue of toddy-palms is deservedly famous, though these gardens cannot compete in grandeur with those of Peradeniya in Ceylon. In one part of the grounds (the Gardens cover 270 acres) are many screw-pines (*Pandanus utilissimus*), but best of all I liked the long avenue of stately *Oreodoxa regia*. At the head of this there is a white marble monument of singular beauty, called "Kyd's Monument." It is by the sculptor Banks, and takes the form of a Grecian urn with figures round it on a tall plinth surmounting a circular platform.

After sundown when all visitors had gone away, as the light of the afterglow bathed it in a soft effulgence, and the wide, long avenue of palms stretched away into mist, the lovely marble seemed to have found perfect setting. As the light waned again the jackals began calling and filled the air with strange melancholy.

Avenue of Oreodoxa Palms, Botanical Gardens, Calcutta.

Reproduced by permission of the Visual Instruction Committee of the Colonial Office.

CHAPTER VIII

MY FIRST SIGHT OF THE HIMALAYAS

When I changed at Siliguri on to the Darjeeling Himalaya Railway, the moon hung high overhead in the morning sky, and the mountains slowly appeared out of the warm rosy mists of the lower air. I was still crossing the lowlands, yellow reaches of paddy stubble dotted with small white storks, wide watercourses and tall clumps of graceful bamboos looking nearly as yellow as the dry paddy stalks.

Then the train entered a belt of dense jungle, a forest track of teak and other large trees. At Sookua Station, bougainvillias and a creeper loaded with orange-coloured blossoms made gay colour. The train jolted and wriggled up the slopes in zigzag curves; creepers hung from tall trees like great falling cascades of little golden leaves. The grade was very steep, and in an hour I was looking back on the plains and down upon the forest-clad lower slopes, over which a few wreaths of mist floated like belated spirits that have outstayed cockcrow and move forlorn in the unwonted day.

Suddenly past Tindaria, 2800 feet up, between the trees overhead, appeared a tea-plantation with its little green bushes in neat serried rows. The forest had now given place to smaller trees, and here and there among the great sweeps of hill were grey and dun patches, bare except for sparse dry herbage and small fern growth. The large leaves of plantains were still visible now and again, and here and there the white hanging trumpets of the poisonous datura. Bare rock became more frequent, and screw-pines appeared among the trees and peach trees flushed with pink blossom. Towards ten o'clock the heat haze gathered over the lower slopes, and the plain with its shining watercourses disappeared in a veil of mist.

Near Kurseong, tree-ferns bordered the line; and almost immediately beyond this station came the first view of Himalayan snows. Only for the next quarter of an hour's run, however, were the white peaks visible. The train then curled along the sides of the mighty hill-slopes, and at an elevation of 6000 feet there were plenty of big trees again with masses of parasite mistletoe on their branches and tree-ferns in their shadows; the leaves of the all-glorious forest glittered in the sunlight like jewels—how Constable would have revelled in them!

All the men at these latter stopping-places were short and thick-set, and the women's ornaments were either gold or gilded and no longer silver like those of so many of the people in the plains. At Ghoom, 7407 feet up, white votive strips of linen with prayers upon them fluttered from sticks upright on all the roofs. At that station a little bearded dwarf came begging—a dwarf with a long pigtail, successor to an old woman who had been well known as the "Witch of Ghoom."

"Woodlands," the hotel at Darjeeling, was the most comfortable I found anywhere in India, and Mr Righi, the young Italian manager, kindly put his private servant, Teenduk, a Thibetan, entirely at my service as guide during my stay.

Teenduk, who told me that Mr Righi 'catched' him five years ago, had under his fur cap one of the most good-tempered faces I ever saw, full of quiet humour and readiness to respond to the faintest smile. He was cleaner than most of the native people at Darjeeling, and certainly washed his face sometimes. This is a thing which Thibetans rarely do, and some people declare that they never take off any clothes, putting on a new garment over the old when that is much worn. The dirt, together with a mixture of pig's blood which the women apply to their faces, gives them a mottled appearance, with black spots over a mahogany ground; but their sense of fun, united to a slow and laconic manner, makes them irresistibly lovable, and indicates that although cleanliness may be next to godliness, humour is the quality which man has added to make mortality endurable.

The high snow peaks of Kinchinjunga and the neighbouring mountains are between forty and fifty miles away from Darjeeling, and seem to hang in the sky as if too beautiful to be altogether of our world. The vast distance and the appearance of sudden leap to such supreme heights, help to give an unreal, mysterious and almost visionary grandeur, which is further increased at this time of year by the fact of their being only occasionally visible.

It was a jolly six-mile ride in the early morning for the sunrise views from the top of Tiger Hill—bright moonlight at starting, with the shadows sharp and clear. I could still see them faintly on the snow as I dismounted at the top just before dawn, and set myself with cold fingers to paint the strange beauty of the sunrise upon the snows. Gradually the cold light of the moon changed to a warm soft glow of golden amber, and that again to rose. The sharp outlines of Kinchinjunga were clear from the first, and presently, much farther to the west, appeared the three humpy peaks of Everest, 120 miles away. Little Righi has been a good way toward the summit of Kinchinjunga. He was one of the five members of the expedition of 1905, when the loss of Lieutenant Pache with three coolies, at a height of 22,000 feet, caused the others to give up the attempt.

As a showman, Righi was well equipped, having that understanding of individual needs so gratifying to the tourist. To the top of Tiger Hill had also ridden for that sunrise a party of Americans, whose one purpose was to be able to say they had seen Mount Everest. Their impatience was considerable, and after arguing among themselves as to which was the summit in question, one lady appealed to Righi to support her selection. "Oh, yes," said he, "that's Everest," and they were well content. "We don't often see it, but I like them to be satisfied," he explained to me when the mountain, by good luck, really appeared later on in another part of the horizon.

There is no regiment quartered at Darjeeling, but the planters of the district make Company A of the Northern Bengal Mounted Rifles (who possessed a Maxim gun before any regular troops in India); and one morning I rode out to the

Lebong parade-ground, above the Runjeet valley, to see a muster. Tea-planters and other business-men thoroughly enjoyed the occasion, and there was a spirited display of tent-pegging with swords instead of lances.

Darjeeling is about 7000 feet high on a ridge above the Runjeet River, which reaches the Ganges via another river called the Teester: and one day I rode with Righi 12 miles down to the Runjeet, and having previously obtained the necessary Government permit we crossed by a suspension bridge to a village in Independent Sikkim, where we were refreshed with native beer made from Marwa, a kind of millet seed and sucked through a hollow reed from a long-shaped vessel made of a section of bamboo.

The river here flowed along the bottom of a magnificent gorge with precipitous sides, and on the return journey I had as wild a ride as I am likely to experience.

Righi had started back a full half-hour before me, and my pony hearing afar off the neigh of his companion, galloped hard along a narrow ledge with a sheer drop below. Full of spirit, and very strong, these Thibetan ponies will gallop up a steep slope where another horse would crawl; and here, on the level, mine went like the wind, kicking loose stones into the flood below.

Near Darjeeling there is a small Llama monastery, a two-storeyed building with a broad foot-wide black border painted round the doors and window openings. Outside stand, in a semicircle, tall poles with long strips of linen prayer-flags fastened lengthwise from the tops downwards, and on each side of the main entrance a row of prayer-wheels mounted on end and fastened to the wall under wooden eaves. The sight of these last carried me back far to the West to a little Gothic church of St Nicholas in Prisiac, where a wooden prayer-wheel of local make, of which I think there are few in Europe, is dropping to pieces with age.

Within the monastery a row of clean-looking brass bowls of water stood in front of some bronze figures, and on each side of a central shrine was ranged a series of pigeon-holes containing the monastery library, while, leaning against the latter, stood some metal trumpets 6 feet long, jointed and telescopic. Upstairs I was shown the large grotesque wooden masks and beautiful brocaded silk dresses for the priest-dances.

I have travelled in many parts of the world now, but I have not yet found any place where there is no dancing. Even inanimate nature quickens into rhythmic movement. The waves dance to the sun and the stars dance in the sea, and in the world of sentient beings birds dance to their mates. It expressed the exuberance of children's joy before ever it became an art, and whether or not Aristotle was justified in his high estimate, dancing is more universal than poetry.

I could not see a Thibetan priest dance, but I did enjoy, thanks again to Mr Righi, a dance of Thibetan peasants, very elaborately costumed and weirdly pantomimic. It was called the "Amban" dance, and represented the homage of a group of Thibetan heads of villages to the "Amban," who was, as far as I could understand, some kind of ambassador or trading representative of the Chinese Government—but mingled with it were imagery and symbolism of local legend and mythology.

The dance was held at night on an open space of grass, and began with the appearance of a little strange flitting figure bearing a stick in each hand which held a white cloth stretched above the head. Up and down like some erratic moth the figure bounded, ran and postured; and presently the "Amban" presented himself grandly dressed on a hobby-horse and wearing a long peacock's feather in his conical Chinese hat. Later in the dance entered two "lions" or "dragons," gigantic creatures made up of two men each, with undulating bodies (hung with white Yak hair), tails, and wildly grotesque scarlet heads with enormous eyes and gaping "practicable" mouths, from which large red tongues flapped or depended. Then came a peacock, a sacred bird, which the dragons sought vainly to harm; and an extremely funny turtle, which they eventually devoured, the child performer slipping out of its bamboo framework before the latter was gobbled up.

Sunday morning is the best time to see the bazaar at Darjeeling, and the types of people from many different provinces. Here was a bearded Kashmiri squatting at his door, grinding seeds in a small mortar; there was a group of Nepauli ladies richly-dressed and accompanied by servants. They wore a strange head-dress, a large circular plaque fastened at an angle above the hair and ornamented with jewels; there were Lepchu men from Sikkim, bare-footed, with hats of felt-like material with folded-up brims and clothes of European pattern under ample cloaks.

The baskets and crates of the vegetable-sellers were often beautiful and more worth attention than the stock-in-trade of the curio shops prepared for the tourist. The best of these latter were the fur dealers, and especially one shop containing some beautiful skins of the snow leopard.

Among the Thibetans the method of carrying great weights on the back is by a strap round the forehead, which throws most of the bearing-strain on the muscles of the neck. Both men and women carried in this way heavy loads to market; but the porterage of luggage from the railway station was almost entirely performed by women, and I saw several times a woman carrying up-hill a heavy American trunk, while her baby hung in front of her suspended in a sling.

Snow fell as I was leaving Darjeeling, and it was in the middle of a snowstorm that, on one of the worst curves of the railway, I caught sight of the words painted in large letters on the face of the rock,—"Prepare to meet thy God." I incline to think that the number of passers-by who derive any satisfaction from such disfigurements of nature is so small that their perpetrators are merely objectionable. The wintry landscape was now exquisitely beautiful; snow dappled the hillsides and lay upon the tree-ferns, making them like large white stars, as if in gigantic magnification of the snow-crystals themselves. Amid such loveliness suddenly appeared evidence of further enterprise on the part of Western religionists. "Heaven or Hell—which?" was painted on another broad surface of rock, and I thought that somehow a legend in Urdu would have been less offensive to my eyes.

After it grew dark, the engine carried a bright kerosene flarelight, which illuminated both sides of the track. As the train wound along the ever-curving road on the steep sides of the hill, the effect was like being in the hilltops with Peter Pan. Peter was not to be seen, but there was something so fairy-like about the beautiful masses of foliage and blossom, clearly and yet softly light against the star-strewn darkness beyond, that I think he must have been just in front of the engine.

At Siliguri I crossed the river, as on the way up, by the ferry steamer. There was a black stream of smoke from our funnel and a level white line from the boat's searchlight. Presently a third streak appeared in the darkness, a line of white sand on the farther bank. It was nearly dawn time and a little faint colour was just showing in the Eastern sky, making the sand look ghostly. The Calcutta train was waiting here; and soon after it started, the disc of the sun rose blood-red out of the level mist.

CHAPTER IX

BENARES

One morning in the train I woke at Buxar, where Major Hector Munro gained a great victory over the Nawab of Oudh in the eighteenth century. On each side of the railway-line I could see paddy-fields, sugar-cane and various crops, as well as a little jute.

By eleven o'clock I was driving from Benares Station through the lines of red brick, one-storeyed barracks, ranged upon the flat pale-grey dusty earth of the cantonment. The railway station is a long way from the town, but at last, nearly opposite a white-spired English church with a "classic" portico smothered in brilliant bougainvillias, I reached Clark's Hotel, and thanks to a friend's introduction, found that a police inspector, one Mahmud Ali, had been deputed to attend me during my visit and show me Benares.

We began without loss of time and at noon were driving along the hot roads, while more leisured mortals slept at the doors of their house on four-post *charpoys*.

Upon the plaster walls of the better native houses there was a good deal of rude figure decoration, generally in red and yellow. We passed Queen's College, which is a Sanskrit College for native students, the Prince of Wales' Hospital, and then an old wall upon which were inscribed the words:—

> "In the garden within this wall were the quarters occupied in the Autumn of 1781 by Warren Hastings, first Governor General of Fort William in Bengal."

Now I always think it is wise to humour a friendly cicerone, and I was not going at the very outset of our companionship to dispute at any length with Mahmud Ali, but somehow or other his mind was confused in regard to history. He declared that he had something of very great interest to show me in the garden and took me to an old well near a farther wall, saying that Warren Hastings concealed himself there during the Mutiny!

The streets were gay and crowded with foot-passengers, camels and horses, sacred cows and native vehicles. We passed one camel loaded with tobacco from some outlying village and just after, a bridegroom of the Hindoo noble caste Khatri, in a pink dress shot with gold, riding upon a white horse amid a deafening noise of drums and trumpets on his way to worship at a temple before the marriage ceremonies.

We were going to the famous Golden Temple and approached it by the bazaar of the brass-workers, where, between lines of tall houses, the sky dwindled to a narrow strip of blue. Far down the bazaar, past the Madhogi Hindoo Temple, a crowd of people huddled together were hurrying along, as if with a common object, under blue smoke which veiled them like a filmy gauze. These, Mahmud told me, were a band of pilgrims making a round of the Benares shrines, and I saw many such groups of native people going about with a leader like a Cook's conducted party.

Presently we came to a small square on the right of the bazaar, shut in by tall buildings, in which the Golden Temple stands and wherein is also the renowned Well of Knowledge. Sacred bulls were nosing about the pavement round a Bo-tree smeared with a red paint called Sandoor and a sweetmeat stall that was protected from the sun by a huge mushroom-like umbrella. Over the sacred well itself, upon its surrounding stone platform about 2 feet high, was built a pavilion of red-coloured stone and plaster, where an old man in a worn and very dirty coat of English cut sat ladling water out of a bucket to anyone who asked. I, of course, was not permitted to step upon the platform, but the faithful also have nowadays to suffer some prohibitions and are no longer allowed to choke the well with flowers.

In the Well of Knowledge, Vishnu the preserver is said to be for ever and behind it and its surrounding shrines of Ganesh and other gods (Ganesh is the good-luck god who was son of Siva and had, of course, nothing to do with Vishnu) the old Vishnagi Temple stands partly in ruins, as it has been ever since it was broken up by the puritan Aurungzebe, and partly turned into a mosque. The old part of this building is yellow-grey sandstone, tawny with age, but the mosque shone brightly in the sunlight with fresh Mohammedan whitewash.

Close by a Hindoo woman was going quickly round and round the trunk of a Bo-tree, which had at its base a lingam and a small nandi or stone bull (both symbols of Siva). She must have gone round at least a hundred times during the few minutes we stopped to watch her, and always in the same direction, but Mahmud said she would not fall as she was always doing it day in and day out.

It was as simple an employment of energy as children make setting themselves just such tasks—walking along the crack between two boards of a nursery floor and back so many hundred times, or hopping on one foot round and round the table, not always with any added zest of competition. It expressed an opposite need to that of contemplation, but in the monotonous round of its activity appeared to symbolize that view of life which shows it as a ceaseless movement along a path that leads nowhere, progressing without change and never arriving save at some part of its many times traversed orbit identical with all the rest. And well may Siva be worshipped in a circle, for the emblem the woman was running round—which invested with religious garments the mystery of perpetual regeneration—symbolizes the Destroyer also since neither Death nor Life can be conceived alone any more than light and darkness or silence and a song.

To enter the Golden Temple is not permitted to Europeans—only to peep through a hole in the wall and also to look at the roofs from the upper balcony of an adjacent house. There are two tall conical roofs shaped—as in so many Hindoo temples—like a common type of mould for ice puddings and a lower dome between them ridged like a melon, and beyond rises the white Mohammedan mosque. One of the tall roofs is red with only little spikelets gilded, but the other is gold all over as well as the lower dome.

As I turned from looking in at the gateway of the Golden Temple I saw just facing it a small Siva temple of stone delicately carved; and near to this, through a pair of brass doors, I saw the shrine of the "Saturday" god—a round face shown upon the upper part of a hanging cloth, without body or limbs, and with two flower-decked emblems in front of it. Then, a yard or two further on, I came to the Cow Temple and entered a cloistered court, where sacred peacocks strutted at their ease and pigeons fluttered. The temple itself was in the middle of this open court, and from its inner sanctuary at the back of its pillared porch or pavilion came the sound of a woman singing in a shrill high voice. A brown cow was licking the wet blossoms off the lingams, and under the cloisters where a crowd of people stood gazing at him sat a particularly ugly fakir. Naked, except for a loin-cloth, he sat looking at the ground with his legs crossed. Mahmud said he was a "Bramchari fakir," and we learned from the gazers that he had arrived early the same morning and had not moved since. He was extremely fat, as fat as the Chinese god of good luck, but with nothing merry about him and a look that was repulsive to me. His long brown hair hung down on to the pavement behind him. He had a piece of board to sit upon, and on the ground in front were offerings of food, but the people said he could not eat anything (he really looked too full). They admired and stared and wondered, and Mahmud said that the fat fakir was an arrant humbug, but then Mahmud was not a Hindoo.

The droppings of sacred bulls seemed everywhere; and when we came out of the Cow Temple and turned down a narrow passage, the way was dirtier than ever, and yet more weird and strange. Through two doors open in the side of the wall a huge red Ganesh, festooned with flower garlands, the lower part of his elephant face covered by a yellow cloth, stared with three eyes, and near him some Hindoos were making butter.

The same afternoon I drove out four miles from Benares to Sarnath to see the Buddhist remains there. Wide spaces of dry mud—dazzling in the sunlight—stretched away from each side of the road, parched for lack of the rain which should have covered them in a mantle of green crops.

The Buddhist "Tope" at Sarnath is an immense and apparently solid mass of brick-work raised upon a stone base and reminding one of the Dagobas of Anuradhapura in Ceylon. Chinese Buddhist pilgrims visited Sarnath at the time when the Romans were leaving England and have left descriptions of this earlier Benares. Excavations on an extensive scale are now going on, and 300 coolies were employed upon them at the time of my visit. The walls and general plan of many buildings, probably monasteries referred to in the account of the Chinese pilgrims, have been unearthed, and a museum is being built to house the finds, which are at present kept under a brick shelter. On a trolley near the latter I saw a very remarkable lion capital from a granite column 45 feet high, which was found lying in several pieces. This capital takes the form of a large quadrupled lion, with an annular relief below its feet of small figures of horses and elephants.

There is a Jain temple close to the Buddhist one; but what little daylight remained I spent in wandering about the new excavations and especially in examining a square chamber just uncovered, which was surrounded by short square columns connected by rows of wide cross-bars or rails of stone, lozenge-shaped in section. On some of these cross-bars there were circular medallions carved with geometric patterns in an arrangement similar to that in specimens in the Calcutta museum. Among the carved decoration there was much incised pattern-work with the spaces cut out, leaving square and not rounded edges.

I did not leave Sarnath till just at sunset, and driving back to Benares it seemed as if a sign came that I should never exhaust the wonders of the world. I saw a star sail slowly and almost horizontally across the sky. It was very bright indeed and had a tail or stream of light behind it and remained visible even after I had drawn Mahmud's attention to it, so that he said, "Yes—it is a star."

Next morning with Mahmud Ali I drove to the river, past lines of shops like tiled sheds divided into open boxes by partitions, past the white buildings of the Maharajah Hatwa's palace, and then past little huts where cactus grew wild against mud walls, sometimes dotted with red spots in crude childish decoration and sometimes covered with dung cakes drying for fuel. The wind blew cold as we crossed Victoria Park, with its grass and flower-beds looking dull under a stormy sky, and followed another long road of dilapidated buildings without one house in which the plaster facing was not half fallen from the tiny bricks. We also passed a square-towered English church, a church for native converts, and then after some long arcades began to meet the crowds returning from the river after bathing. On the water storm was now driving from Mirzapoor, and the river was all whitened with crested waves.

A police boat was waiting for us at the Dessasumay ghat, which was thronged with pilgrims. We went first up the river to the end of the chief ghats, then turned and came slowly down. The wind was bitterly cold and the boat rocked wildly as we began the time-honoured progress down the long line of majestic palaces, gloomy under grey skies, and the flights of wide innumerable steps, down which a ceaseless stream of pilgrims came to bathe even on such a day in the icy water. Four miles long is this vast line of masonry from the Assi Ghat at one end to Raj Ghat at the other near the Dufferin Bridge, and all that way the other side of the Ganges is but white sand without a single stone.

So many times have travellers told about it, this river-front of Benares, and more times yet new travellers will describe it.

Near the great Mosi Temple is one of the strange vast observatories made by the founder of Jeypore city, Sawar Jaya Singh. It was converted to such use from a great palace built by one of his forbears, the Rajah Man Singh, about 1600; and from its roof (to which we climbed to examine the strange gigantic instruments, the Samrat Yantra for finding time and declination and the hour angle of a star, the Chakrayantra and the rest) a wide and distant view is obtained of city and plain.

At the Mier Ghat, farther on, the masonry looks all falling to pieces and broken through from the foundations sloping at all angles as perpetual reminder that the sacred river is capable of wrath, and in times of flood can devastate as well as sanctify no whit less surely than Siva the destroyer can create anew. Octagonal towers lean and gaps of river stairways yawn as if some earthquake had shaken them, and Mahmud declared that an old man had told him it was just in the same state a hundred years ago—I suppose by report of his fathers, for even the most righteous of the devotees at the small Mohammedan bathing temple beyond scarcely live so long. As we continued through the choppy waves a burning ghat for poor folk came in sight. One body was being burned and another, a woman's, shrouded, lay with the feet dipping in the river.

As we went on I could now hear above the wind the sound of thousands of voices as we neared the Mano Kanka (or Karnika) Ghat, the most sacred of all in Benares, with its holy well of Vishnu perspiration into which Devi (the wife of Siva under another name) dropped once an earring.

More palaces followed—that of the Maharajah of Gwalior and that of Nagpur; then the Mahratta's building and the vast Panch Ganga Ghat, with the tall minarets of Aurangzebe's Mosque above it, built on the site of a Hindoo temple that intolerant puritan destroyed.

Near a Jain temple I noticed a strange colossal recumbent figure which Mahmud called Bean Sing, whom he said was one of the four brothers who were great men in Benares. The huge figure, very rudely shaped, was painted a pink colour with yellow loin-cloth and moustaches of inky blackness. Then there was the Nepaul Temple with its carved woodwork and grotesque little indecencies, and a pair of snake-charmers with quite an assortment of animals—cobra, python and other snakes as well as scorpions.

A temple to Siva's blood-loving consort about a mile from the town is one of the shows of Benares, attractive to Europeans on account of the number of monkeys which live in protection about it. On the way I saw an old mosque to which age and decay had given much beauty. The red brick showed all along the base and in part of the minarets where the plaster had dropped away. Little grey squirrels were running about the walls, green cactus was growing on the yellow earth against the red brick, and in front of it rose a palm tree with can attached high up under a cut in the trunk, catching the liquid from which the spirit called toddy is made. Mahmud told me that all the palms in the district were contracted to one man, and that each morning the cans placed in position the day before were ready for collection.

I left the carriage to walk round the old mosque and saw beyond a fence some potters at work. There was the clay being kneaded by women into lumps of suitable size, and the potter sitting on the ground and turning his simple horizontal wheel with one foot, while with skilful touches of both hands he shaped the vessel. Almost every village in India possesses a potter. He is as essential as the holy man who blesses the fields for harvest, and in country districts is generally paid in kind, getting a definite quantity of grain per plough each harvest for providing the necessary supply of earthen pots to the household, and the shapes of his wares, as well as the method he employs, are probably at least two thousand years old.

Opposite to the mosque across the road was a new *Idgar* with half the ground paved and at one side the steps of the *Kasbah* to the *Mimbar*, on which the Mohammedan preacher stands. Under a shelter or roofed shed near the Idgar a processional car of Juggernaut dozed through the idle months and declined to notice more hard-working bullock-carts which groaned past, laden with rough stone for road-making or long sarput grass for thatching houses.

Farther on was the Central Hindoo College, founded largely through the efforts of Mrs Besant, and now accommodating 500 students. The original building, to which much has been added, was presented by the Maharajah of Benares in 1899:—"For the education of Hindoo youth in their ancestral faith and true loyalty and patriotism." In the large playground of this college some Hindoo youths were playing football.

Beyond the white buildings of the Maharajah of Vizianagram's palace with their high-walled gardens and cool-looking pavilions, and the houses of native bankers, surrounded by orange trees laden with green fruit, and yet another temple called the Mahram Barhal, the Durga Temple appeared at last.

A young man had just brought a little black kid for sacrifice. He was dressed in tan leather shoes, a long fawn coat with a pattern on it and a small black cap on his head. He had an orange red caste mark freshly painted on his forehead, and round his shoulders hung a flower garland. He had just recovered from an illness, and for that reason was making sacrifice. Planted in the ground stood a square post, to the base of which a woman, who was sister to the executioner's wife, was helping to tie the unoffending kid. Black flies were swarming round as the woman pulled the hind legs of the goat, and the executioner, with an absurdly large sword, wide and curved, cut off the head at a blow. Monkeys leering and chattering played about all round, and several lean-looking dogs darted forward to lick up greedily the blood spurting from the little body, which was flung down a few yards away. The head was put on a small altar facing the entrance to the inner shrine that the god might see it, and then the executioner and the woman (who, by the way, was tattooed) cleaned and prepared the carcase for cooking, that the young man might take it away with him for home consumption.

The sun was setting behind the Durga Temple as I walked across a beautiful garden called the Anundabagh, between red blossoming Arhol bushes to see a man named Merthil Swami, who succeeded ten years ago one of the most famous "holy men" of modern India, the Swami Bhaskarananda Saraswati. The garden was presented to Bhaskarananda by the Rajah of Amethi, who continues to send money for its upkeep. Swami Bhaskarananda was born of good Brahman family, and after a youth spent in diligent study of Sanskrit and the Vedantic philosophy, renounced the world and became a wandering ascetic, roaming from one end of India to the other clad in a single garment; and at last believing that he had attained "knowledge," settled in Benares for his remaining years, "waiting his deliverance from mortality."

In a little house with brass doors I saw in the garden a life-size marble statue of this old man squatting naked, as he had done in life, with serene and peaceful countenance though with a slight raising of the eyebrows that creased his forehead, and curiously outstanding ears. The statue was made during his lifetime and is said to be very like him. On the bald head lay one red rose.

"Every Maharajah," said Mahmud, "came to pray to him," and he might have added every foreign visitor came to see him, for Bhaskarananda always welcomed English and other European visitors, and gained their appreciation and respect both by his learning and his courteous manners. *Tam cari capitis*.

A disciple named Gaya Purshad who lived in Cawnpore had given a lakh of rupees to build a tomb of white marble for Bhaskara, and it was nearing completion on the spot where he used to sit with his legs crossed and where, being holy beyond all purification of fire, he was buried in the same sitting posture. The tomb, against which leaned a wide bamboo ladder, is a small square building with three windows of pierced marble screen-work and one door opening, and the workmen were busy upon a lovely marble arcade surrounding the whole mausoleum. Inside, on the centre of the floor over the place of burial, there is a little plain slab of stone on which lay a wreath of pale and dark marigolds.

Merthil Swami, the man who was chosen by Bhaskara to take his place in the Anundabagh after he died, does not abjure all clothing like his master, but was dressed in a long plain woollen gown. Smiling courteously, he received me on the veranda of the house in the garden where he had been talking to a number of young men. He has deep brown eyes, a wide forehead and a narrow chin somewhat disguised by a slight grey beard, and his skin is light in colour.

I asked Merthil Swami of the present state of Bhaskara, and Mahmud interpreted his answer:—"Bhaskara's spirit will be in no more man; he has gained Heaven and is with the god Brahma."

It must be a difficult task to wear the halo of a saint so generally revered as Bhaskara, and I was not surprised to hear that Merthil Swami is not yet as popular as his predecessor.

Late that evening a heavy hailstorm made terrifying play on iron roofs with large stones, and blustering weather continued the next day. I determined to try to paint in spite of it, and went early to the Aurungzebe Mosque. Far above the river on the paved space outside the mosque at the top of the great ghat, a fakir was sitting on a bed of iron nails. They were iron spikes about four inches long, and he perched on one end of the bed, with a loin-cloth which afforded considerable protection. As the spikes were very blunt and close together there seemed to me no great difficulty in the man's performance. For eight years, people said, he had sat there; but a few yards from him, under a peepul tree, was a low umbrella tent closed to the ground on every side, and into this the fakir is carried on his spike bed every night. Mahmud gave no account of him, and although I had no religious bias he looked to me a peculiarly nasty person. "He hides his money somewhere under the ground like other fakirs," Mahmud added, "and if it could be found after his death it would be Government property, as he would have no heir," which may or may not be true.

Swallows were flying back and forth in the mosque. The stone walls were whitewashed, and the ceilings within the cupolas were decorated with a dull red pattern on plaster once white and now a creamy grey. This is the mosque which shows from the river, with its minarets high up above the vast flight of steps of the Panch Ganga Ghat, the best known scene at Benares. I painted it from the water, but the wind was too strong to keep the boat still, even close to shore, while occasional sudden showers of rain increased the difficulties.

The last time I went upon the river at Benares was one evening just after sunset, when the clouds were dove-coloured above the long line of ghats and palaces, sweeping along in a majestic curve which continued above the white flat sand of the farther bank. Mahmud and I had reached the Ganges at the Assi Ghat, the farthest upstream, and on the opposite shore rose the palace of the Maharajah of Benares, one of the few buildings upon that side. A police boat was waiting—and leaving the carriage by a golden tract of mustard to drive round and pick us up lower down the river, we were taken swiftly down-stream by four Hindoo rowers. In the far distance over the curve of sand the Dufferin Bridge was visible. The water looked blue-green and clear, and I thought that evening the usual accounts of its pollution must be exaggerated. Swiftly the rowers urged the boat along till I stopped them at a palace of yellow sandstone, in which some old Delhi kings yet drag out with their harems and opium pipes squalid pensioned lives. We pulled up to the great steps called Sivati Ghat, where a man sat cleaning his *goriaya*, a Benares pipe. Pigeons were flying about the walls and cupolas above, and a faint rose-colour just flushed the clearer spaces of the sky. On the wall a marble tablet was inscribed:—

> "This was the residence of Rajah Chait Singh where he was arrested by the order of Warren Hastings, on the 16th August, 1731 (*sic*), and where, on the same date, after the massacre of two companies of native troops with their British officers, he was rescued by his adherents."

There was the window by which Chait Singh escaped—he went off on an elephant.

Re-embarking we sped down the stream again past the Hanuman Ghat, above which showed the neem trees about the largest of the temples in Benares—that to Hanuman, the monkey-friend of Rama, who rescued Sita, his wife, from a king of Ceylon who had carried her away. On—past a little burning ghat called Masan with broken steps and past the Kedar Ghat and the building of one Tivwa, a rich Bengali, and a large charity house for fakirs, and past little lamps that floated on the water in front of a stone lingam on the wall. All along the edge of the river many similar lights were now twinkling. People were putting them to float for worship, lamps with butter and not oil in them. In the twilight lines of pilgrims were still distinguishable trooping along in robes of green and rose and white and purple. Temple music sounded, drums and cymbals and wind instruments. Against the walls like great targets hung now many of the huge mushroom-like grass umbrellas of the selling stalls. The same obese fakir I had seen the day before in the Golden Temple sat now gazing at the sacred river with a crowd of gapers watching as before.

We passed more neem trees, and then in rapidly increasing darkness once more approached the famous burning-ghat. One pile was almost burnt out, while another was flaming high. Two of the dead man's relations tended the fire; higher up the steps fifteen or twenty of his relatives and friends sat watching the last scene of his life's little drama.

"Eight maunds of wood for each," said Mahmud, "cost two rupees, fourteen annas (one maund equals eighty pounds), but for a rich man's body to be burned by sandal wood at the Rajah's Ghat costs 150 rupees."

The darkness gathered more and more and the pale white figures sitting in rows on the upper steps of the ghat were almost lost, except when now and then more lurid flames rose, dancing up to light them; the rowers bore us on again past more and more little lamps on the water. This time not Hindoo but Mohammedan hands were setting them afloat, and Mahmud said:—"Mohammedans worship all rivers, Hazarat Khizar."

We passed the burning-ghat of rajahs, with its odour of sandalwood and the Vishnu footprints, and once more that holy tank of the Manokanka Ghat, of which the water is believed to be sweat of his body.

CHAPTER X

LUCKNOW

At Lucknow it was Race Week. I had already heard from the famous "Wutzler's," the best hotel, that they had no room; and when I arrived one evening at the capital of Oudh I called vainly at others in a scale of reputation which diminished in accord with my hopes of a bed. I had left Benares the same morning, and after passing land green with various crops, including a great deal of mustard, the train had carried me over plains of grey monotony, only occasionally broken by patches of cultivation, herds of long-eared sheep, long-legged pigs, large black vultures and stray, weary-looking camels.

Surely all Anglo-India had come to Lucknow for the races. I had left a small crowd of English people at the railway station, who had given up hope of finding shelter and were only waiting for a train to take them away again: and believing in the possibilities of canvas, I sought out one after the other, "The Civil and Military," "The Imperial" and "The Prince of Wales'," and then roaming still "without a guide" tried for a tent at the "Eclipse," and at last found one at "The Empress." This last was managed by a thin Mohammedan, who was apparently destitute of any notion of mutual benefits, but rich in appreciation of the fact that every other hostelry in Lucknow was over-full. I certainly obtained a "lodging for the night" at "The Empress," but the fact that with travel-habit I was able to sleep soundly should not be taken as testimony to good accommodation.

The next morning at an early hour I was bargaining with a gharry-wallah who demanded 17 rupees for the day because of the races, and after paying some official calls I went off to see the Residency.

The events of the Mutiny days are so closely identified with every brick in the old red ruins that it would be almost impossible for an Englishman to consider them apart from those associations, but I think if it were possible they would still have more appeal than the extravagant vulgarity of the ugly palaces and other architectural eyesores that were reared so lavishly in Lucknow early in the nineteenth century, and remain for the traveller to stare at for his sins—huge curios of debased art, wearisome to visit and desirable to forget.

One William Ireland, who told me that as a boy of ten he was among the actual defenders of the Residency, being attached to the fourth company of the 3rd Battalion East India Company's B.A., showed me the many points of vivid interest connected with the memorable siege.

Trimly-kept walks surround those hallowed walls, bright in the sunshine with gay pink masses of bougainvillia and golden clusters of bignonia benarola. Every guide-book tells you the heroic tale and the Baillie Gate, Dr Fayrer's house, the Begum Kothi and the rest are household words in England. There are many monuments and memorial tablets at the Residency, and I will quote but one and that the inscription on an obelisk just *outside* its precincts:—

To the Memory of
The Native Officers and Sepoys
of the
13th Native Infantry 41st Native Infantry
48th Native Infantry 71st Native Infantry
The Oude Irregular Force
Native Pensioners, New Native Levies
Artillery and Lucknow Magazine
Who died near this Spot
Nobly performing their duty
This column is erected by
Lord Northbrook
Viceroy and Governor General of India
1875

Let us never forget those loyal hearts who withstood the insidious influences of a wide-spread crusade of mutiny which combined the appeals of military grievance, race hatred and religious zeal.

The chief bazaar of Lucknow, which forms one of the six wards of the city, is called the Chauk. Here still thrive jewellers and silversmiths, though the quality of their work is deteriorating. The prices are low and the wages are low. A rupee a day is not enough to satisfy the best artists, nor is four annas enough for a highly-skilled workman. *Bidri,* a kind of damascening lately revived, brasswork, ironwork and wood-carving, all go on here as well as a special local industry, the modelling of small coloured figures from clay worked into a paste with babul gum, belgiri, and sometimes brown paper and cotton-wool.

Then there is the carving of wooden blocks for printing patterns on cloths, the making of musical instruments (see that long sitar hanging in the shop-front) and the beating of gold-leaf and silver-leaf for eating. Indeed, it is true that people at Lucknow eat both gold and silver-leaf. I watched the thin piece of gold-foil being put between two leather leaves and then hammered out on stone, very slowly expanding to thirty times its original size. It is sometimes taken for disease of the heart, but it is not so much in cases of sickness but rather as a general fortifier to give additional strength to the whole body that the metal-leaf is swallowed, and after all the practice is more universal than one thinks at first. Children of many lands have a great fondness for tin trumpets—and I remember a New Year's Eve in London when a certain English Government Official offered me floating gold-leaf to drink for good health!

The first time I drove through the gates of the Akbariderwazar at one end of the Chauk a long swing bar, with upright wooden spikes two feet high, lay across the roadway. This was to close the bazaar to vehicles from two o'clock to eight in the evening (in summer from three to nine), the busiest time for shopping. No gharries or ekkas (another kind of wheeled vehicle) are permitted to enter during those hours, except by a special pass of the city magistrate, such as I carried. Were it not for such regulation, the narrow thoroughfare would every afternoon be nothing but a wedged confusion. In the larger Indian cities there is so much traffic that such a narrow street practicable for pedestrians and horse-riders, palanquins and litters, becomes jammed at once if open to wheeled vehicles in the busy hours.

An arch crosses the street at each end of the Chauk, one pointed and the other round—both without mouldings, and along each side a runnel of water flows in an open gutter. There is no profusion of delicate tracery about the projecting windows and other parts of the house-fronts as in many cities, and much tawdry and common workmanship; but looking back through the opening of the pointed archway beyond the near figures of the ever-moving crowd, sombre in the shadow of the houses and blended with the subdued sumptuousness of stuffs and wares, the outer roadway and a few buildings beyond contrast in simple spacious majesty—bathed in the glow of Eastern afternoon.

It was the first time I had noticed cowrie-shells being used as money—as a common medium of exchange—and nothing in India seemed more significant of the frugality of the mass of the people. Upon the brick and stucco platform, about 3 feet from the ground, that fronts many of the houses, there squatted upon a worn dhurrie a cowrie money-changer in a printed cotton dress and a little white cotton cap, and in front of him lay the heaps of shells, seventy-two in each. One anna is, of course, equal to four pice, and here at Lucknow while the gharry-wallah was demanding seventeen rupees for a day's hire, each of the four pice that make an anna was divisible into seventy-two cowries. Imagine yourself being able to divide a farthing in Whitechapel into seventy-two parts!

I had an anna converted into cowries without any lapse on the part of the changer from his accustomed gravity, but it was one of the few occasions on which Tambusami was thoroughly amused. I insisted forthwith on seeking what I could purchase with the shells, and a little further along the bazaar I bought for eighteen of them (the equivalent of a fourth part of a farthing) some salt, some spice, some tamarind and a portion of cooked grain-flour called pakori.

The Lucknow Races might have been on Epsom Downs for any evidence thereof in the Chauk that afternoon. A woman with a burka—a Mohammedan begging-woman in a white garment that covered her from feet to crown of head, having two round holes cut for seeing through—relieved us of the balance of our shells; and the police inspector, who accompanied me, drew my attention to a house of more pretentious decoration than its neighbours. Within, he declared, lived a *Paluria* or dancing-girl, who made 1000 rupees a month; and the fancy came to me out of that mesh of contrasts, where sun and shadow were so closely interwoven on the loom of life that warp and web seemed to become each other's fibre,—what if the unknown woman hidden beneath the ample folds of that snowy burka were, after all, a disguised *Paluria* of yesterday, accepting alms in white oblivion?

Such women of light hours often, I was told, at Lucknow are those who have lived with some Mohammedan in the curious temporary connection called *Mulaa,* which is a local practice instituted, as far as I could learn, to permit the addition of more wives without indefinite responsibility, the connection being terminable at the will of either party. The women of this class have often a considerable band of retainers, and the professional singing-lady who entertains strangers usually provides fiddlers, drummers and *manjira* or cymbal-players, who all receive a portion of her fee.

In a side alley leading off the Chauk there is a factory of otto of roses. Lucknow is famous for its perfumes—and one distilled from jasmine is highly popular, as well as an oil from roots of the Khaskas grass.

Lucknow, apart from the native quarters of the town, is a place of wide roads well laid out (after the destruction for military purposes of many houses at the time of the Mutiny), parks, gardens and other open spaces. I made a toilsome round of the chief show buildings, the jejune palaces, the mosques and the ungainly meretricious tombs. There was the Great Imambarah, built under Asaf-ud-daulah, whose tomb it is, as a relief-work in the Chatisa Famine of 1784 (for there were famines in India before the present administration). The interest here is a mechanical one, in the successful construction of an enormous roof in coarse concrete without ribs, beams, pillars, abutment, framework or support of any kind, except from the four surrounding walls. Rather over 160 feet long by 50 wide and 49 feet high, this vast apartment houses the canopied tomb which stands a little oddly, as it is placed with its axis in the direction of Mecca, to which the sides of the hall are not parallel. Near to it stands a huge tinsel *Tasia* carried annually through the streets at the time of Moharam.

The walls of the Imambara are very thick indeed, with innumerable passages and stairways in them which lead to a veritable maze on the roof level, and it is from some of these passages that the little "loges" or tiny box-like balconies high up in the walls are reached, from which purdah ladies could look down on function or ceremony, as English women from the ladies' gallery in the House of Commons.

I saw the handsome three-domed mosque of the Jama Masjid, with blue and purple decoration painted in line on walls and ceilings, except on the ceiling of its middle porch which was coloured in green. From the platform of the Jama Masjid I could see the ornate Husainabad Imambara, another tomb built in the year of Queen Victoria's accession, by the same king as the great mosque itself, as a burial-place for himself and his mother. A red-brick modern clock-tower showed some distance beyond the tallest of its gilded cupolas. The Husainabad Imambara, built almost entirely of painted stucco, is gaudy and vulgar in decoration and feeble in design. Its great hall contains some tons weight of glass chandeliers and common German ornaments. An enclosed court with paved walks and flower-beds contains a long rectangular piece of water, on which a barge with life-size figures of a man and a horse upon it is pushed up and down by one of the attendants. Coloured glass balls hang from arches of bent ironwork, and the railings along the flower-beds are all fitted with sockets for lights, while the stucco faces of the building are furnished with a multitude of small hooks for the same purpose. The stucco itself is of a peculiarly bright quality, and illuminated at night by thousands of fairy-lights, these buildings have evoked much admiration; but so also have the plaster decorations of Cremorne, Vauxhall or Ranelagh, the white palaces of Shepherd's Bush and the *cafés chantants* of the Champs Elysées; and, after all, it was race-week, and since Lucknow had its "Grand Prix" if only these far from venerable mausoleums could be turned into an "Ambassadeurs" or a "Jardin de Paris," they might cease to be troublesome!

A less offensive building is the Kerbela of Dianatud Doulah, of old red sandstone, rosy in the sunlight, surmounted by another gilded cupola, but marred horribly by a new porch roofed with corrugated iron. The Kasmain also, a copy of a sacred place in Baghdad, had much beauty in the coloration of its arabesque patterns of pale celadon greens, buffs, reds and smoky greys.

Seeking a little rest in the cool basement of the Lucknow Museum I came upon a lovely piece of sculpture, the very sight of which was as refreshing as a plashing fountain in a waste of sand. It was apparently the upper portion of an octagonal pillar, and was found amongst the ruins of Asaykhera, a small village in Etawah, on the right bank of the Jumna. Eight dancing-girls move in a circle slowly and rhythmically, and although their feet are supported by brackets their attitudes are full of easy movement. They wear jewelled bangles and anklets and a string of jewels encircles each of their necks, passing between and round the breasts to fall in front of the otherwise undraped thighs. The heads of the figures are broken, but their loss seems hardly felt in the delightful movement of the group. I found a luxurious sense of calm and quietude in contemplating this sculpture and for the time forgot the Imambaras and the noisy chaffering of the Chauk Bazaar. I think Cellini would have liked it; he must have enjoyed the carving even if he had deemed the group too homogeneous; certainly Lorenzo would have admired it.

But the strong spirit that holds the English visitor to Lucknow is certainly not the sensuous magic of æsthetic charm. "It is the due admixture of romance and reality," said Sir Henry Lawrence, "that best carries a man through life,"—and the heroic days of the Mutiny have left at Lucknow memories so compact of both that the stranger can but heed them and drink in the tale with ever-growing eagerness.

I turned my steps towards the old Sikandra Bagh, beyond the horticultural gardens, to see the little that is left of the walls through which Private Dunlay of the 93rd, on the spot now traversed by the road to the river, was the first to enter that stronghold of the rebels. On the way the flattened dome of the Shah Najaf, another great tomb, appeared against pale rosy clouds, a red flag clinging to its mast above walls of such tremendous thickness that they withstood both naval guns and Captain Middleton's battery. But it is another flag that keeps in my mind whenever I think of Lucknow—that one from the old staff on the Residency tower. A new one flies from it every year, but its pattern does not change. We last a few years longer than the shred of bunting and others will succeed us—may the high and noble courage of our people in the past be constant still enduring after us!

CHAPTER XI

CAWNPORE

"To-day that's Oudh—to-morrow it may be Cawnpore—the boundary line is the main stream of the Ganges and that is ever shifting." Thus spoke the manager of a great woollen mill as I stood beside him on an embankment in front of it, looking at the vast expanse of open plain beyond the river which flowed past us. The wind was blowing the white sand in clouds over the plain. Lines of long grass planted at intervals slightly broke its force and gave a little protection to the young crops, when any crops were there.

Cawnpore is fast becoming the Manchester of India, and I was visiting some of its large mills and factories. Part of the wool comes from Australia via Calcutta, but most of the raw material used at Cawnpore is Indian. It was being unloaded at the railway siding, and near by women were sorting—picking it over—and men pressing it down with their feet into large sacks.

Just at the moment this firm had in hand a Government contract for 11,000 coats, and had just finished an order of 33,000 coats for the police of Hyderabad, Deccan.

In an upper storey of the factory a vast floor was covered with khaki; it had been chalked all over from patterns, and Indian cutters were now shearing away at it. A bell rang in the weaving-shed. This was attached to the machine for making the warp. Every time a length of warp of fifty yards is made the bell rings automatically. Then it is taken off on to a roller beam and transferred from the warp-mill to the loom.

Near the cloth-mills there is a leather factory. The skins, mostly buffalo, had come to that raw hide-shed from all over India. Some were simply dried, some arsenicated and some, white-looking skins, had been salted. I was shown a special feature of this tannery—its method of tanning in latticed drums, half submerged in pits. The hides hung lengthways from the rope within the lattices, and at the end of each huge gun-metal or copper drum there were eight arms and a manhole.

In a yard outside bark was being unloaded from railway-trucks, ready for grinding up and infusing with "leaches." Three sorts of bark were being delivered—Babul (*acacea antica*), Sal (*shoria robusta*), and Rhea (not the native Rhea). There was a special and elaborate plant for making extract of bark, a process which was conducted *in vacuo*, so that the colour should not be affected by the boiling. In the same yard there were piles of sacks containing myrabolams from the Central Provinces, and in a corner I caught sight of a group of people dressed in strange sulphur-coloured cloaks, which covered head as well as body, leaving holes for the eyes as in a Mohammedan woman's burka—dresses that made me think of an *auto-da-fé*. The air about them was full of a cloudy yellow dust. "And what are these?" I asked the polite gentleman who was conducting me. "Those—oh—ah—they were not working the other day when the factory commissioners came round!" he said, laughing, and took me to look at something else. The bark extraction, as I said, was conducted *in vacuo*: this other process was evidently carried on *in camera*.

I do not think there is any near danger of India being turned into a machine, and the iron fetters of industrialism may even be welcome to a people living habitually at grips with starvation, and besides—has not one of the largest of the Cawnpore manufacturing companies set noble example in building a model village for their 3500 employees?

The manager was sorely exercised about pilfering propensities, and how much have I heard from Englishmen as to native thieving! I was assured that a Hindoo will so gently tickle with a straw the face of a sleeping traveller that he will turn his head just enough to permit abstraction of any valuables he may have placed under his pillow, and will then tickle the other cheek till the traveller turns back his head to its former position and sleeps on unharassed by any tiresome dreams. No such experience was ever mine, and in fact throughout my stay in the country I was never, to my knowledge, robbed of anything, and the only instance I encountered in India was that of a young French count who was relieved on the railway of much gold by a European train-thief. I wish, indeed, I could think such allegations all as unfounded as the accounts of the imaginary rope-trick.

In Lancashire I have seen many a crowd of mill-hands leaving work, and wanting to compare the similar moment at an Indian factory, I waited outside one of these at Cawnpore a little before closing time. Presently the men began to come out, at first in small batches and then in quickly-growing numbers—but what peculiar gymnastic exercise were they going through at the gates? A horizontal bamboo pole was fixed a couple of feet above the ground, and as each man raised his legs to step over this a chuprassee passed his hands over the workman's sides. Presently one was stopped and bidden to stand aside till the rest had passed. It was an ordeal by search and one of the various devices used to aid detection of the pilfering that I was assured is constant.

Through a small bronze gate, cast from one of the guns of the *Shannon* (those guns which bluejackets dragged all the way from Calcutta), every Englishman who goes to Cawnpore enters an octagonal sandstone screen in the middle of a small public park. Within, heavy and commonplace, Marochetti's marble angel stands in the centre above the closed well-head. There is not in the recorded history of any people a tragedy at once so terrible and so inimitably sad as that of the Cawnpore massacres: and on emerging from that small enclosed plot with its too ponderous angel, there can hardly be an Englishman who does not carry in his face the expression of a deep emotion. There are many churches in India, but there is no shrine so sacred to her rulers as the Cawnpore Well. Not far away stands the neem tree, on which some of the rebels were hung, and two larger trees are pointed out by the side of which sepoys were blown from the guns. The House of Massacre has long since been razed to the ground, and its site is now only marked by a block of black stone surmounted by a white marble cross and bearing an inscription in gold letters.

A road, shaded by some of the very same trees that hid the Nana Sahib's men on the 27th June 1857, leads to the brick-built ghat and its stone steps. They descend from each side of a small whitewashed Siva temple now, I think, no longer used. The steps are long and walled at each side: when I stood upon them no water lapped beneath. The Ganges was low and its main current had shifted away across the white stretch of sand beyond this narrower meandering stream. To the left the red brick piers of the Oudh and Rohilcund Railway Bridge paled in the heat haze to a faint pink colour. On the opposite shore a few lines of tall Kassa grass dry and dead, were ineffectually trying to protect patches of ground sown with melon seed. Overhead a peepul tree, an old tree—witness of all that terrible past—stretched a canopy of leaves that shimmered in the sunlight and danced in the little breeze, and while I stood there a Hindoo woman, ankles and wrists loaded with heavy silver bangles, went down the steps and over the sand to the water—that sacred water—to bathe and to wash her white garment.

CHAPTER XII

THE HOUSE OF DREAM

I lay quite motionless on my back upon the little stone platform that faces the south-west window—lay quite still and listened. In the intense noonday silence I could not hear even the chirp of a cricket. Often had Akhbar the Great reclined upon this stone bed of the place called Khawbgah, the House of Dream, and mused with roaming mind on government and power, the jealousies of sects and ministers, the ingratitude of dissolute sons, the tale of all the littleness of men and on his own ambition to build up a better and more perfect state.

Here had he mused and here had slept—but now in what strange contrast to the suspended consciousness of sleep is that deep soundless vacancy within the channels of the dead man's brain! Akhbar's decaying bones within stone slabs lie at Sikandra, but his great idea of universal toleration did not die with him.

Immediately above in the roof was a carved medallion, and a little blue pigment still remained upon the red sandstone. My head was towards the north and my feet towards the south: there are four openings in the walls, and when I looked towards the north I could see across the women's court to the Diwan-i-khas, the private audience-hall, and when I looked to the south I could see the low-pillared Record Office. The pilasters of the chamber are carved with grapes and pomegranates, and on the red walls fragments of painting are still visible. I made out on the north a Buddha, on the east a winged angel and two women, and on the south a god with a large tail. On the dado I made out a man dancing, a boat with six people in it and one boy climbing up the mast, and a walled city behind a Hindoo temple.

Over the doorways there are Persian verses in golden letters, and one, Riaz Ahmad, translated these for me during the afternoon, as follows.

Over the south door is written:—"The Imperial Palace is beautiful, pleasant and elegant, it is made to represent Paradise."

Over the east door is written:—"May the floor of thy house become the mirror for the eyes of the Janitor of Paradise, and may the dust of thy threshold become the black powder for the eyes of heavenly houris."

Over the north door:—"The foreheads of those who bow down in adoration and touch the dust of thy house will shine like a Zohra." "Zohra," said the kindly Mohammedan, whose patience I tried hard, "is Venus, the name of a very shining planet."

Over the western door is written:—"The Imperial Palace is more beautiful than heaven because of its gates. There is no doubt in this matter that it is Paradise itself."

The room below was painted all over, walls and ceiling, by Chinese artists with flowers—almond blossom, lotus, tulips, lilies and roses.

This House of Dream is but one among the buildings of the royal city of Fatehpur-Sikri, which was built by Akhbar towards the end of the sixteenth century, and after some years' occupation was abandoned through the continued difficulty of obtaining a good water supply. It has never since been occupied and consequently remains to-day almost exactly as it was when lived in by Akhbar and his court.

I had driven the twenty-two miles from Agra in a decrepit gharry, which turned over on one side on the way back. There was a wealth of bird-life along the roadside in the early morning—large storks, king-fishers, hoopoes, the ubiquitous minah, crows, kites and little green birds with one of the tail feathers twice the length of the others. Then there was a delightful bird about the size of a chaffinch, with black back and wings but golden-red breast and tail, doves such as Jemshid watched with his princess, white vultures, wagtails and plenty of green parrots.

We changed horses half-way near Mowgwa, a grey village on a low grey hill, where I watched a squirrel collecting material for his big nest hanging high up in a tree.

Rather over twelve miles from Agra there is an old isolated gateway of red sandstone which my driver (for whose accuracy I cannot vouch) declared "is a city gate of Agra brought here broken."

Among mango trees Naggra, another village, nestled on the left and then one called Kirowdi on the right, and all this road was bordered with beautiful shade-giving trees. At last I could distinguish a long line of crenelated wall, and we reached a gateway choked with a crowd of donkeys laden with dung-cake fuel. Within, roads diverged and we followed one that led direct to a second gate called Naubathkana, the musician gate, where drums were always beaten in token of respect whenever the king entered the palace precincts. Here I left the gharry and walked into the open quadrangle in front of the Diwan-i-Am, the great court of public audience. From the cloisters along the wall projects the king's place of judgment, a building with five open arches on a highly-raised basement and a hand-rail over low stone-carved screens. At my feet as I stood on the other side of the quad a stone was bedded deep in the ground with a circular hole cut through it, which everyone is told was the elephant ring to which the four-footed executioner was fastened conveniently for trampling condemned prisoners.

More celebrated is the Diwan-i-Khas, the private audience-hall, square in plan with stairs in the walls leading to galleries which cross the building at the second floor level to the capital (elaborately bracketed) of a central column. Cut on the floor of one of these galleries I noticed a stone-mason's mark, in the form of a bow and arrow, the arrow being fitted in place across the strung bow. The huge head of the centre column is a very king of capitals, and although it appears much out of proportion if considered solely in relation to the column, it does not seem so when properly regarded as part of the whole conception of this curious hall.

The short massive crossing arms of the gallery, which the column supports, give the feeling that they themselves help to hold up that huge cluster of stone brackets below them, and our eyes are affected as if its weight were partly borne by the shaft beneath it and partly by the crossing bars above.

It is in that central space at the crossing of the galleries that Akhbar is reputed to have sat discussing religions and philosophies, and nothing I have heard more convinced me of his tolerant disposition than the choice of such a very restricted space for argument.

Another privileged seat was that called the Grukimundi, under a small stone canopy outside one corner of a building known as the Ankh Michauli. This seat was allotted to a Hindoo teacher who, said Riaz Ahmad, instructed Akhbar in the doctrine of the transmigration of souls. Then there was the pachisi-board in large squares on which girls stood as pawns in the game played from a blue stone cross on the centre of the pavement. I was indeed shown by the assiduous Riaz Ahmad all the many sights of this dead city of Akhbar's court—House of Miriam with its garden and its bath—Palace of Birbal with its rich intricate and elaborate carving—Palace of Jodh Bai with an exquisitely latticed room projecting over Miriam's garden, and the Panch Mahal with its five colonnaded storeys on the first floor of which there are fifty-six pillars, each differently carved.

The court ladies used the Panch Mahal as a kind of playground, and I walked along part of a covered passage way which led thence to the Khawbgah. Then there was the great mosque, very lofty, and the Dargah Mosque with the tomb of Salim Chisti exquisitely beautiful with white marble screens of the most delicate fretted tracery, shutting in the tomb itself under a domed roof.

Salim Chisti himself was the hermit saint whose prophecies led Akhbar to build a city in that very arid neighbourhood, and Riaz Ahmad was of his family.

When I had looked long at the lovely tints of worn decoration and the rosy colour of the red sandstone, we left the blue carpets and polished marble floor of the mosque and sat for a while under the shade of some trees in an enclosure at the back.

I have heard of people being much pestered at Fateh-pur-Sikri by would-be "guides," but not only did I escape any such experience there, but Riaz Ahmad, whom I engaged as cicerone for the day, proved a very agreeable companion, not at first over-communicative but as the hours wore on becoming more so.

Under a little astambole tree near us, as we sat resting, were two tombs, one under a small pillared canopy and the other by its side without any covering. Both were small and one was exceedingly tiny, so that it was not large enough to contain more than a kitten or a very small doll. It is probable that confirmed information is obtainable about both, but there was a certain naïveté about Riaz' talk which pleased me, and it seemed more illuminating than a mere repetition of authenticated fact.

"The small tomb," said Riaz, "is that of the infant son of Salim Chisti, of whose family I am. The child died at six months by the power of his own mind, just to show a miracle, and the very small tomb close beside it is that of a tooth. Akhbar, childless, came to Salim Chisti and some say that to give Akhbar a son the child of the holy man was sacrificed; but that is not true, for the babe, of its own mind, ceased to live that a child might be born to Akhbar. As for the tooth," he went on, "there was a woman who lived in our family a long time ago (we may not tell the names of our women), whose husband went away with Jehangir when the king sent an army to capture Nour Jehan. Now this man who went with Jehangir died in battle, and because his body could never be found and his wife happened to have one tooth of his which had come out, the tooth was buried in memory of her husband."

And this is how Riaz Ahmad told me the story of Jehangir's marriage as we sat in the shade by the mosque wall.

"Nour Jehan was found by a traveller—abandoned upon the road when she was quite a baby, because her parents could not bear to support her on account of the poverty, and she was presented by the traveller to the king because she was beautiful, with the report that he had found her upon the roadside. And as he also found her to be of extreme beauty the king ordered her to be nursed in his palaces. When she became twelve years old Jehangir, who was about the same age and had played with her as companion, became enchanted with her beauty and loved her." I thought of their padding feet as they chased one another in children's games about those paved courts—playing "catch me" over the pachisi-board, and of Nour Jehan shrieking safety as she reached a crossed square where the pieces are not permitted to be "taken."

And Riaz continued—"But Akhbar would have none of this, and to keep her away from Jehangir, married her to Shareef-Ghan-Khan, the Governor of Bengal. Now Nour Jehan had never loved Jehangir, but had only played with him in friendship. When Akhbar died, Jehangir at once sent to Shareef-Ghan-Khan demanding his wife, but was refused. Then sent Jehangir an army in which that man of the tooth was one of the officers. After great fighting, that Shareef was killed and Nour Jehan was forced to come to the Imperial Palace, though she said she would have been more contented to be the wife of a common soldier than to be queen with a husband she did not love. For six months she lived in the palace in a separate house with the mother of Jehangir, but at last when she did not see any way to get rid of him she accepted his love, became queen and obtained such influence over her husband that he put her name upon the coins."

This story led us to talk about women and Riaz Ahmad said, in spite of the tale of Nour Jehan—"God gave the man more power than woman, so she is the inferior; she is not like man. She has the right that we should be just to her, to clothe her as well as we clothe ourselves, and not to give away her right to another woman. We may not say of one of our wives—'she is the more beloved'—they must be equal, otherwise it would be a sin to have more than one wife." Perhaps emperors may have preferences!

Before leaving Fatehpur-Sikri I went to see the magnificent Gate of Victory.

Inside, the inner portals are carved with wonderful skill, letters upstanding upon the red sandstone. At the top words are carved in Arabic, which Riaz translated for me thus:—"That one who stands up to pray and his heart is not in his duty, he remains far from God. Thy best possession is to give in alms and thy best traffic is to sell this world for the next." Then a Persian Rubaiyat:—"What fame could you gain sitting on a throne in a silver mansion? The beauty of the world is simple, like a looking-glass. Behold yourself when you look at it." There follows the name of the carver of these verses—"Mohammed Mason."

Riaz Ahmad followed strictly the ideas of his forbears, and would not hear of any relaxation of the seclusion of women. In this he was very different from a younger co-religionist whom I had met at Agra at the Moharam Festival, and who was very anxious to talk to the English stranger about what he considered the unfairness of Government regulations. He belonged to what he called the reformed Mohammedans, and said that his sisters were quite free to go about unveiled where they would. He complained of the lack of freedom of the press in India, claiming that it should be just as free as it was in England, and was much surprised when I told him that in England we should not permit any newspaper to publish direct appeals to assassinate the sovereign. He was quite a young fellow, two-and-twenty, and just out of college, hoping to get a billet in the post-office—although he declared that the English clerks are paid higher salaries than natives for the same work.

I think it would be an excellent thing if some good English publisher made it his business to arrange for the translation into Urdu of some of the best English fiction. This young man, for instance, said he had read all he could get and informed me that "Reynolds" was our greatest novelist and that a large number of his books were published in Urdu. I asked him the names of some of the chief ones and he mentioned *Mary Price, The Star of Mongolia* and *The Mysteries of the Court of London*. He added that the last-named had been prohibited by Government, but that of course such copies as had already been issued had naturally been treasured by their possessors. He urged the desire of himself and his friends to read the books that are read by well-educated people in England, and I think the range of books available is very restricted. He talked to me about Indian poets, and said that the best modern ones were Dagh of Delhi (poet to the Nizam of Hyderabad, Deccan) and Amir of Lucknow, both of whom died a few years ago, and I hoped the standing of their works was higher than that of *Mary Price* and *The Mysteries of the Court of London*. He told me of the writers of Marsias also—Amias and Dabir of Lucknow and added, "I cannot myself write good Marsias, so what is the use of writing at all? But I do write *Gazal*, which have two lines, and *Rubaiyat*, which have four lines, and also *Kasida*, in praise of any famous men."

He certainly had some imagination, for he went on to inform me, laughing, that His Highness the Nizam prided himself upon the swiftness of his carriage-horses which went so quickly that only his moustache could be seen; and after he had passed, no one was able to say what clothes he had had on because of the fleetness of those horses.

We went together to the great mausoleum Nour Jehan built for her parents in the days of her power, and he also accompanied me to Sikandra, the tomb of Akhbar. We drove thither from Agra one hot day, till tall white minarets appeared on the right of the road some miles away across golden fields of mustard, and we soon found ourselves in front of the outer gateway.

Filling a wide band round and over the arch and making very handsome and indeed perfect decoration, are some quotations from the Koran, and added at the base of the left side are the name and date of the carver—"Kutba Abdul Hal Shirazi, year 1022, Hijra."

The whole interior of the great building of Akhbar's tomb is one dark vault 74 feet high. Ending just above the marble of the grave itself there comes down from the darkness the thin chain of a lamp, which is lighted only at the annual festival of Akhbar's death, called in Persian, "Barsi." While two Khadims (servants of the mausoleum) in white turbans and white dhotis held hurricane lanterns for me and the young Mohammedan, a little daylight filtered through the long stone entrance passage, and above, from one of four openings in the wall, a clearer shaft crossed the great void, illuminating part of the chain and falling upon the opposite wall in a pale shade of blue. There is no decoration in this vault—only the plinth of the tomb has one chiselled pattern along its edge. The body—Akhbar's body—wrapped in a white cloth, on which lavender, camphor and other scents had been scattered before it left the palace, was laid upon stones some three or four yards below the floor level and then, after other stones had been placed at the sides, one long slab was laid across the top and earth put over it. The older of the two Khadims said that the rings would have been taken off the king's fingers. He had been thirty-eight years at Sikandra but remembered no strange thing ever happening in the mausoleum. There he has held the lantern for people of all degrees and many countries—people of the West as well as of the East; Edward the Seventh (when Prince of Wales), the Tsar of Russia (when Tsarevitch), the Amir of Afghanistan, as well as our present king.

As I walked slowly round and was looking at the chain—part of which now told as a sharp black silhouette against the light patch of wall beyond—and the broken end hanging to its ring, the young Mohammedan chanted for me some passages from the Koran, his musical voice echoing sweetly in the great dome.

Facing the main gateway to right and left of the central vault are the tombs of Arambano, a daughter of Akhbar, and of Mehrin Nisa, the learned daughter of his great grandson Aurangzebe, who used to write Persian poems. Above the domed central vault with its prisoned air and darkness, reached by a long stairway, is a square court open to the sun and surrounded by cloisters of which the outer walls are marble screens carved in intricate geometric patterns, through which the light comes softly.

Along these cloisters, on the side facing the centre of the court (where a block of white marble bears the ninety-nine names of God), each spandril has a Persian verse above it, and contains a rosette in which is cut part of a poem. These are so interesting that in all twenty-five people, lost in the pleasure of reading from one spandrel to another, as they moved round, have fallen into one of the unprotected wells of the stairways and been killed!

I walked round with the young Mohammedan—keeping one eye open for the stair-wells—while he read me the verses, of which here are several:—

> "Think not that the sky will be so kind as Akhbar was."
>
> "His life was free from every kind of fault."
>
> "All kings which were, or which are, or which will be upon the earth are not so great as Akhbar was."
>
> "He gave justice to all his people."
>
> "The sky is not so elegant or so lofty as the throne of Akhbar."
>
> "No one is saved from the hands of Death."

CHAPTER XIII

DELHI

Meerut itself, where the Mutiny first broke out, is but forty miles from Delhi, and when the rebel troops reached the old capital, Delhi became the centre of revolt. It fell entirely into the hands of the mutineers, and when the combined forces defeated the enemy at a village six miles north of Delhi they gained possession of the "Ridge" (where the red sandstone comes to surface in strata of about forty-five degrees), only to find that they who would fain have besieged the city were to become themselves besieged and suffer heavy losses before General Nicholson could reach them with reinforcements from the Punjab.

The storming and recapture of Delhi is one of the chief examples of stubborn determination in the teeth of heavy odds, and one of the principal chapters in the history of British arms.

The various sites connected with those events are familiar from frequent description to many who have never been east of Lowestoft Ness, and from innumerable photographs the Kashmir Gate must be nearly as well known in London as Buckingham Palace.

Near it, and just south of the cemetery where he is buried, there is a capital bronze statue of General Nicholson (by Mr Brock), in a little park named after him.

The building that became the Residency after the Mutiny and was then occupied by Sir David Ochterlony, has been more recently converted to the uses of a Government High School for boys. It was originally built by Shah Jehan as a library for his son Dara Shikoh in 1637, and its spacious rooms suit rather well the purpose of a school. The headmaster, who happens to be a Dutchman, took me through the various class-rooms and introduced me to a number of, doubtless, learned pundits—the special masters for Persian, Sanskrit, Arabic, Urdu, English and "Science" subjects. In a class called the 5th High, at the time of my visit, native youth was being lectured upon Nelson's blind eye.

Delhi was the capital of the Moghul Empire before Akhbar removed it to Agra, and it became again the seat of Government under Shah Jehan; so that some of the chief examples of Saracenic work in India are to be found in its buildings. Under Shah Jehan was built Delhi's "Great Mosque" and the Palace within the Fort. The former differs from others of its style in its external grandeur, one of the more usual characteristics of mosque building being the elaboration of the interior rather than the exterior.

Great flights of steps lead up to the three splendid gateways of the large open quadrangle, surrounded on three sides by pillared cloisters. The three divisions of the mosque proper are roofed by magnificent marble domes with black vertical lines inlaid upon them, and on each side of the centre archway long graceful stems rise up and up to end above in tops shaped like a lotus, beautiful from below, but no less so at close quarters, seen from half-way up one of the two tall minarets which flank the building at the north and south. I was well repaid for climbing to the top of one of these by the splendid views from it. To the west I could see the Fort and the river beyond, with a long bridge, and to the north-east the city and the numerous small domes of the so-called Black Mosque, with the mighty Tower of Victory, the red Kutab Minar, in the far distance rising from the ruins of old Delhi.

Down below I was shown the treasures of the mosque, which included a hair of the prophet (a red hair) and some words in his handwriting. On the other side of the marble basin in the centre of the quadrangle there is a sandstone pulpit, paler in colour than the red of the steps and walls, and beyond this, at the back of the interior of the mosque, the wall of marble, through slight inequalities of surface, looks like mother-of-pearl.

Architecturally these glories of Delhi are shared by the Fort and the series of palace buildings within its precincts. The great walls of red sandstone, the magnificent entrance of the Lahore Gate and the long vaulted arcade through which one approaches the interior of the great enclosure are, however, to my thinking, nobler and more impressive than the marble halls of the palace within.

This Lahore Gate is in the middle of the west side of the Fort. On the east flows the Jumna, and at the southern end is another gateway called the Delhi Gate, with a colossal dark grey stone elephant—delight of English children at Delhi—on either side of the entrance.

Among the palace buildings the noblest is the Diwan-i-am or Hall of Public Audience, containing at the back a raised recess where was formerly the famous Peacock Throne of solid gold inlaid with rubies, emeralds and diamonds, backed by two peacocks with jewelled and expanded tails. The glory is long ago departed, but the walls of the alcove on the upper level are still partly covered with inlaid panels of small subjects worked in stones of various colours. Among these, high above the doorway in the upper wall at the back, is one called the Orpheus Panel. Guide-books state that it represents Austin of Bordeaux, one of the foreign architects who helped to adorn the Moghul Court—but the Orpheus is represented as quite a youth, whereas Austin of Bordeaux would have been old at the time.

I was climbing up a bamboo scaffolding to examine this spirited and delightful panel, in which the poet son of Calliope, plays to a group of listening animals, when I met a little fair Italian to whom, through Lord Curzon's efforts, the restoration of the damaged panels and the addition of new ones to fill blank and broken places had been happily entrusted.

For many months the Florentine craftsman had lived here cutting and polishing, and although he sometimes longed for the Arno as he looked out upon the Jumna River, he was of such a gay and merry disposition and took so much delight in his own incomparable skill, that it was a joy to meet him. Of the twenty-four original panels he felt very sure which were of native and which of Italian workmanship, for there were at Delhi, he told me, four unknown Italians doing this work when the decoration was first undertaken. His art is not of a creative kind and he has little invention, but carries to an extreme of skill the imitation in polished inlay of bird or beast or flower. At its worst his work was seen in a piece he showed me as a *tour de force* of manipulation, imitating a popular painting of a merry monk, but in his panels for the Diwan-i-am he kept quite happily to the spirit of the earlier designs.

I was curious to learn from what far places the stones were gathered which he cut and rubbed, and I noted as an instance those composing one small panel of a bird which he had just completed. These included Green Esmeraldite from Australia; Corniola from the Jumna; Abri and Jal from Jeypore; Black from Liége; Chalcedony from Volterra; Colombino from Val Mugnone; Lapis Lazuli from Colerado; Malachite from St Petersburg; other Colombino from Fiesole; other Lapis Lazuli from Persia; other Malachite from Siberia, and a grey stone from Cairo.

In Florence near the Ponte Vecchio the Italian craftsman's sister keeps a shop going during his absence for the sale of inlay work, and at the same time exercises her own more meticulous talent in making microscopically fine mosaics and miniatures from scales of butterflies. Such a man as her brother is without either the sorrows or the dreams of a great artist, but he seemed as happy in his craft as the Gentle Pieman of the Bab Ballads, and I have little doubt that something he exclaimed—which was too much for my limited knowledge of Italian—might well have been translated by the pieman's words:—

"I'm so happy—no profession could be dearer—
If I'm not humming 'Tra! la! la!' I'm singing 'Tirer, lirer!'"

But what shall I say of the Diwan-i-Khas which forestalls the highest reach of compliment by calling itself Heaven in a distich? Its marble walls and jewel-petalled flowers, its carved graceful arches, and all its spacious grandeur, appeared woefully deserted, and from this hall of heaven all the dear delicate little angels have long since fled, so that I could not find the tiniest feather. In the Rang Mahal near by I had a more tender impression. This is where the chief Sultana lived, and the painted decoration on the marble walls is of exquisite colour. Pale blues mingle with paler tints of green, and soft red-edged flowers seemed still to brim their cups with memories. Here leaned a woman's shoulder: here pressed a cheek wet with very human tears, and on that marble stamped a little foot, jealous and angry, while light laughter rang, or baskets of ripe figs from the bazaar were searched in breathless hush for hidden messages of love.

To see old Delhi at closer quarters than such a distant view as that from the minaret of the Jama Masjid, I drove east from the city by many great dome-topped tombs, mostly in a half-ruined condition as in an Indian Campagna, and visited on the way the Mausoleum of Humayun, which divides architectural with historic interest. The design of the building is similar to that from which the Taj was later evolved. In its general proportions the total height appears too little for the great and high-terraced platform on which the triple octagon of the great building stands. Underneath this platform I walked through a low dark passage to the vault where the Emperor Humayun was actually buried. With the help of matches I could distinguish a plaster plinth one and a half feet high, and upon this a plaster tomb. I noticed one great hole in the plaster base and another in the ground beside it, and learned that these were made, not by any latterday members of that most repulsive of all Hindoo sects the Aghoris, but by porcupines which I was assured might be seen in numbers on any moonlight night, and one of whose quills I picked up from the floor.

Humayun's tomb is now identified in the pages of our history with a deed of no doubtful daring which was too swiftly followed by one no less doubtfully unwarrantable. It was here that Hodson of Hodson's Horse, with a few troopers and superb audacity, summoned an armed crowd to lay down their weapons, while the King of Delhi surrendered himself.

I should not leave the neighbourhood of Humayun's tomb without referring to the delightful use of blue and green-glazed tiles in the roofs of some adjacent buildings.

The next stopping-place that day was at the shrine of Nizam-ud-din-Aulia, a holy man who died early in the fourteenth century. High diving from a roof-top into an unclean water tank failed to interest me greatly, but the tomb of Amir Khusran, a poet, within the same enclosure as that of the saint, delighted me as a perfect monument of dignified respect. Quiet and peaceful it looked in the cool shadow. The walls were marble screens fretted with close patterns, and the entrance door was of brass in four upright strips, so that the two halves folded back upon themselves. Outside, heavy-quilted purdahs hung over the marble to keep out dust, and the whole was surrounded by an outer wall of pierced sandstone, which had been whitewashed. At one end of the grave a copy of the Koran lay open upon a wooden reading-desk, and ostrich eggs, covered with written texts, hung from the ceiling.

Close to this poet's tomb is that of a daughter of Shah Jehan, named Jehanara, in a tiny enclosure, with bare earth over the place of sepulture and one upright marble slab with Persian verses inlaid in black marble.

Driving on past domes and ruined walls for some miles farther I came at last to the great Tower of Victory, the famed Kutab Minar, and to the ruins of a magnificent mosque with a series of superb arches, and a courtyard of cloisters divided by Jain pillars.

In height the red sandstone monument, called the Kutab Minar, is less than a fourth of the Eiffel Tower in Paris, less than half the Washington Column, or Cologne Cathedral, and not much over half of the Great Pyramid. It was built in the early Pathan period, before 1320, and a few decades earlier than Giotto's Campanile in Florence. The latter never received the addition of its intended spire, but as it stands is already fifty feet higher than the Kutab. This actual height is largely discounted in appearance by the close proximity of Brunelleschi's tremendous dome, and the Campanile becomes as was intended but an apanage of the

Cathedral. Near the Kutab Minar no rival enters the vast arena of the upper air, and neither the noble arches of the adjacent mosque, gigantic though they are, nor its cloisters with their richly-ornamented pillars taken from the Jain buildings the Mohammedans replaced, do more than dignify the splendid monument of Victory. It gives an impression of soaring strength unrivalled in any building I have seen, an impression practically impossible to be received from pictures or photographs or any representations upon a diminished scale.

The Kutab Minar and the Iron Pillar, Fatehpur Sikri.

By successive storeys banded with balconies and the decorative characters of Arabic inscriptions, the red sandstone building rises up and up, ceasing at last in two tiers of white marble, which seem to the beholder at its base rather entering Heaven than ending anything. From the roof of the mosque the lowest band of inscription can be seen with sufficient clearness to make out its intricate beauty and perfection of decorative design.

Almost blue in colour against the warm sun-lit red sandstone of this mighty tower, the Iron Pillar, fifteen centuries old, stands within the precincts of the ruined mosque, no more than four times a man's height, smooth and undecorated, save for a small inscription on one side and a simple capital with a fluted bulb surmounted by a little flat square slab. A man standing on this, unclothed save for a loin-cloth, looked like a bronze statue. Sometime, it is said, an image of Vishnu stood there.

Next day on the other side of Delhi, between the Flagstaff Tower and the Mutiny Monument, on the rough ground of the Ridge, I was looking at another curious pillar, one of the stone "Lats of Asoka," which is said to date from some centuries before Christ. An inscription at the base of the column states:—

> "This pillar was originally erected at Meerut in the third century, B.C., by King Asoka. It was removed thence and set up in the Koshuk Shikar Palace near this by the Emperor Firuzshah, A.D. 1356, thrown down and broken into five pieces by the explosion of a powder magazine, A.D. 1713-1719. It was restored and set up in this place by the British Government, A.D. 1867."

There was a tearing horrible wind and clouds of dust blowing along the Ridge. The Mutiny memorial is not beautiful.

Tucked away among narrow streets of the old city, where blood-red handprints marked the white walls (I think in some connection with the imminent "Holi" festival of the Hindoos), I found the most strange as well as one of the oldest of Delhi's Mohammedan buildings, the Black Mosque, the numerous small domes of which I had seen from the minaret of the Jama Masjid. It belongs to that sloping style of architecture which seems kindred to Egyptian work, and gives an appearance of massive strength. A wide flight of twenty-eight steep stone steps leads up between two tall cones of masonry, which flank the entrance and rise above its battlements.

I had the great pleasure at Delhi of being welcomed by an old friend in the I.C.S., to whom I owe many an interesting screed from India since our school-days—letters written in the scant leisure possible to an Indian judge. I found Alfred Martineau but little changed—full of the same contented humour he has always possessed. Such cordial hospitality as he and his charming and gifted wife extended to me during my visit came with that welcome contrast to accommodation at hotels and dak bungalows that only travellers can understand, and from the hour when I found him waiting at the railway station on the arrival of my belated train to that of my departure from the Moghul capital, these good friends seemed to think no effort too great to further my pleasure and convenience.

When I look now at the hollyhocks in my own garden I remember always those other English hollyhocks grown with such eager care about a home in Delhi.

CHAPTER XIV

DEHRA DUN AND LANDOUR

A grey squirrel dropped from the roof on to the table, scrambled over the papers beside the magistrate's hand, and scampered away into the adjoining room.

I was sitting in the Deputy-Magistrate's Court at Dehra Dun, waiting beside the D.-M., while he discussed a matter of land compensation with a stout gentleman in gold-rimmed spectacles, and I learned that "Government" pays compensation of fifteen per cent. plus the market-value, of land taken for engineering works. Our chairs were upon a raised part of the floor, divided from the other two-thirds of the room by a wooden railing, behind which a number of people waited audience, and among them I noticed the round face of a little Goorkha Subadar, with the silver badge of crossed knives on his forage cap. Dehra Dun is the headquarters of the Goorkhas, and, thanks to the kindness of Colonel Crommelin, I was able to see the smart bayonet practice and physical drill of the Second Battalion of the 9th Goorkha Rifles.

Among the military forces, however, a mountain battery interested me most. Dehra Dun is not, of course, a hill station, but there is plenty of hilly ground close to it, and this No. 32 Battery was put through its paces for my benefit on a steep piece of rocky ground, the mules kicking and bucking like creatures possessed.

The guns, painted a pale coffee colour, are worked by Punjabis, and one of these posed for me to paint him in the blazing sun with extraordinary patience. I was told that these troops very rarely suffer from sunstroke, but that when some of them went to China a regular epidemic of heat apoplexy was experienced, due probably in large part to the power of suggestion aroused by two or three cases of such an unusual trouble.

In his khaki turban the Punjabi wears a roll or crest of scarlet cloth which glows far more brightly in the sun than can be represented on canvas. Beside this burning red the most brilliant tint I could command was as far from the true pitch as the dry watercourse in the valley was different from its flooded aspect after rain.

It is not only the Punjabi turban that cries gaiety aloud at Dehra Dun. I saw the dak tree here which bears large scarlet blossoms, and when in flower finely justifies its popular name of "Flame of the Forest." There are many kinds of trees to make the Dun beautiful, and when I started early one February morning for Mussoorie I drove in a tumtum at first through tall bamboos, eucalyptus, fir trees, mangoes, sal, peepul, plum, cherry and a host of others. Before me the great foothills of the Himalayas blushed warm and rosy, and along the crest of the higher ridges above, the white houses of Mussoorie showed in streaks and lines and patches as if a little snow had remained unmelted after a recent fall. I passed the tents of the X-Ray Institute of India and drove steadily on to Rajpur, gradually acquiring a considerable escort of boys from that village mounted on ponies, which they urged me to engage for the ascent to Mussoorie.

Rajpur consists of one long straggling street of small shops, and here I left the tumtum and hired two coolies, to carry my baggage, and a horse for myself. On this road I passed again and again living embodiments of toil—men carrying baulks of timber on their backs. They looked almost dramatically terrible, not like Leighton's exultant Samson bearing the doors of the city gate in triumph to the hilltop, but weary in mute submission to the burden of mortality.

In this matter of bearing burdens of physical material weight the part is played with more universal similarity even than that of going without food. Jean François Millet was reproached with painting his men carrying a calf on a litter as if they were carrying the Host, but the truth is—as he explained in one of his letters—the expression of men carrying depends upon the weight, and whether they had the Ark of the Covenant or a calf, a lump of gold or a stone, the same expression would be the result; the weight of timber was just near enough to breaking strain for these men's bodily tension to produce an air of slow solemn travail impressive as a religious penance and appealing as an heroic endurance.

Landour is higher than Mussoorie, and as I wanted to see the mountains at early morning, it seemed better, if possible, to sleep at Landour. An American missionary on a pony was buying dried peas at a shop in the bazaar, and after explaining to me that he was a vegetarian, as if that were an original idea and a condition of personal merit deserving of awe, he advised me to try for shelter at a certain Mrs Sharp's who had, as he rightly supposed, a suite of rooms to let.

This good woman, a nurse by profession, had living with her three grandchildren, a girl of twelve and two boys rather younger, neither of whose parents (of pure English blood) India born, had ever been out of the country. These children were the first examples I had met of a second generation of English born in India, and a very healthy and merry trio they were. The father had been an engine-driver, and the mother, since his death, had had to get work at a distant town. These bonny, apple-faced youngsters certainly showed the possibility of healthy rearing of English children in India, but they had spent their little lives as yet entirely in the healthy mountain air of Landour, and far from enervating influences.

Mrs Sharp was a genial old lady of optimistic temperament, whose chief anxiety seemed to be to keep on good terms with her native cook and to make other people happy. A young railway guard was staying with her for a short holiday, and in the evening I was asked to look in on a homely party in their living-room, where a young English girl from a Mussoorie milliner's store played a piano and sang songs called—"We're all the world to each other, Daddy."—"For I've got you and you've got me," and "I'll love you, dear, for ever." The last-named brought easy tears to the eyes of Mrs Sharp, who declared with heaving unction "that's my favourite song." The more treacly the sentiment the more they all enjoyed the words, and the whole scene with the badinage and byplay of the English lower class was a curious contrast to the Indian life I had been seeing.

Happy and innocent people they were, with all their affectations on the surface, through which sterling qualities peeped unobtrusively—people (whose æsthetic sense was far less than that of a bower-bird) lacking all delicacy of either eye or ear, lacking any faintest spiritual conception beyond a heaven of solid twangable golden harps and paper decorations called Jacob's Ladders, open and honest as the day—feeding all the stray cats of Landour as well as the five they delight to own—in a word so essentially British that in a distant land one of the same nation is moved first to smile at meeting them and then to run his fleetest!

It was an easy stroll in the morning to the top of Landour where my feet crunched dry hard snow, and it was cold—very cold work to sit painting. I spent most of the day up there. Looking back over the plains all was haze in the afternoon and mist in the morning, and in the opposite direction clouds covered the snow-peaks of the Himalayas. The best view I had of the plains, however, was on the next day from Mussoorie, lower down—Mussoorie, that growing collection of bungalows and hotels soon to be filled for the season by the annual rush from below for health and cooler air.

Just beneath me I could see St Fidelis, the Soldiers' Orphanage, the St George's College, boarding-school for European boys, and beyond in the distance the dry zigzag bed of a tributary of the Ganges. Dehra Dun sat in the valley, and far away to the right, very faint indeed, rose the Siwaliks, the hills where once roamed monstrous elephants.

I walked down to Rajpur and being directed upon a wrong path was involved in a tramp of fourteen miles instead of the six taken by the old road from Mussoorie. There was little to vary the monotony of the road—a flock of white sheep—an English lady and her children being carried up in "dandies"—a tree fallen across the path. All through the hottest hours of the day I kept steadily on, and Tambusami, if he was not actually done up, pretended to be so, and when I insisted on watching a native tightrope dancer at Rajpur instead of getting into our tumtum, he was as near active revolt as his peaceable nature would permit.

CHAPTER XV

AN EVENING OF GOLD

About the time when many obscure fishing-folk in the British Isles were reaping rich harvest from Spanish galleons dismantled by storm and tempest, and the chief literary glory of England was paying scores at the Mermaid Tavern for men whose humour his genius turned to undying springs as it splashed on him from their cups, a woman in India who carried her husband in a basket, he being maimed and without hands or feet, placed him within the shadow of a tree while she sought alms from a neighbouring village. Now the man was no sluggard and had his eyes about him, and a lame crow, by reason of his own calamity, drew his attention. He watched the bird fly to an adjacent pool of water. To his amazement the crow no sooner dipped its legs than they became cured, so that it could walk, and its plumage turned at the same time to a milky whiteness. Rolling out of his basket the poor cripple himself reached the pool, and on his wife's return showed her a restored and perfect husband, with normal extremities, sitting upon the basket. At first it is said the woman declined to believe his identity, but Mr Buta Singh, the Amritsar bookseller, who tells the story in his *History of the Golden Temple*, asserts that "she was subsequently satisfied when the Guru attested the power of the Amrit" (which is the water of immortality).

I think there were possibilities of pathetic developments, and that although the addition of one hand or foot at a time might have been tolerable, it would have been altogether too much for any wife, while she had turned her back for the morning's shopping, to find the helpless subject of her charity able to walk over her, and her domination destroyed for ever. Be that as it may the story serves for the origin of the sacred tank of Amritsar and its far-famed Golden Temple. The Guru digging upon the site of the miracle is said to have come deep in the delved earth upon a mysterious chamber, housing an old ascetic seated in devotional posture, with grey hair grown long. There are still older legends of the holiness of the spot, for it is told that Buddha, passing through the country, stopped in the jungle by this same pool of water and said—"This spot is best for the Bhikshus to obtain salvation and far superior in that respect to other places in the East, but it must have time for its celebrity."

And when the time came the temple arose and all Amritsar. The great shrine itself stands in the middle of a large square tank, and its precincts include the whole of the wide pavements that surround the water. On these pavements one must go barefoot or wearing velvet footgear, supplied at a small boothlike office at the entrance to the square enclosure. This is attached to a police station, which boasts a speciality in the way of Indian clubs. A row of these, gigantic in size and of considerable weight, stands outside the door, and a Punjabi is ready (for a consideration) to display his splendid muscles like the "strong man" generally to be seen along the quays of Paris near the Institut de France.

A marble causeway bridges the water to the Hari Mandar (God's Temple), starting from a large gateway on the margin of the tank. By the side of this, when I first saw it, a Hindoo was sticking wet rose-leaves and marigold petals on to a wall-painting of a four-armed and four-headed Brahma. Entering the gateway I passed through two doors plated outside with silver and within inlaid with ivory upon the polished wood. A man stood at this portal holding a long heavy silver wand and looking, but for his turban, rather like a verger in some English cathedral. Many people were walking to and fro upon the causeway, but I pushed ahead to the open doors of the temple where the Granth Sahib, the sacred book of the Sikhs, lies covered with a cloth of gold and canary-coloured silk, under a great violet-lined canopy, from the centre of which hangs a golden tassel.

Immediately behind the Granth sat a high priest taking his four-hour turn of duty. A large bundle of peacock feathers lay to hand for dusting; but pigeons, catholic as to the place of their droppings, flew constantly in and out.

"And this is the watch given by Lord Curzon," said a self-appointed guide in my ear, pointing to a large clock set incongruously in the gilded copper wall over one of the four doorways.

A white drugget, held down by carved marble corner-weights, was spread over the centre of the marble pavement. On this, in front of the Granth Sahib, were three silver vessels for offerings of money, and about them lay a heap of loose cowries and pice, while some of the rosy-eyed pigeons pecked away at rice which had been scattered over the drugget. On making offering to the temple one is presented with a sugar cup—a half sphere of coarse white crystal sugar (the size of half an orange), of which I do not know the significance. Men called "Marrasis" on one side were playing stringed instruments and singing words of the Granth.

Up to a height of about six feet the walls were of white marble lined with black, and at the corners inlaid with mother-of-pearl and cornelians; there was a little flower pattern, but above this height the whole interior with its gallery was gilded, and the gold surface intricately patterned over in red and blue.

Outside, across the long causeway with its marble balustrade and rows of lamps, the entrance gate faces an open stone-flagged square surrounded by buildings, the chief of which is the gilt-domed Akal Bunga where, I was informed, "Sikhs are made." This institution is partly subsidized by Government and partly depends for income upon the offerings made by those who come to be initiated. It is a kind of house of investiture and ordination, and contains various historic treasures—"irons" of old time including weapons which belonged to some of the Gurus. Every orthodox Sikh must wear five things, and these are—first, the Kunga, a comb of wood or ivory; second, the Kara, a circlet of iron; third, the Kash or loincloth; fourthly, Kesh (pronounced Kaish) which means long hair, and lastly, a Kard or knife, a miniature specimen of which was given to me when I was garlanded in the Akal Bunga.

Extremely beautiful was the constant procession along the causeway of the temple votaries in bright dresses, and the dazzling brilliance of the golden building itself reflected in the surface of the water, one moment as still as a mirror and the next all quivering in a thousand ripples.

I walked round the border of the tank past various other "Bungas," built by princes and rajahs for their use when visiting Amritsar, till I reached the side farthest from the causeway; here, entering a garden, I passed an enclosed well and came to the tall tower called Baba Attal and climbed its seven storeys.

When I had reached Amritsar the evening before the whole place was under a pall. Dense clouds of white dust, choking and almost intolerable, swept along on the wings of a strong wind, hiding the side of the road like a thick fog and even driving along the passage-ways and corridors of the hotel and entering at every door and window; so it was with anxiety that I looked out next morning and with much relief beheld bright sunshine through a clearer air. Though, however, the wind-storm had abated, as I stood on the top of the tower, a pall of dust still hung over the city spoiling what should have been a wide and distant view.

The tower was built to commemorate a son of the sixth Guru who recalled to life a playmate who had died. The Guru is said to have been very wroth with his son for this act, whereupon Baba Attal lay down and died saying he gave his own life to his friend. The inside walls of several of the storeys are covered with painted frescoes, and on one floor true fresco painting upon wet plaster was actually going on. Small boys were grinding the colours, and an artist of skill and invention was covering the surface with scenes of crowded life illustrating sacred stories. His naïveté made me think a little of Benozzo Gozzoli, especially in his frescoes at San Gimignano, but this work was on a very much smaller scale and, for an Oriental artist, strangely lacking in design.

I returned late in the afternoon to the flagged square facing the entrance gate through which the marble causeway leads across the water. I said the pavement was stone—it is all of marble. About it sat many flower-sellers, men in white, red and black robes with baskets heaped with orange-coloured marigolds, blue cornflowers, pink roses and scarlet poppies. The silver doors stand open, and through the white marble gateway a constant stream of people come and go along the causeway with its rows of golden lamps on short marble standards leading to the Golden Shrine itself in the middle of the water.

Close by, from octagonal marble bases rise two tall masts of gold, at least sixty feet high and ending in spear-heads; a yellow flag hangs from each, one pale canary colour and one dark like the marigold flowers. Ropes keep these masts firm, ropes with grand curves that sweep from the iron collars, necking the masts high up, to iron rings fixed in the surrounding buildings.

Under a little shrine in the wall sits a blind man. The water of the sacred tank may bring him inner vision, but to-day has no such virtue as to cure aggravated cataract. A stranger stops a moment at the shrine, and when he is gone the blind man rises and gropes with his hands to feel if any pice had been put down on the small marble ledge that projects before the painting of a Guru.

The sun has now just set and a light that seems to cast no shadows spreads and grows, suffusing all the scene in soft effulgence. Most of the women are dressed in long trousers, close fitting from the ankles to the knees and then bagging out loosely. They all have long veils which they wear like a hood; some are white but others scarlet, crimson, or orange, and some of green silk tissue strewn with silver stars and bordered with a ribbon of bright gold. It is the hour when even humble clothes take on luxurious tints, and richer stuffs show all their utmost beauty in enhanced perfection. One passes near wearing trousers of pale blue with silver pattern, a silk coat of deep rose-pink, and over all a veil of pale canary-coloured tissue painted with roses and bordered deeply with gold. I thought "Was Solomon in all his glory..." but just then some children playing with a ball butted against me in sudden collision, and at the same time I encountered a Sikh gentleman who claimed direct descent from the second Guru, spoke English softly, and in leisured talk deplored to me the vanity of women.

In front of the building called the Akal Bunga, which faces the entrance to the causeway, a great drugget stretched from the upper branches of a tree heavy with leafage to staples set in the wall. The leaves shook and the drugget swayed a little. Old priests with long white beards sat at large window openings chanting—thousands of windows were in sight, but never one pane of glass though sometimes wooden doors or gaily-painted shutters. A woman passed arrayed like some princess of mediæval France, wearing a golden head-dress shaped like a sugarloaf and tapering slenderly to a point whence yards of pale blue tissue floated in the air behind her. In the same clear air a child's kite high above caught glints of light. Oh! golden, golden hour, how often on a wistful thread my thought like that child's kite will float away, borne by easy airs of memory, into that distant scene and dream it all again!

CHAPTER XVI

"GUARD YOUR SHOES"

A wide, sandy plain with trees and a little scrub. Here and there camels were feeding on this poor herbage or, where they could reach them, upon the leaves of trees.

I was on my way from Amritsar in the Bombay mail-train, and after passing Wazirabad and Lalamusa the country changed from flat plain to irregular humps and hillocks of mud, as far as eye could see. Mud everywhere—grey, desolate, monotonous mud. I passed mud towns. Here and there accumulated stores of great mud-coloured logs lay near the line river-floated from the hill forests of Kashmir. Then slabs and ridges of grey rock thrust out of the mud. I could see away over a plain of pathless distances to where a range of mountains slowly grew. Then, as in a world of crumbling fossil cities, all the grey desiccated land was dust. Presently, wild yellow grasses appeared near the dry beds of former pools and quivered a little in the faint evening breeze.

I reached Peshawar a little before dawn and got out at the cantonment and not at the city station. A powerful electric light illuminated the wide platform. It gleamed on the white sides of the carriages and caught with light the creepers on long strips of wooden trellis between the upright posts of the long station veranda. A man huddling a blanket round him was leaning back against the bookstall, and as he turned his head, his beard shone fiery red. In a drizzling rain (thrice blessed for previous shortage) mail-bags were being pitched from the train into a trolley-box. In the stationmaster's room a group of great-coated men with rifles crowded round a fire. The city station had been raided only one week before, and although the cantonment was safer "than houses" there was an invigorating air of excitement.

I drove to the Alexandra Hotel and slept for a few hours in a tent in the compound, as the rooms were all occupied by the wives of officers returning from a military expedition.

All that day Peshawar seemed a veritable slough, but the night was clear and starry and the following morning sunshine reigned. Snow glittered on the distant mountains, white cherry-blossom gleamed in orchard and garden. English children, some on ponies and some in "prams," were out with their ayahs, and the wide tree-bordered and well-kept roads through the cantonment looked not unlike English parkland in spring.

I entered the city by the Kissa Kahani—the Peshawar Lombard Street—

through the pointed arch of the Edwardes Gate, the Kabuli Dariwaza. This led me to the Kotwali, with its own wide gateway leading off at right angles into the silk market and the older parts of the city. Immediately on the other side of this white-washed police station is a wide and busy space. The Kotwali faces an octagonal rest-place, called the Hastings Memorial, with seats on a platform some ten feet above the road at the other end, and between the two was a dazzling scene.

Red and white and yellow, hung out to dry in the sun after being dyed, were a myriad skeins of silk (brought hither from Bokhara and from China), on long lines up and down one side of the oval space. Opposite to these, bordering as it were the central way, were stalls of bankers and money-changers—four of them side by side and each with their large pile of rupees and other coins (which is really a mud-cone covered outside to look like a solid heap of silver). Then at the back, behind the silk on the one side and the money stalls on the other, were the lines of bazaar shops.

I turned right from the Hastings Memorial and presently reached a building called the Gor Khatri which stands on a piece of rising ground, and here I found Mr Agha Khan—not the celebrated head of the Aligar College, but a junior Tehsildar who had been deputed to show me Peshawar.

We went first up to the roof of the building from which there is a fine view over both country and city. Mr Agha Khan was a short Mohammedan with a black beard, many clothes, and a large stick. He pointed out to me a small Hindoo temple about forty yards away called the Gorak Nat, the name of a Hindoo saint who lived there many years ago and gave the name *Gor* Khatri. This building was originally a guest-house built by Nour Jehan, Jehangir's queen, and is sometimes called still the Sarai of Nour Jehan Begum. Its greatest title to fame, however, lies in its having been occupied for many years and largely added to by the Italian General Paolo Crescenzo Martino Avitabile, one of the most romantic characters in history and, under Runjeet Singh, Governor of Peshawar, which he was the first man to keep really in order.

Walking on the flat roof with Agha Khan I looked over all the city. In the distance to the right rose Mount Tartara from the line of hills that surround Peshawar on three sides like a horseshoe. Cutting through the flat-roofed town, and coming straight to our feet, was the long sharp shadow of the Bara Bazaar. To the left I could see the red-brick Mission Hospital; the large cupola of the mosque of Dilawar Khan, a Kardar in the time of Chaghatta; and still farther to the left, a tower called the Burj of Said Khan; while far away beyond Peshawar, a dip in the nearer hills, marked the position of Jamroud guarding the entrance to the Khyber Pass. Behind us, across the compound of space belonging to the Gor Khatri, was another of its buildings used at times of Mohammedan festival and as quarters for any representative of the Amir of Afghanistan coming to Peshawar.

The Gor Khatri itself is now used for municipal offices. The unglazed window spaces are fitted with dull red wooden shutters; shoes were lying about everywhere in the large rooms, and the brick floors, covered with rush matting, were littered with books of paper made in the Peshawar gaol—that revered building which gives compulsory shelter to so many saintly characters. Amid a heap of documents officials squatted with reed pens, each under his own particular cupboard let into the thickness of the wall.

Here upon dhurries spread over the rough matting sat the "Siahnavis" who keeps the general revenue accounts of the Tahsil. Opposite to him, also on the floor, sat the cashier, the "Devidial" (salary 15 rupees per month). Then at 20 rupees per month, in the midst of a huge litter on a red and blue striped dhurry, sat the Wasil Baganavis, keeping the accounts from the separate villages of the Tahsil. Opposite to him again was the "Ghulam Mahdi" (15 rupees per month). He keeps accounts of income tax and wears silver studs. "Every man who makes a profit of 1000 rupees or more in a year," said Agha Khan, "has to pay income tax."

In the next room, Mr Faujuin, a Pathan, fair, and speaking some English, keeps for 20 rupees per month the Urdu records of cases, criminal, civil revenue, and judicial revenue. He is called the judicial "Muharrir." Then I came to the "Kanungo," the highest of these minor officials who keeps (for 40 rupees per month) records concerning crops and agricultural matters. In this Tahsil, the Kanungo informed me, among the chief things grown are rice, maize, cherry-maize, bajra, sugar-cane, cotton, chilis, cabbages, carrots, turnips, wheat, barley, grain and sesamum—also a little tobacco and, among fruits, grapes, pomegranates, melons and water-melons. There are eighty-two patwaris, lesser officers for the villages in this Tahsil and four field Kanungos who bring in the village reports. Finally, I was introduced to the Tehsildar under whom, with his two assistants, all these other officials work. The Tehsildar owns to 200 rupees per month and the assistant Tehsildars to 60 rupees each.

Inside the main gateway of the Gor Khatri, in a room behind iron railings, were a couple of prisoners. In cases of non-payment of taxes the Tehsildar has power to keep a prisoner for ten days before sending him for trial before the Deputy Commissioner, who may then sentence him to a month's imprisonment. In criminal cases the Tehsildar can himself sentence up to six months.

Mr Agha Khan and I now drove half-way down the Bara Bazaar and then walked up a very muddy side street called the street of Hakims (native doctors). We stopped to talk to one sitting on the raised floor of his shop with its rows of strange bottles and drug jars.

Mr Agha Khan and I were getting on famously. He did not seem at all wearied by my questions, and appeared to enjoy my happiness in being in what is largely still an Afghan, if not a Persian, city. But the doctor—this old turbaned, black-bearded magician with so much spare drapery! I would not ask his name lest I should be told it was not Abenazer and that he never had a nephew, but I did ask what money he charged for his advice and drugs. And the Hakim answered, "A rupee if I go to the patient's house, but if the sick man come himself to the shop only the medicine do I charge him for and the cost of that would be three to five rupees." I wondered if the latter price was in expectation of any possible demands of my own and remarked, "That would surely be a very great deal if the sick man were a poor man." "If the illness is serious," said Mr Agha Khan, "he will be able to pay—otherwise he will not."

Near by was a barber's shop, combined with a bathing establishment. We went inside and as I wished to see the baths the barber got a small lamp and took me to the back of the shop where the baths were: stone boxes like tiny cachots with wooden doors. There was just room for a man to stand upright or squat upon the floor, and in the middle of the wall on one side was a small hole in which the bowls of water could be placed from without.

A woman at the corner of the street was cooking or "popping" maize. She put the maize into a bowl-shaped depression over the fire with some black sand which was afterwards sifted back from the corn. She was paid by retaining a small portion of each lot brought for her to cook.

Near by was the mosque of Dilawar Khan, of brick-work and decorated plaster, and a tank of turbid green water in the middle with red goldfish swimming about in it. Mr Agha Khan said that Dilawar Khan was a Khardar of the Chaghattai kings. I noticed a long wooden trough *inside* the mosque. "It is to put the shoes for safety," said Agha Khan; "there are many thieves here who would take them if left outside," which indexed one side of the Peshawar character and showed that the Pathan's passion for thieving is greater than his respect for religious observance.

We watched some goldsmiths for a while and then a baker making round flat cakes called "gird" of wheaten flour and water and others of the Afghan pattern shaped like a flat spoon. These are called "Nan," and have ghee (butter) mixed with the flour so that they cost two annas each whereas the girds cost but two pice. The oven is like a spherical kiln in the floor with the fire inside on the bottom and a small round opening at the top on the floor level where the baker sits. When he has kneaded the dough and marked his cake with various thumb-marks for decoration, he takes a *rafida,* a kind of small stiff pillow, wets it and on it puts the cake. Then, reaching down through the oven-hole with his hand, he slaps it up on to the curved wall and leaving the cake adhering brings out the pillow again. Then when the bread is cooked, with a hooked bamboo stick called a kundi he brings out the baked loaf. "I am very wise and clever to do this work," said the baker, "this is not easy work."

Next we called at a dispensary where a native doctor, trained at a medical school at Lahore, told me he sees an average of 200 patients per day. Eyes and throats were the most frequent trouble. We saw another mosque—one founded by Gangeli Khan, another official under the Chaghattai kings—with a fine old Imam. The Imam must be ready at all times to go to the house of one dying and read the Arsin as well as to wash the body and perform various ceremonies after death.

In another part of the city I went to see a house in the street called Undar Shahr which had been recently raided by Zakka Khels. Two bankers, Nan Dan and Chela Ram, had the upper floor where the raid took place. Going through an open passage-way in this building I came into an Afghan merchant's go-down, where raisins brought from Kabul were being sampled by a group of men sitting upon the floor. Among these merchants, bargaining with them, I saw, somewhat to my surprise, an enterprising Teuton!

With regard to the raid and the probability of its having been engineered by friends living in the city, I was told the following native proverb:—

"Chori Yaru naukri
Baj Wasila nahi."

Of which the meaning is:—

"Theft, love and service
All require a go-between."

Near the Katchari Gate is the Government High School, a large red-brick building next to a white Hindoo house. I went in one day and found the lowest class sitting in a circle on a large dhurry in the garden, the boys' shoes taken off and carefully put aside. The classmaster, Abdul Rahim, was teaching reading and writing. These children pay from one to three annas per month, while boys in the higher classes pay from three to eight rupees each. Some higher classes were doing gymnastics in the playground. They were all Mohammedans except four and very few of them were married, marriage in the North-West Provinces being usually later than elsewhere. While Mr Hargreaves, the enthusiastic headmaster, was telling me this, a small boy in black velvet came up to him. The boy brought a message from two others in one of the classes in the schoolhouse. He said he wanted "leave" for Chan Bad Sha (which means moon king) and Phul Bad Sha (which means flower king), because the sister of Chan Bad Sha's mother was sick. I was then shown a boy whose father, the Shahzada, Abdul Karim, was King of Kokand, the district from which Babar came. This lad, who wore a long-sleeved Chitral coat, talks five languages—Turki, Urdu, Persian, Chitrali, Pushtu and English. "My home is two months' journey from here—from the way of Kabul, Bokhara and Samarkand," he said.

Another clever youngster was Fazal Rahman whose father was a C.S.I. Fazal was enormously fat and appeared proportionately good-tempered. Many of the boys show an altogether precocious and surprising memory. Mr Hargreaves told me he had caught them knowing by heart, without understanding it, an epitome of English history they had got hold of surreptitiously to save all bother of studying the proper history book.

Several men and a boy who had been waiting some while for the headmaster's attention now received audience. The youth was an Afridi, whose name had been crossed off the books for continuous absence and who wanted to be re-admitted. He was very fair, with beautiful brown eyes unusually large, and declared he would never be absent again if they would take him back. He had been sick—very sick—but was well again. His white turban was dirty. His lungs had been wrong since June, but at last he had been put in a freshly-flayed sheepskin for some hours and was quite cured!

Outside the school I passed an old Hajji who had lately come from Mecca and was on his way home. A number of his fraternity, waiting for some days in one of the Sarais, had just cost the schoolmaster twelve annas for rope. The cause was as follows:—Moti (which means Pearl) was the name of an exceptionally ugly buffalo whose only labour was the daily drawing of a little water on a piece of land belonging to the school. Moti was well fed, and at night was always taken by the man who had charge of him to sleep in the Sarai, now crowded by the ponies of the Hajjis. The buffalo resented the unusually close quarters and in the silence of the night, charged right and left into the Hajjis and their ponies. The pilgrims thereupon attacked Moti's guardian with sticks and belaboured him soundly, and thus it was that Moti's keeper required 12 annas for new rope wherewith to bind the outraged buffalo.

The schoolmaster introduced me to a great friend of his, an American archæologist, Dr Brainerd Spooner, whose charm is only equalled by his energy and whom I found in one of the trenches at Shahijikidheri a little way from the city where he was superintending excavations in search of the great Buddhist stupa of Kanishka or its foundations.

A thorough organization of archæological survey in India was one of the fruits of Lord Curzon's viceroyalty and Dr Spooner, who is a specialist in ancient Oriental languages, was superintendent of the survey in the North-West Frontier circle.

Kanishka, according to Vincent Smith, lived about A.D. 125, and is supposed to have erected near Peshawar the most lofty and important stupa of all India, so celebrated indeed that it, or rather its adjacent monastery, was occupied for a thousand years. "We are trying to prove," said Dr Spooner as we tramped along deep trenches and clambered over mud hillocks, "that this is really the spot where Kanishka did build." I saw some masses of masonry and lines of wall which had already been uncovered, and later, at Peshawar museum, some pieces of sculpture and plaster reliefs showing very strong Greek influence; but since my visit, far greater success has rewarded Dr Spooner's labours including the discovery of the Buddha relics which have now been presented to the Buddhists at Rangoon.

CHAPTER XVII

"A GATE OF EMPIRE"

Mr Agha Khan had undertaken to send me early on a certain morning a "suitable" vehicle in which to drive to the Khyber Pass. It proved to be a heavy old phaeton with a pair of big lumpy horses and a driver named Junno Kuchwan. It was not possible to get any other conveyance without some hours' delay, and as the "fitten" as he called it was already behind time (it was 7.15 a.m.), I started in it for Jamroud and the famous Pass.

A military expedition was just over but convoys of stores had still to return, and when I obtained permission to enter the Khyber and make a painting of the fort of Ali Masjid, the pass had not yet been re-opened.

Four miles from Peshawar and five from Jamroud I stopped near some big tamarind trees. The place, a military border police fort, was called Harising Poor, and from it I could see the big fort of Jamroud on the level plain and to the left, violet in the morning light, the hills of the Khyber through a V-shaped dip in the horseshoe of mountain that nearly surrounds the Peshawar country. Very far to the right, snow mountains watched over the nearer hills and away to the left, where raiders come from above, was a small blockhouse where twenty-five men were kept.

As I drove nearer to Jamroud the native hamlet appeared, with a tall tower of the usual village type, at some distance from the Fort, and the long wall of the Sarai where passing caravans, coming from Central Asia and Afghanistan, stop on the last night before they reach Peshawar.

I saw a company of the Khyber Rifles being drilled in an open space near the Sarai. I watched them marching in fours—marching in fours to a flank and company opening fire in close order. The men were Afridis of various tribes and the Subadar, the senior native officer of the company, was a Malikdin Khel Afridi—all good fighters, cunning thieves and as light-hearted as children. A great Jirga was about to be held at Peshawar and armed tribesmen were dribbling in to attend it.

Before going on to the mouth of the Pass I looked into the Sarai. The men in it were mostly Kabulis waiting to go up and not down. They were taking tea, sugar and general supplies from Peshawar, having sold there the raisins they had brought in from Afghanistan. Their camels were of the long-haired Central Asian type, stronger than the Indian camels and very different in appearance.

The Fort of Ali Masjid, in the Khyber Pass.

Reproduced by permission of the Visual Instruction Committee of the Colonial Office.

My permit having been examined at the fort, and a khaki clad sepoy of the Khyber Rifles told off to accompany me by way of escort, I drove on towards the mouth of the pass. The road enters by a sweeping curve along which the wind blew strongly. Here the "fitten" horses began to jib, and in spite of all Junno Kuchwan could do they flatly refused to go forward. Kuchwan, who had been on foot for some time, at last began to heave rocks at the horses which was still unproductive of the desired result. It became clear that we could never reach Ali Masjid with these animals, and there was nothing for it but to get back to Jamroud and try for a chance "tumtum," having come out from Peshawar earlier in the morning. We found, however, there were only two and both were booked for immediate return. It seemed hopeless and I was beginning to arrange for the next day when the officer in command of the fort pointed out another "tumtum" just emerging from the pass and exclaimed, with an eager twinkle in his eyes, and a peculiar straightening of the back, "There's a lady in it."

There were two ladies in it—they had driven from Landi Kotal, having made the journey from Kabul in eleven days. The younger said she was a lady doctor just leaving the Amir's service, and they were both persuaded to let me have their vehicle and drive on themselves to Peshawar in my phaeton.

In addition to my Hindoo servant I had now with me the sepoy escort, and throughout the rest of the journey there was a running squabble because the tumtum driver contended that he ought to walk. The rifleman was a Kuchi Khel Afridi, and his most obvious characteristic was a passion for shaking hands with me. Whenever vituperative argument seemed extra strong, the Kuchi Khel appeared to cap the other man's invention and turned to shake my hand grinning and nodding his head. This occurred at about three minute intervals during the afternoon. I might be gazing at the landscape or noting cave dwellings on the hillside—when I would feel my hand suddenly seized and wrung hastily; he was a very friendly man this Afridi!

We passed altogether quite a number of people along the road. In one place where I was walking some tribesmen invited me to share their food, and I ate with them—bread, coarse brown sugar in lump and Indian corn. Then I passed an officer of the Amir's army with a convoy of mules bringing the goods and chattels of the lady doctor.

The fort of Ali Masjid crowns what looks like a steeply sloping squat cone of hill in the middle of the pass, about half-way that is between Jamroud and Landi Kotal, with the main line of hills on each side. It is of tawny yellowish stone of much the same colour as the ground. I climbed up to it from the roadway but found no one within. Hot and dusty with the clamber I walked round the walls, banged at doors and shouted loudly to any who might be inside, but to no purpose, and it was only later that I learned how it was that no one was stationed up in the fort itself. The reason was that the camp remaining from the expeditionary forces was pitched below by the side of the road on what had been a few wheatfields belonging to an adjacent village of cave-dwelling Kuchi Khels.

My permit demanded early return that I might be at Jamroud again well before dark, and after an hour or two I started back little knowing how soon I was to see Ali Masjid again.

What happened was that we came to a place where there was a sick camel on the road, and the tumtum horses both took it into their heads to shy violently and become generally rampant. The bamboo shafts of the vehicle were not very strong and when, through the sudden plunging, they both suddenly snapped short off at the body of the tumtum and left two splintered ends I, being in front, was thrown upon one of the rearing ponies. I managed to get clear without any hurt and none of us were harmed as much as the driver himself, who was a bit bruised and had one finger torn. His face, by the way, was disfigured by an old scar which he said was through a former break-down.

Now whatever it was the tumtum driver said to the sepoy at this juncture it roused his deepest feelings, and a torrent of execration raged between them. It was clear that the whole affair was being laid upon the Afridi's shoulders, and I don't know how long he would have kept his hands off the driver if two young officers on their way back to the camp had not reined up to know what was the extent of the damage. Dusk was not far away and they insisted that I must ride back to Ali Masjid and spend the night in camp with the 59th Scinde Rifles Frontier Force. I say insisted, but I was nothing loth.

At first, however, it only seemed to be a case of "out of the frying-pan into the fire," for the native bred horse called up for me started off at a hurricane pace, refusing to obey the reins. I left the officers far behind, and every time the road turned I was at some difficulty to keep in the saddle. The more I pulled the faster the horse went. I wondered afterwards whether this impetuosity was intended as an expression of joy at his new burden or annoyance. He gave in at last and gradually became amenable, but I am convinced that no warrior of any of the conquering armies that have entered by the Khyber Pass ever rode so swiftly towards India as I galloped away from it.

Heaped about the camp was a great quantity of booser bales, and in the wind, which was steadily rising, the chopped straw of the booser blew everywhere. The very walls of the mess were built of booser bales for there was no tent—only enough sailcloth to make a roof (absence of tents and "travelling light" generally had greatly helped the success of the recent expedition). After dinner, with the wind still rising higher and higher, straining at every cord, tearing and ripping everything that could be torn or ripped, howling so loudly that even coughing camels could not be heard through it, most of us sat talking while the surgeon and another played picquet by the light of a hurricane lantern.

There had been some of the enemy's people among our own troops (they had had option) and stories were told of them. One tower in the Bazar valley belonged to a Jemadar among the party about to demolish it. "Would you like us to let your tower stand?" he was asked. "Oh! smash it up, sahib, I shall get compensation." Apart from personal or family feuds it really matters little to the Afridi which side he is on so long as there is a sure chance of fighting; he loves it more than life. When they came to the Jirga what was the first question asked by the "enemy"?

Some Zakkha Khels went up to the General and asked him, "Did we fight well, sahib?"

It was said that compassionate members of Parliament, knowing as much of a Zakkha Khel's mode of life as that of the ruling class in Mars, had begged at Westminster that their gardens and orchards might not be destroyed, and that their women and children might not be turned into the *streets*. These things cheered the camp at Ali Masjid, however irritating they might have been to authority. The women and children had all been moved to places of safety before the expedition started. A blind about "manoeuvres" was well understood in the Peshawar bazaar, though the unusual rapidity of the movements did surprise, and, as objected at the Jirga, the use of smokeless powder was baffling.

At first no newspaper correspondents were allowed to come near, but one or two young men who reached the expedition later certainly did their little part to increase hilarity. One reported that Lala Chena (which he did not know was another name for Ali Masjid) was destroyed with heavy loss, and another that a regiment of Goorkhas (who pride themselves on doing everything possible quietly by signs) entrained with much noise and shouting.

"If I'm charged for transport on this kit I refuse to go on service again," said a man with a green eyeshade. Four conversations were going on at the same time and all were fighting with the noise of the wind. "Fourteen aces and fourteen queens," called Hubby the surgeon from the depths of his sheepskin coat. "I expect Hubby's going to pay for his transport," cried another, and one, reading from regulations—"Any class of transport animal may be provided except elephants." And one telling yarns of Tommies and the vernacular—"I dunno wot 'ee says, sir. Look 'ere, I'll call my mate—'ee can bowl over bat" (bol, *i.e.*, speak, and bat, *i.e.*, language). And of thirsty Tommy on a railway platform—"Now, then, bring that there pani—don't be lumba or I'll break your confounded seer," and again—"Know their lingo? No, sir, I axes 'em once in English and then I brings the lakri."

Of camels—"We were going along a very narrow path with a steep drop on one side of a thousand feet or so and a sheer rise on the other. Suddenly one of the camels slipped and rolled down. We halted and looked over the edge and saw the poor beast ever so far below. I sent some men down to cut off what baggage had remained on the animal and to collect as much as possible of the rest, and the man who looked after the camels went down to cut the tail off to show the owner that he had not sold this one. He took his knife out and was just getting 'home' when that camel gave a spring and made for the ledge. We loaded him up again and—Oh, yes, the tail was all right!"

Then of Afridi feuds and of the sepoy who would go on firing after an officer rode up and told him to stop as the distance was much too great. How he entirely ignored the officer and continued to fire, and then to a sharp remonstrance only said: "Do let me have one more shot, sahib; it's my uncle."

Among these hillmen there are very binding unwritten laws. No man may kill his brother while he holds the plough in his hand. The blood-feud is the life of the Afridi, but they prefer some reason in the start. Thus when a certain rifleman ran amuck, and it was necessary that he should be shot, some of his relatives appealed to the officer in command, begging that to them might be given the killing of him since were it done by any not of his own family a feud must be started and many deaths ensue.

At night I was given the luxury of a hospital dhoolie, whereby I was much better sheltered from the wind than the others. Officers and men vainly sought sleep, and booser whirled everywhere about the camp. The young moon swung in the starlit sky: signallers at a blockhouse flashed their tiny sparks to a party up on the ridge: in the darkness of the hills unseen and far rested a hoof-mark of Mohammed's steed. I put my head out for a last peep at Orion and soon was in a dreamless slumber.

In the morning I was out early watching the camels in the wind and later, in a little shelter, I painted a portrait of Nasir Khan, a Subadar of the 59th Scinde Rifles and a Eusaf Zai Pathan. He had a beard of fiery red, which I was told is the result of using black dye and not being able to renew the treatment.

On the hillside above the camp was a Kuchi Khel village of cave-dwellings. I asked my sepoy escort to climb up to it with me but he firmly declined, explaining that it was his own village and that he had a feud on, so one of the officers accompanied me.

The hill, called Asrog, which means the veins of the horse, was now in bright light. The fort on the round molehill shape in the middle of the pass appeared sharply against a drift of cloud. Beyond it, towards Landi Kotal, the silhouette of mountain was black purple, with two growing patches of yellow light, where the sun got through behind the fort. And all the while the wind, the Khyber wind, hustled and tore and screamed through the camp.

The loose shale glistened in the sun and the low bushes looked silver grey as I again left Ali Masjid, following the little stream that spates in June when the snows melt. Then these caves on the hillside will be empty and the Kuchi Khels will be all away up in the Tirah hills.

CHAPTER XVIII

THE CAPITAL OF THE PUNJAB

"Hatee Aiah! Hatee aiah!" — "The elephant comes!" cried the children running, and one small scamp danced in front and shouted, *"Hatee kuta machi bucha"* — "The elephant is a dog bad beast," and fled to escape consequences of such boldness. I was now seeing Lahore city from the back of one of the Lieutenant-Governor's State elephants which had swelled with pride the heart of Tambusami, my servant, when in all the bravery of scarlet trappings it came to fetch me from the hotel. Tambusami's respect for "Government" was almost sublime. He rarely showed the faintest interest in shrines or temples, but invariably reflected every manifestation of official interest in, or attention to, his master. On such occasions the whole strain of his body seemed differently keyed, and on the back of that elephant he gave himself the most amusing airs, tilting up his chin and appearing to bask in an atmosphere of luxurious importance for all the world like a child playing at chief minister to some Haroun al Raschid, who had thrown off disguise and shown himself to the public in proper grandeur.

With me was a delightful Pundit Omaid Chand, Superintendent of the Punjab Government Records, who accompanied me during my stay at Lahore. "My native place," he told me, "was Saharanpur in the United Provinces; but now I am a nationalized Punjabi because I have been here fifty years since I was eight years old."

We entered the city by the Delhi Gate and filled the narrow street so that there was consternation among the shopkeepers and joy among the children all along our route. Elephants are no longer used so much as formerly, and at Lahore even the Lieutenant-Governor only keeps two now instead of eight.

When we met a troop of buffaloes there was a mighty hubbub. The shopkeepers squealed and jibbered much that I am sure was impolite as the frightened beasts plunged and pressed upon their goods. Many of the taller buildings with elaborately carved woodwork belonged to well-to-do Mohammedans, who have their homes away from the city, and use such houses in the intervals of business, and for friends of an evening. They do not usually go home till after nine o'clock at night. We were, of course, on a level with the projecting balconies and carved oriel windows. Here and there awnings were stretched across the street between the opposite houses, and once or twice we had to wait while these were hauled up to let us go by. Passing through another gateway we halted before a beautiful mosque, wondrous with exquisite tints of blue and green in the old glazed tiles that were all about its front and minarets. Its elaborate inscriptions were in blue, with yellow and green ornament on a white ground. Baked daily in the sun for nigh three hundred years the beauty of this glazed inlay was only enhanced by time, and well may it last unharmed through future centuries! The narrow streets, in spite of all their charm, will be swept away as the townsfolk gradually alter their standards and ideas, but the traveller of the age to come should still find this fair mosque to please his eyes.

Out of the city at length we came to the now open space about the crenelated walls and bastions of the fort, and the Badshahi Masjid with its four old capless minars. Midway between the west gate of this mosque and the walls of the Fort stands the graceful pavilion called the Baradari. The stone is mostly red Agra sandstone, Jehangir's favourite building material, recalling Kenilworth in colour, but the mosque has three domes of white marble.

Descending once more to earth I walked all over the fort, with its Pearl Mosque of white Jeypore marble (much, so much less fine than the Moti Masjids of either Delhi or Agra) its white Nau Lakha, its Diwan-y-khas, looking ready to tumble to pieces, though now in the restorer's hands, and its Shish Mahal.

Near these last, to the right of the same quadrangle, is the armoury. In Europe the traveller is often shown instruments of torture—rack or boot or "maiden," and in England what village of tourist attractiveness is without either stocks or pillory? In India, however, such relics are rare, and those shown at the Lahore Armoury, including a machine for pulling off thieves' fingers, invented by Dhuleep Singh, only remind one of the general absence of such stepping stones to civilization.

There is a great variety among this choice collection of weapons, and although it cannot compete with that of Turin, Valetta or Hertford House, it would prove at least a valuable addition to any one of them. Here are recalled the times of Ranjeet Singh, the one-eyed monarch, who had the genius to gather under him European officers of such calibre as Avitabile, Allard and Ventura. Here are cuirasses, imported by General Ventura for his French legion of 8000 men, bearing on their fronts the Gallic cock with laurels and standards on a star of steel, and beside them Sikh shields with copper bosses. Here are swords from Iran, with ivory hilts and blades engraved with mottoes calling on the help of "Ali." There are combination swords and pistols, Afghan knives, old flint-lock and match-lock guns with barrels damascened, old four-chambered match-lock revolver guns, musquets (short carbines or blunderbusses) carried by the Gurcharahis, (Sikh cavalry 4000 strong), tir kaman (bows and arrows), tarkash (quivers), Abyssinian shotels made with a double curve and wielded with the point downwards, Mahratta swords, farangs—straight swords adapted by the Mahrattas from the Portuguese, Khandahs, those long Sikh swords made broader near the point, a Persian mace of the time of Rustem—a gem for any collection—tabai (battle-axes) gokru, the crowsfoot—caltrap of ancient Europe for throwing down to stop cavalry, a Burmese Dha or Dhas, a fakir's baraggan or short sword-stick leaning on which some "muni of the ages" has sat in meditation in the jungle. There are Goorkha kukris and Hindoo Katars, the iron-shod stick of a Chaukidar, a powder-flask of golden thread, back-plates and breast-plates and helmets of steel and brass.

The armoury is certainly more interesting to-day than the Shish Mahal opposite wherein, as in a certain chamber at Versailles, it is said that begums and a man would shut themselves for weeks together. Here there is indeed no armoury of love—is it because the weapons of that warfare were of a kind inseparable from those who wielded them—the charms that vanished with their owners? Or can it be that their enduring pattern has never been improved upon, so that each blade and buckler of the past is still in full demand for current wear?

I went up to the roof of the Shish Mahal for the view of Ranjeet Singh's tomb and the Badshahi mosque, and between its minarets towards the west could see the silver band that is the Ravi River, and then before going back to the elephant I looked at Ranjeet Singh's tomb on which certain bosses are carved in the marble with curious significance. Eleven of these are grouped round a large centre, and of the eleven four are for Ranees (who are married women) and seven for concubines, while at two of the corners of the slab are detached smaller bosses to commemorate a pair of pigeons burned in the funeral pyre.

What a contrast, I thought, on returning to the spacious roads of the modern town outside the city gates, between the new order and the old! On arriving at Lahore the first thing that the stranger notices is the fortified railway station, then a tank and an old mosque covered with green-glazed tiles with others about it of bright peacock-blue; and then, as he drives from the station in a gharry, through white dust, past quite handsome modern buildings in pale red brick, comes the "Upper Mall," a perfect road with an ideal lay-out for a modern town—wide and trim with electric-light standards painted a clean grey on brick-edged grass strips which separate the centre roadway from a riding track that, in its turn, runs parallel to a footway; while on either side stretches a line of gardens. It is all as handsome as the Boulevard Anspach at Brussels, and as different from the more lovable streets in old Lahore as can well be imagined.

I had seen in front of the museum Zam Zammah, the old gun with a long history which Rudyard Kipling played round as a boy long before Kim was written, and had watched the urchin scrambling on its back when the policeman was not looking. Having heard that the character of Mahbub Ali of *Kim*—"known as one of the best horse-dealers in the Punjab"—was drawn from a man named Wazir Khan (not that minister of Akhbar after whom the Chauk of Wazir Khan is named, but an old horse-dealer who is still alive), I took some trouble to inquire for him. The old man was on the road, however, having gone to a horse-fair at Jhelum, but I found his son and asked him to show me the old Sarai where his father used to sleep on his visits to Lahore. This is called the Sarai of Mahomet Sultan and belongs to the Maharajah of Kashmir. It is a wide quadrangle, about 60 yards square, with round-arched cloisters on all sides; and the son of Wazir Khan showed me, shut off between pillars, the place where his father used to sleep in the old days. The shadows of a large shisham tree flickered over the broken white plaster of the wall. There was a well in the centre, and near it was a group of horses from Waziristan. Out through the gateway ("the Gate of the Harpies who paint their eyes and trap the stranger") I could see the Lunda Bazaar and a woman squatting on the edge of the footway washing her face with soap. Near her was a tamasha wallah, a boy with a cage of green parrots, and a Hindoo woman cooking chupatties over a fire of dung-cakes, and from one of the houses there was singing in Pushtu.

I returned to the old gun and entered the building of the "wonder-house" in front of which it stands.

The Mayo School of Industrial Art, which is attached to the Lahore Museum, was founded to revive arts now half forgotten, and generally to develop the Industrial Art of the Province. I went thoroughly over its various departments, its schools of modelling and design, architecture, engineering, wood-carving and carpentry, repoussé and blacksmith's work—and I do not think the importance of this college, as an educational institution, could be exaggerated. Its ambition to turn out a constant succession of the best possible craftsmen, rather than theoretic students, makes it the best means yet arrived at of moral and mental development inseparable to my thinking from the purely utilitarian value of handicraft training. Among the students were pointed out to me lads from distant villages and outlying districts, some in receipt of Government stipends, others supported by District and Municipal Boards and others again by Independent States. A well-regulated boarding-house is connected with the school for the accommodation of such pupils, a large proportion of whom find immediate employment on the completion of their course at the school and so continually add to the popularity of its training.

The energy, talent and success of Mr Percy Brown during the many years in which he has developed and enlarged the scheme initiated under the late Mr Lockwood Kipling, are beyond praise, and I only hope that his recent translation to Calcutta may bring an extension to other provinces of India of practical application of the same educational ideas.

The museum is justly proud of its Buddhist sculptures, the best of which is one in black hornblende schiste (from the Yusafzai country near Peshawar), of Buddha after his forty-nine days' fast. Carved with extreme delicacy and refinement, this wonderful sculpture seems to carry one rather to Renaissance Italy than the North-West Provinces. Who were they, these sculptors? How much or how little were they identified with the people whose gods they carved? Would Alexander of Macedon have had in his train men of sufficient eminence in their craft to account for the apparent Western influence?

One of the latest additions under Mr Brown's curatorship is a collection of paintings and drawings of the Moghul Emperors and people of their times, which includes many exquisite illuminations and old water-colour drawings of extreme fineness and delicacy and yet full of character, design and amazing distinction. Appreciation of such things since the days of their production is only beginning to be re-awakened, and they are still purchasable in India at such prices as the museum can afford. Mr Brown told me that I was the first who had yet looked at this collection with enthusiasm to justify his own in buying them, but "who knows the spelling of Du Guesclin?" They are as wonderful as Holbein's drawings, their detail would have enchanted Altdorfer, and their exquisite line might have delayed the death of Aubrey Beardsley! Such are the Mullah Do Piaza, the picture of Akhbar's jester and his thin Rosinante, or the beautiful drawing of Humayun,

Babar's son, out a-hunting.

India is a land which changes any sympathetic traveller to a set of strings on which its spirit plays through all the working-hours. Every day is crowded with new wonders, and no sooner does he sink to earth, as if fallen from the hands of one player, than he is snatched up again and every fibre wrung by some new loveliness he knew not of.

One afternoon I drove out with the pundit to Shaddra where Jehangir is buried and Nour Jehan. We started to the west of the city on the high road to Peshawar, past the Mohammedan cemetery and the Hindoo burning-ground, outside which some women in white and yellow robes sat waiting while their men-folk burned a body within.

In the time of Ranjeet Singh, the pundit told me, the river used to flow past the Badshahi Masjid, a large red sandstone mosque, which we next passed: but in India the rivers are not so constant as the stars in their courses.

A little farther on we crossed the dry bed called the Ravi Nullah and then, driving through the Ravi Forest, reached the bridge of boats that spans the Ravi River at a little distance from the railway-bridge. A merry old Kuka Sikh on a white donkey was waiting at the bridge toll-gate for someone from whom to beg the money to cross. It is a long bridge and very narrow, so that two vehicles cannot pass one another and a bullock-cart, which had just started to cross from the opposite bank, seemed inclined to take an infinity of time about it; but the Kuka Sikh was in no hurry, and when we had paid his toll joked with the pundit to beguile the time. This boat-bridge has to be dismantled in the rainy season, from June to August, when the river is swollen.

We left the Peshawar road soon after crossing the bridge and presently reached Shaddra and Jehangir's tomb, a large and elaborate affair with much space about it and great entrance gateways and lines of narrow water tanks in the gardens within. Dismounting from the gharry we walked over the great open space of the Sarai and through the eastern gateway, with its honeycomb vaulted ceiling and soft warm flower decoration on its pink stucco-covered brick-work, to the water channels of the tomb garden, past the central tank and on to the Mausoleum itself, an exquisite low building with four tall minarets, half of white marble and half of the red Agra stone, of which Jehangir was so fond.

We walked up the steps and crossing a pavement of badal stone entered the inner chamber through an arch with a dado of old glazed inlay. Within, a flat oil-lamp upon a metal stand, threw flickering light in a bright path upon the marble floor. There was rich inlay of agate, cornelian and amethyst, the ninety-nine names of God and the titles of Jehangir, all but the most important title—that of husband of Nour Jehan. She is buried, the Queen who ruled him and his people—only her own brother she could not save from his wrath—about half a mile away and I was surprised to find the place in a state of utter neglect. It is awkward to approach and I expect is rarely visited.

When we reached it the sun was very low. A cow was stalled in one part of the neglected tomb and, as I approached, a Mohammedan fakir, rising from the ground to his full height, tall and thin, shook his hands at the sky and cried in Persian—*Al Mout! Al Mout!* ("Everyone must die—everyone must die!")

"But this is a stable," said the pundit, whose learning perhaps did not include Bethlehem. It is true that the tomb was railed round, but the railings were broken and the sturdy rogue of a fakir had settled himself comfortably with his charpoy, his goat and his cow. His beard was grey and his unkempt hair peeped out in tufts from his roughly-tied turban, once white and spotted with dark blue. The things he continued to shout were curious, but the pundit agreed with me it was mere wildness and no scheming for backsheesh that prompted a reference to England. Waving his arms round and round he cried—"The English will rule all over the world," and then—"One God to rule over us all. He created Adam and Eve: *bismillah heraai mornana heem la ilia illillah.*"

I walked up some broken brick steps and passing through a series of low-pointed arches, down on the other side of a low circular wall, I stood before two tombs. The one nearest to me was that of Nour Jehan, who had been called Rose of the Harem, Light of the World: its neighbour was that of her adopted daughter.

The tombs are quite plain plaster-covered brick-work. In the outer passages there remain some traces of painted ornament—but because she had no children, and her stepson, Shah Jehan, was not on good terms with her when she died, there is here no decoration, no inscription. Not for her tomb are the ninety-nine names of God!

Through the arches on the farther side I could see the trunks of date palms and old, old mango trees in the Begumpura, a garden Nour Jehan had loved. I went underground to the crypt-like chamber below the tomb, and with the help of matches made out that there was nothing upon the floor—only in the ceiling one inset space corresponding to the cenotaph above. The pundit thought the body was probably very deep in the ground—I know not.

When we came out above ground the last of daylight was making golden play among the palms and mango trees. They were in flower—and next June fruit would be upon them.

CHAPTER XIX

AT THE COURT OF HIS HIGHNESS THE RAJAH OF NABHA

His Highness the Rajah of Nabha is a noble old Sikh chieftain, distinguished among the native rulers of India, although his territory, one of the Phulkian States, is but small. Through the kindness of the Punjab Government and of His Highness, I was given an opportunity of visiting the little court.

To reach Nabha, my train from Lahore was the Bombay mail, and I have rarely seen greater confusion at any railway station than reigned upon its arrival. Every class of carriage was already full, yet there were a number of first-class passengers waiting with title to berths booked in advance as well as second and third-class ticket-holders. The train was already of the maximum size permitted and, after half an hour's uncertainty, a third-class carriage was actually emptied of its fifty or more occupants, taken off the train and replaced by an empty first-class coach. Few more striking instances could be found of purse privilege. It would correspond in England with the dumping on a Crewe platform of the third-class passengers by the Scotch express from Euston to make room for first-class passengers waiting for the train at Crewe. It was not a case of native and foreign, or English and Oriental,—for plenty of native gentlemen travel first-class and it simply meant that having a seat in a third-class carriage in India does not insure your finishing the journey by the train in which you started.

My servant was left behind on this occasion and was consequently not forthcoming when I reached Nabha Station in the morning. Poor faithful Tambusami had not understood whither we were bound, but for some reason or other thought it might be Patiala, and when I returned to Lahore three days later I found him weeping on the platform after vain endeavours to track me.

At Nabha I was met by three of the Rajah's ministers and driven in a luxurious victoria to a large guest-house painted red and blue and standing in quite beautiful grounds. A pair of horses drew the victoria, but a kind of wagonette which followed with my luggage was pulled by two camels which always have rather a circus air in harness.

The red brick-work of the building was all picked out with white, like the walls of a doll's house, and on each side of the wide arch at the entrance there was a life-size painting of a turbaned soldier presenting arms.

His Highness the Rajah of Nabha.

[From a painting by permission of the Visual Instruction Committee, the Colonial Office.]

His Highness's private secretary could not speak English, and a native gentleman, Mr Hira Singh, who was a schoolmaster in the town, had been deputed to attend me as interpreter during my stay.

I was taken first into the reception-hall, which was hung with small portraits in gouache of former rajahs and famous Sikh monarchs, such as the Rajah Bhagwan Singh (the late Rajah of Nabha), the late Rajah Ragh Bir Singh of Sandoor and the Maharajah Ranjeet Singh, who was painted in a green dress with a halo round his head and mounted upon a brown horse. In large letters on one wall appeared the motto:—

"May God increase your prosperity."

Breakfast was served me in a large room adjoining the great hall. Over the carpet a white drugget was spread and the chairs were all covered in pink chintz.

Mr Hira Singh suggested that I must need some rest and should sleep awhile, so I was taken to my bedroom which was another large apartment. It was a blend of the genuinely Oriental and the Tottenham Court Road. The washstand was humbly and yet aggressively British, while the wide bed was gorgeously upholstered and covered with a beautiful silk coverlet of canary yellow, and was furnished with two tiny hard cushions or pillows in the middle, as well as an ample allowance for the head. I was certainly tired with the journey and nothing loth to lie down. Outside one of the open doors of the room I could see the red-and-blue lance pennon of a sentry appearing and reappearing as he passed to and fro in the sunlight. His footsteps were quite noiseless, and wondering whether after all it was the real sentry or one of the painted ones from the archway wall I fell fast asleep to wake an hour later and find that Sirdar Bishan Singh, Vakil to the political agent of the Phulkian States, a stout, pleasant-looking little man, and Sirdar Jawala Singh, His Highness's minister of finance, taller and darker, were patiently waiting for me in the reception-room, sitting side by side on chairs, with their feet primly together and silently looking before them.

His Highness had graciously consented to give me an hour's sitting the next morning, and these gentlemen had come to drive me to the palace where the painting was to be done to choose a position of suitable lighting. So down I walked again by the five long steps between the blue columns and out through the archway to the victoria, and the painted sentries were still presenting arms and the live one stood at attention. We drove first to the Diwan Khana by the Winter Palace, and going up a long flight of steps to an upper quadrangle I was shown the rooms of the State Treasury and the old heavily-bound boxes containing the wealth of Nabha.

The Diwan Khana itself is used for durbars, and the whole of the upper part of the great room is one continuous forest of chandeliers, mostly of green cut glass. On the walls of this Durbar Hall I noticed four beautiful old miniature portraits of rajahs, with real pearls fitted in for necklets and precious stones and gems on the horses' trappings as in eikons of the Greek Church and a painting of a feast, larger, but worked in the same style as the miniatures. The building was erected in the time of the Maharajah Jaswan Singh of Nabha, and the very florid carpets were certainly not of any earlier date.

As we drove away I saw many pigeons and green parrots about the walls of the Winter Palace, and noticed that all over the building niches had been left for the birds.

Mr Hira Singh told me that the population of Nabha town is over 15,000 and that it is "quite a busy city" with steam cotton-mills (I had seen the tall chimneys near the railway station). The city gateways I passed through are quite stately buildings and in an upper chamber of each gateway, with its silk covering hanging out over the window-sill, is kept a copy of the sacred *Granth* of the Sikhs.

Driving through part of the city and out again we passed a Hindoo temple with a spacious tank, over one end of which spread the twisting branches of a beautiful "beri" tree, and before long came to Elgin House, a newer building than the Winter Palace, with a very large Durbar Hall, having at one end a painting of Queen Victoria. It was here that the sitting was to take place, and after choosing a suitable position in which His Highness's gold chair of state might be placed ready I went over the rooms of Elgin House and also upon the roofs of the upper storeys.

The Vakil showed me the chief treasures with great pride, but among them all there was not a single beautiful thing of native craftsmanship. Instead of this there were huge modern German vases—pictures sliced into one another by a mechanical trick, so that as you moved along in front, the Princess of Wales changed gradually into the Prince. Mechanical singing-birds of most expensive accomplishment were made to warble for my delectation and greatest of all wonders at the Court of Nabha, a clock-work group of figures behaved quite like real people and a band of musicians played operatic airs while a ballet dancer stood tiptoe on one leg. The mechanical singing-birds had already made me think of Hans Andersen's story of the nightingale, and here was the heroine of another of his tales re-created after the burning she endured with her beloved tin soldier as devotedly as any Hindoo widow of suttee days.

The formal gardens were pleasantly arranged, but managed to avoid the beauty of an Oriental Bagh without achieving that of the European style they sought to imitate. The proportions were good, but there was no grass and one longed vainly for spaces of lawn or greensward to contrast with the elaborate carpet bedding.

On leaving Elgin House we drove to the Gurdwara of Baba Ajabal Singh. A tall and handsome black-bearded priest of thirty-two years showed us over the building, but what most interested me was a wild-looking figure I saw hanging about the cloisters. He was armed with a sword and dressed entirely in black garments, with a huge black turban twisting in and out of steel circlets and irons, and bound over and round in its turn by a metal chain. This was an Akali, one of that still privileged sect of fighting fanatics who became famous in Ranjeet Singh's time under the daring and picturesque "Gardana Sahib"—Alexander Gardner (born on the shores of Lake Superior in 1785).

I had heard that the Akalis wear blue garments to perpetuate the memory of the blue clothes the Guru Govind Singh wore as a disguise, on the occasion of an escape from Moghul soldiers, and part of which he gave to one of his disciples to found a new order—that of the Akalis in question, but this man's habiliments were as black as a crow's feathers. Like their famous Rajah, Ranjeet Singh himself, this latter-day specimen of the bhang-drinking cut-and-thrust "immortals" had only one eye, and I asked whether he had by chance lost its fellow in a fight. "I have never had a chance of a fight," said the Akali—adding consistently with the tenets of his sect—"if I did I would never give in." While we were talking a thin old Sikh limped towards us; he had once been taller than the average man, but was now bent and emaciated with constant opium-eating. Mr Hira Singh told me that he took one "masha" (equal to 16 grains) at a time and took it twice in every twenty-four hours. The old rascal, his deep brown eyes twinkling, put to me a special petition that the Government should grant to all real opium eaters a large quantity gratis at regular intervals to make them happy. He said also, on my asking him what he dreamed about—"In my dreams I think of the Creator, and I feel very earnest to go to a better field and to fight there," which, as I was assured the man was an abandoned scoundrel, may be taken as Oriental humour expressed with an eye to backsheesh.

Driving back to the guest-house we passed an arena where wrestling matches are held, with six circular tiers of high stone steps as seats for the spectators, and a square "loge" built in the middle of one side for the notables, and here is conducted the only physical "fighting" that takes place at Nabha nowadays. The day of the Akalis is over, and while their brother Sikhs make some of the best material in the Indian Army, the devotees of this narrow sect have become wandering mendicants, privileged to carry warlike weapons, and truculently direct in their demands for alms.

The portrait sitting was fixed for eight o'clock the next morning, and ten minutes before his time the noble old Rajah stepped from his carriage and walked almost jauntily up the steps of Elgin House, where I was already installed with palette and canvas.

Gorgeously apparelled in a costume that was like a kiss between two halves of the Arabian Nights, and wearing upon pale greenish silk a galaxy of decorations which included the G.C.I.E. for his part in the last Afghan War (he is now an honorary Colonel in the British Army) and stars and medals from many great Durbars, the Chief of Nabha wore at the same time an air of vigour and joy in life that made the years sit lightly on his shoulders, years that a wrinkled forehead declared numerous.

One of his ministers told me through Mr Hira Singh that at the last Delhi Durbar His Highness had delighted every one by the spirited and boyish way in which he had galloped his horse along in front of the assembled princes. May he appear as hale and vigorous at the Durbar of December next!

After he had shaken hands with me and beamed cordial smiles, we walked through the Durbar hall to the room where I had set up my easel, and the Rajah sat, as arranged, in a chair of gilded brass with lion arms, and directed his gaze at a particular flower vase upon which we had fixed to keep his head in correct position for the portrait. The pupils of his eyes were brown, with a faint grey rim, and he had long waving moustaches as well as a long yellowish white beard. He carried a sword with scabbard of pale green and gold, a steel mace with spherical head, and a contrivance by which, when a catch was pressed at the end of the handle, a number of short sharp blades started out from the head, and also a steel trident of new pattern. The old man was bent upon having as many arms about him as possible, and sent for a large shield of black metal with four bright bosses and a crescent, a favourite rifle and another trident sceptre, so that I had all I could do to dispose these about him in such a way that he could sit comfortably and keep his head still. He seemed especially proud of the mace with the trick knives, and after explaining the mechanism to me with gusto he continued at intervals during the sitting to manipulate it, at which the whole court laughed heartily. They were grouped on either side in all the glory of official costume and included the Commander-in-Chief, who came to England for the Coronation of Edward VII., the Foreign Minister, the Finance Minister, the Chief Justice, the Medical Adviser, and various generals and councillors.

To paint a portrait in an hour! Well, I was not sorry that His Highness had arrived before the arranged time, and that I had already set my palette, and though it would have been intensely interesting to have talked with the Chief of Nabha through the excellent interpreter, when once the weapons were arranged to incommode him as little as possible, I went at the painting with the fury of an Akali and contented myself with smiling appreciatively at his occasional ejaculations.

Every now and then he made a peculiar coughing noise, which began softly and rose to a crescendo, sounding as formidable as the traditional catchwords of the giant of the bean-stalk. It was like "ahum, ahum, ahum—ahhum," and kept his ministers in lively attention.

As nine o'clock struck (for there were clocks at Nabha as well as at Elsinore) I laid down my palette and am glad to say His Highness expressed with Eastern courtesy great delight at the sketch.

Before going he sent for his favourite grand-child, Sirdar Fateh Singh, a boy of about twelve years of age, who shook hands frankly with me. On hearing that I must positively leave Nabha that afternoon—in spite of his kindly pressure to stay at least a fortnight—the Rajah gave orders for the finest of his State elephants to be sent round to the guest-house that I might see an ingenious device by which fountains of water from a hidden tank played from the front of his head to lay the dust. The elephant, unlike his vigorous old master, is weak and ailing, but I found him still a magnificent beast and arrayed even more gorgeously than lilies in sunlight-carrying scores of crystal lamps as well as the fountains.

Mechanical arrangements of all kinds seemed specially to delight the Rajah and he again showed me one of the singing birds I had seen the previous day. Just before leaving Elgin House His Highness paid me the pretty compliment of asking if he might have permission to go.

CHAPTER XX

IN SIGHT OF AFGHANISTAN

I left Lahore soon after eight o'clock one evening and when I woke in the train next day found myself smothered in dust and traversing the great Sind Desert, that almost rainless tract, which depends solely for any possibility of cultivation on irrigation from the Indus.

An important trade route from Afghanistan and Persia coming through the Bolan Pass has its base at Shikarpur, in Upper Sind, a few miles from the great cantilever bridge, called the Lansdowne Bridge, which joins Baluchistan to India crossing the Indus between Sukkur and Ruk.

An engineer was waiting at Sukkur railway station to show me the great bridge, and as I had to continue my journey the same evening we were obliged to face the heat of the sun and started back towards the river on a trolley worked by hand levers. We passed a kite's nest close to the railway on the perpendicular face of a mass of limestone rock.

Sukkur is a good-sized town of more than 30,000 inhabitants, but its buildings seemed to be all of wattle and daub, though three and even four storeys high, and they were grey in colour, uncomfortably monotonous in the terrific heat.

A single span of the bridge joins the Sukkur side to Bhakkur Island, a mass of limestone rock fortified centuries ago. The keys of the gates were in charge of a signaller at the blockhouse and a bridge inspector. While they were being obtained I read the inscription upon the bridge—

"Erected by F. E. Robertson and M. S. N. Hecquet, 1887-1889.
Girders made by Westwood Baillie & Co., London. J. S. R., 1887."

It is one of the great monuments of Queen Victoria's reign, one among the many bridges, waterworks and railroads that have so far monopolized in modern India all architectural aspiration. Splendid in its utility, an inspiring instrument of commercial development, it looks like the creation of some great Arachnid but stretches its iron network so far into the air that it is as much larger than any spider's trap-net as the highest of the Himalayas exceeds an ant-hill. I walked a little way on Bhakkur Island and stood on the sand under some high walls looking at the Ruri end of the bridge. They were the walls of an old nunnery called "Suttian," I think for widows who had declined to be burned with their dead husbands. The engineer told me in connection with "Suttian" that a man named Mosu Shah was said to have built a minaret we could see with the object of spying upon one of the nuns with whom he was in love.

Out in the stream in front of us two men were "pala" fishing. They had swum out each with an immense metal chattie to keep him afloat and, resting upon these, fished the river with nets on long slender poles, putting the fish inside the chattie as they took them from the net. The fish come up to spawn and the men float down stream with their nets in front of them.

They drifted through the very reflections of the vast cantilevers just as a train was steaming over the bridge and made one more of the innumerable contrasts of the old and new order I had seen in India.

Regaining the trolley we crossed to the Ruri shore and walked some distance over the wide burning sand for the best view of the bridge. A number of cattle were down upon the sand near the water-edge seemingly well content, as I have seen great herds baking in summer heat on level sand on the West Coast of Ireland at the edge of the Atlantic. Here at Ruri, however, the sun beat with greater fury and a group of Sindi boatmen and their families, who had been busy mending sails spread out on the sand, had all stopped work till cooler hours arrived.

In the summer, that engineer assured me, the thermometer reaches 240° and even 250° *in the shade*! "I have been here twelve years," he said, "and during all that time we have had six rainfalls." He pointed out to the right of the bridge the magazine where dynamite was stored for blasting purposes, and, farther to the right, another small island with a very old temple on it. This island is called Khwajah Khisah and the temple shrine, although the building is in the form of a mosque, is frequented by both Hindoos and Mohammedans.

There is a very important project in hand for damming the Indus just above this temple so as to raise the water-level and so feed the canals during the dry season as well as at periods of flood. I could make out the head of the Begari Canal, then quite dry, in the distance between Khwajah Khisah and the island of Bhakkur.

When I returned by the trolley to Sukkur there was a local train in the station and the carriage in front of the waiting-room where I sat resting in the shade seemed to contain the most obviously authentic prototypes of that famous Asiatic "forty," more celebrated even in Europe than the French Academy. Red faces with large mouths agrin between thick moustaches and short bushy black beards, blue turbans and dirty finery—the very perfection of stage villains, but Morgiana? No, I could not see her and the music of the opera, *The Barber of Baghdad*, with its superb iterations of that lady's name came drifting through my head.

The reflections of the dull red girders of the bridge were now almost green.

I again slept in the train that night and woke up in the Bolan Pass in British Baluchistan. At half-past nine in the morning the sky was very pale and although the shadows of the hill-clefts were clear they were not hard. On each side of the line there was a flat boulder-strewn plain which was stopped abruptly a quarter of a mile away by steeply rising heights of rock. Then suddenly the flat plain itself would be trenched and split into huge cañons, clefts going deep down into the earth. A few grey dried plants, almost the same colour as the stones, were the only visible signs of vegetation.

In the early morning at Sibi Junction I had branched off on the Western (or Quetta) arm of the great loop which extends from Sibi to Bostan Junction. By ten o'clock the train with two powerful engines was ascending a gradient of one in twenty-five beyond Hirok. From the window I could watch, upon the old Kandahar Road below, the old slow-creeping progress of a camel caravan. The pass was now narrowing, closing up on each side and the cliffs rose steeply where at a sharp turn I caught sight of a square block-house perched on a jutting crag.

At Quetta I had the double annoyance of missing luggage and of being taken, on account of my dark beard, for an expected French spy. The latter misunderstanding was put right by a subdivisional officer from Chaman (the present terminus of the railway beyond the end of the Kojak Pass) whither I was bound and where, having left the loop at Bostan Junction, I arrived the same evening to get a peep across the border into Afghanistan—to set foot in the Amir's country, that land of Mohammedan freebooters, waiting and waiting in vain for an autonomous India whereunto their co-religionists would be able to welcome an invading army.

Going out into the sunlight from the gloom of the dak bungalow everything seemed at first only brightness, as if the external world were like a cup brimmed with a throbbing intensity of light. Then, as my eyes accustomed themselves, I saw that near the bungalow were peach and apricot trees holding sprays of blossom, rose and white against the pale blue of the sky, and that in the distance on every side mountains rose out of the plain, not grey and cold but warm with faint tints of amethyst and delicate red, and that snow lay upon their higher peaks.

Chaman lies in the plain within a horseshoe of mountains, and the space of clearly seen country is so vast that the mountains look almost as if drawn upon a map. The little town is entirely of wattle and daub, a grey blanket colour with just a little paint and whitewash about a Hindoo temple, and here and there a peach tree in flush of blossom. The main street is very wide and in front of some of the shops there are tiny enclosures, five or six feet square like miniature front gardens. Two patriarchal looking old Pathans were walking along in front of the shops. They wore the same kind of stout leather boots, and from above the turban peeped the same type of conical head-covering that I had seen worn by pedlars in Ceylon and throughout the length and breadth of India. They were Achakzai Pathans and one, whose name was Malik Samunder Khan, said he was eighty years old.

Seeing the entrance of a caravanserai I was going in when Tambusami demurred. It was a long way truly from his home near Tuticorin, and he gave these Northern folk his favourite epithet calling them "jungle people." Seeing that I was going into the sarai in spite of his remonstrance, he said submissively, "Where you go I come," but added, "Where you not go I not go."

There were not many camels within, but in one corner some Afghans were pouring raisins into heaps, and inviting me to eat, gave me larger and finer dried grapes than I had ever seen. The raisins were called "abjush" and the men were Popalzais (Candaharis). Alas! we could exchange no talk but they made me welcome, and while we squatted silent in the sunlight and the clear delicious air, one, taking up a stringed instrument called a "rahab," sang to its accompaniment. It was certainly not a song of fighting: there was gladness in it—even passion now and then—but no fury—I think it was a love-song. It was not a song of fatherland: there was pride in it but no arrogance. Nor was it assuredly a song of religion: there was faith in it and adoration, but no abasement. Yes, I'm sure it was a love-song.

Quetta with its gardens and orchards, its fortified lines and its command, by reason of natural position, of both the Kojak and the Bolan Passes, is one of the most important of Indian Frontier posts. I returned to it from Chaman and drove and walked about its wide and well-metalled roads such as the "High School Road," the "Agent Road," and the "Kandahar Road." Trees, as yet bare of leaves, lined the sides, and fruit blossom looked gaily over walls and fences.

The "Holi" festival of the Hindoos coloured these days. The throwing of red powder or red-tinted water seemed pretty general, and hardly a white dhoti was to be seen that was not blotched with crimson or vermilion splashes. People danced in the streets, and one came suddenly on a crowd watching folk wild as bacchanals, both men and women dressed in gay finery, garlanded with flowers and dancing with strange fantastic gestures in obedience to the universal song of spring's new advent. I went early to bed in another dak bungalow, having somewhat of a fever about me since the blazing hours two days before at the Lansdowne Bridge, and awoke in the early hours. My great-coat had fallen down at one side of the charpoy, and I felt as if a cold plaster lay upon my chest. Tambusami was crouched in front of the fire and had fallen asleep covered in his blanket. From the blackened broken hearth a little acrid smoke puffed fitfully into the room. On the floor lay a torn and extremely dirty dhurrie which had once been blue. Between the dhurrie and the damp earth mildewed matting showed here and there through the holes. A decrepit looking-glass in a broken frame stood upon one rickety table against the wall, and on another an iron tray of uncleaned dinner-plates added to the general air of dirt and squalor.

Leaving Quetta by a morning train I was again passing through a region mountainous on either side beyond a plain white with leprous-like tracts of salt. It resembled neither frost nor snow, but was a strange blotchy incrustation as if the earth were smitten with some fearful pestilence.

On one side the mountains were grey with violet shadows following their clefts and scoriations, spotted in places by dark leafless shrubs, and on their summits lay a little snow. On the other side the hills were red with only soft warm hints of shadows, and beyond them was a band of filmy blue almost as light as the sky. Soon, as the train raced on, the intervening plain became strewn with small loose boulders and isolated tufts of dry dead prickly bush. Two long tents like giant slugs hugged the ground with their black bodies, and near them a few scattered sheep hunted the sparse nourish of aridity.

Again I passed Bostan Junction, this time, however, instead of going on towards Chaman, turning to follow round the Eastern arm of the loop by what is called the Harnai Route. The landscape had quite altered, but was still strange and unhealthy looking. A veritable pigment seemed to exude from it, varying in different parts of the same field of vision. The outlines were noble but the colour, instead of being the effect of light and air upon masses either of local uniformity or varied by differences as of flowers or vegetation, was by this frequent change in the hue of the earth itself too prismatic for majesty and too trivial for grandeur. A rugged pile of grey rock will receive from the procession of the hours indescribable glories, but a mass of mixed French fondants squashed into the same shape could never capture a tithe of such beauty. In chalky half-tones the landscape ran the entire gamut of reds, yellows, blues and greens, with an appearance of false sweetness as if the face of earth had been smeared with pigment destroying all natural glow.

And yet—and yet—as noon grew nearer and the hovering heat made all things hazy and indistinct, where all merged and was lost, and nothing began or ended, surely that was beautiful—earth mother—mother-o'-pearl.

After leaving Mangi Station the train approached the famous Chappa Rift where a vast and sudden break in the mountain makes a wide stupendous chasm, with steep perpendicular sides. I was permitted to ride upon the locomotive for this part of the journey and watch this wild and desolate magnificence of nature's architecture unfold its terrible titanic grandeur. At one point the railway crosses the rift by an iron bridge called after the Duchess of Connaught. Entering a tunnel in the vast wall of rock the train emerges again at one end of the bridge, and after crossing the gulf turns along the other side so that for some long time this narrowest part remains in sight, the maroon red ironwork of the bridge staring dramatically in the centre of a desolate landscape of silver grey. No patch of grass or shrub or any other live thing is to be seen—only the immensity of the scale is marked by one small block-house, a minute sentinel which shows against the sky on the tallest height of cliff.

As the journey continued, the rocks took more fantastic shapes and above a steely gleaming river and its grey beach of stones, the cliff became like serried rows of crumbling columns as if some cyclopean Benares uplifted by earthquake reared its line of petrified palaces against the sky.

CHAPTER XXI

RAJPUTANA

Jaipur was stricken by plague: the number of deaths had gone on increasing and the living were thrown into a state of bewilderment. The Rajput princesses had fled in panic to the old palace of Amber and strangers were, for the time, asked not to visit that ancient capital. The dinner-table that evening, spread in the open courtyard of the hotel, became heaped with moths attracted by the lamps and dying through their ardour, and it almost seemed as if some spiritual light were attracting in the same way human souls to leave their bodies tenantless.

In company with the Nazim (district officer) I started out betimes in the morning—passed the large grey bungalow of the Rajah's chief minister, the lunatic asylum, long cactus hedges and gardens in which white-domed cenotaphs of buried chiefs gleamed among graceful acacia-like Aru trees, while peacocks arched their jewelled necks upon the walls,—and entered the city by that one of its seven gateways called the Moon Door (Chand Pol), crenelated and covered with painted decoration which included a guardian figure on each side of the entrance, turbaned soldiers with fixed bayonets supported on different shoulders in the artist's desire for symmetry.

The gateway was really like a large square tower with considerable open space inside, thatched huts leaning up against its outer wall. Inside the city the wide well-paved streets looked so clean and spacious and the pink-coloured stucco of the houses so bright and gay, that Death seemed a cruel intruder there without excuse. Yet three corpses were carried past us while we stopped for a moment. "The one in yellow is a woman," said the Nazim. I asked why a group of Mohammedans sat in the courtyard of a house near us, and the Nazim said: "Someone has died there—these are friends met to read some of the aphorisms of the Koran."

The day before there had been fifty-four deaths in the city, which was some decrease as the daily toll had quite recently reached one hundred.

In the Chand Pol Bazaar there were not many people about, though to the stranger there was no evidence of calamity beyond the occasional passing of corpses. The sunshine was so bright and the air so pleasant, and a crowd of pigeons fluttered and strutted with such animation round a sacred bull! Near us a small peepul tree hung over one wall of a red sandstone temple—the Sita Ramjika—like a fountain of green and gold.

At the famous observatory Mr Gokul Chandra Bhawan Raj Jotshi, who is in charge of it, showed me round the strange gigantic instruments. We examined the largest sundial in the world, with gnomon 75 feet high; and standing in the paridhi, the circumference of the dial, I could see, above some pink dwelling houses, the clock in the palace tower which is regulated by the old dial.

Very curious are the twelve houses of the Zodiac (Rashi Valya) each with a little painting of its celestial landlord upon the thickness of the wall under its four-centred arch.

The Nazim took me on to see the Maharajah's Palace, and in its lovely gardens, near a tree of Kachnar in full bloom, we came upon the tomb of a pet dog whose memory had been honoured with a sculpture of his canine incarnation carved in black marble and protected by a dome-topped marble kiosk. The Nazim said the dog had been loved for his extreme obedience, and there was a tale of some gold bangle lost in a billiard-room which he had restored to a despairing owner. It was a graceful monument in beautiful surroundings and a great contrast to the unpleasing tombstones in that crowded little canine cemetery near the Marble Arch in London, but there was another piece of sculpture in that garden which I was more anxious to see, but which, alas for me! was hidden that morning.

Gobindaji, said to be one of the most beautiful of the carved figures at Muttra, was brought here for safety by the Maharajah Mon Singh, and is apparently treated as if the stone has quite corporeal needs, for the Nazim said: "True he lives at the bottom of this garden. He has his hours: sometimes he has just taken his food and sometimes he is sleeping. Just now he sleeps, so you are not able to see him."

I love most gardens where old statues sleep, but without any wish to disturb their slumbers possess some little of Aladdin's curiosity—or Coventry Tom's; besides, had I known Gobindaji's hours I would have timed my visit more opportunely. As it was, in this garden where dogs have monuments and statues lunch, I could at least enjoy the jasmine flowers and the blossoms of the pomegranates and the grapevines trailing over rough stone uprights.

At the bottom of the garden we passed through a door in the wall, and walking down a narrow flight of steps beheld the Rajah's crocodiles under the windows of the zenana quarters. The keeper of the crocodiles was an old white-bearded man, extremely tall and thin—so thin in fact that his charges must have long ceased to wait with any eagerness for indiscretion in too near approach. The spacious tank was enclosed on three sides by a wall, and on the fourth by the palace itself. We had descended by the steps from a terrace and stood on a small piece of muddy ground on to which the thin keeper enticed his huge charges by throwing a bundle of rag towards them and withdrawing it by a string. In the middle of some beautiful public gardens close to the city stands Jaipur's "Albert Hall," a large building in white marble, which contains a durbar hall and a fine collection of examples of Indian art and industry. Its courts are decorated with mottoes translated from Persian and Hindoo literature, and as maxims for guidance they are not at all easy to reconcile with each other. From the *Hitopadesa,* for example, on one wall is quoted:—

> "Fortune attends the lion-hearted man
> Who acts with energy; weak-minded persons

Sit idly waiting for some gift of fate."

And on another from the same source is written:—

"He has all wealth who has a mind contented.
To one whose foot is covered with a shoe
The earth appears all carpeted with leather."

After all they represent different aspirations and only mystify because they are marshalled here as from the same authority. One man would rather have a rough road tearing his defenceless feet as he treads it with a purpose, while another would prefer to watch a garden sundial marking contented hours that leave no record behind them. And the first might fall powerless on the wayside, and the second shatter a kingdom by the report of quiet words.

There are aviaries of beautiful birds in the gardens about the museum—rose-coloured flamingoes and Rajput parrots with heads like peaches and pale grey "Mussulmans" from Mecca, with primrose crests and orange cheeks.

At his bungalow not far away I had the pleasure of a chat with Sir Swinton Jacobs, the dear old engineer and architect who has done so much to keep alive traditions of Indian craft-work, and is one of the very few Englishmen who has not flown from India when white hairs came.

In all India no spot has been so rapturously praised for its beauty as Udaipur in Rajputana and its lake-reflected palaces. Travelling towards it from Jaipur I found myself a day later in the State of Mewar, passing fields of the white opium poppies for which the State is famous.

Udaipur is a white town and comes quite suddenly into view after you have been watching from the train a lovely range of hills, warm and glowing. The bright railway station is a grey stone building with a square tower, and the lower part of it is half smothered in pale convolvulus. The flowers are glorious at Udaipur, and I found the white house of the British Resident bowered in magnificent bougainvillias. This gentleman kindly promised to ask the Maharana to grant me a sitting for a painting.

Driving over a bridge past crenelated walls, a road hedged by dense broad-leaved cactus, led me on to a forest of leafless trees softer in colour than an olive wood. It was like a forest from a fairy-tale, with troops of wild long-legged swine and peacocks, their bright tails rushing through the branches like a coloured wind. Then I came out upon the waterside where the white group of palaces with their long sloping ramps, their many flights of steps and galleries, their towers and cupolas, rose up majestically, unrivalled save by their own reflection in the lake. What part was plaster looked like marble, and what was marble glowed tremulously warm like some white mineral counterpart of flesh.

Four rowers pulled me in a long boat to the Jag Mandar, one of two palaces which, completely covering the small islands on which they are built, appear to be floating upon the water. I landed at some wide steps at one end of a terrace on which four stone elephants stand with raised trunks saluting. A band of darker colour upon their legs and on the walls showed that the water was at a lower level than it sometimes reached. There was a garden within the walls of the palace from which three palms rose high above the rounded shapes of lower growing trees.

The Palace of the Maharajah of Udaipur. [Drypoint Etching.]

The Maharana had consented to give me a sitting of one hour at four o'clock in the afternoon. A two-horse carriage took me through the city to the lake-front and then along under the white walls of the palace. More than ever as I passed close beneath them was I struck by the similarity in general shape of one great series of towers to those of old Baynard's Castle; but never have the waters of the Thames reflected so white a building! And the beauty of that vast whiteness destroyed for me forever the old argument which tries to explain the former strong coloration of Greek architecture by saying that large surfaces of white building would have been intolerable under Southern sun.

After I had arranged my easel in the room, which had been fixed upon for the painting, the Maharana entered, carrying a long sword in a green scabbard. We bowed to each other and after moving to the chair which had been placed for him he motioned me to be seated also.

Of all the native princes in India, the Maharana of Udaipur has the longest pedigree, and his kingdom is the only Rajput State which can boast that it never gave a daughter in marriage to a Moghul emperor. This tall and dignified chieftain is High Priest of Siva as well as ruler of the State of Mewar, and is revered for his religious office no less than for his temporal sovereignty. He is thoroughly and proudly loyal to the British rule, but a brother of the Englishman who did his utmost (in accordance with expressed wishes from high quarters) to bring him to the Coronation Durbar of 1903, once told me that on the morning of the great function "my brother found Udaipur on the floor of his tent, stark naked and ill with fever, so that he could not go."

His beard and moustache were brushed upwards and stained with some dye which made them a metallic blue colour. A small turban came down over the left temple. He wore no orders or decorations, and his only jewellery consisted in a double row of pearls round the neck and one diamond ring on the right hand. A long gown, with close-fitting sleeves, made of maroon-coloured cloth, and bound at the waist by a belt and a white sash, clothed him from the neck to the velvet-shod feet.

He had agreed to sit for me for one hour but I thought, in spite of his gentle dignity, the first quarter was for him a long while going. During that time no one had spoken, and I asked whether he had not in the palace some teller of stories who might keep him from feeling the irksomeness of sitting so long in one position. When the interpreter explained my suggestion he smiled and asked whether it could trouble me if he talked with his ministers; and two of these, coming forward at my acquiescence, talked with him throughout the rest of the sitting, and as he still kept well his position for me the change was mutually agreeable.

To my left, beyond an outer gallery, lay the beautiful lake, and, crowning a hill immediately opposite, shone the whiteness of the Summer Palace.

On my way back from Udaipur I stopped at Chitorgarh, fifty miles away, to drive to the famous fortress city of Chitor, the former capital of Mewar.

The hill of Chitor lies on the flat land like a long mole or hog's back. All along its crest old tawny buildings with towers and turrets stretch in a broken line as if they formed the ridge of some old saurian's back with many of the spines broken. Rather beyond the centre the Tower of Victory, yellow and tawny as the rest of the buildings, appears sharply prominent. Trees circle the hill at its base and rising from among them the road leads steeply along and up the side of the cliff in one long zigzag. The slopes of the hill looked grey as I approached.

The tonga I had engaged to drive me from Chitorgarh crossed by a stone parapeted bridge the almost empty River Ghamberi, in the bed of which the bare rock jutted up in sloping shelves. We passed a cemetery and several fields of green barley, and the zigzag road up the hill looked more imposing the nearer we drew, with its eye-holed curtain wall, its bastions and towers. Still in the plain below, we now entered through the pointed arch of a gateway the bazaar of modern Chitor. It was full of dogs, pigeons, cattle and people,—a narrow crowded street at right angles to the hill. We turned by the large white Kotwali and a beautiful temple porch and passed houses with elaborately carved fronts having stone balconies with grey reliefs of elephant processions.

Then we entered the "fort" itself, and began our progress through the long series of its seven gateways that close the zigzag road at intervals. First came the "Padal Pol" of Akhbar's time, and then a new gate with two monuments and the sacred emblems of Siva. The third was the Gate of Hanuman, the monkey friend of Rama. Set within a grand stone arch, the old wooden doors covered with large iron spikes were dropping to pieces with age. Between this and the preceding gateway Akhbar himself is said to have shot the besieged leader in the great siege of 1568. The Ganesh Gate followed, and just at the turn of the zigzag far above our heads the rough masses of bare rock—here, blood-red ochre, and there, pale purple grey—reared up and up to yet higher steeps of masonry to the line of the great road wall above. Here and there stunted trees clutched the stones or straddled some projection with clinging roots. The fifth gateway was the Jorla Pol with a rough stone house built over it. The Lakshman Pol was close to this last, and had a group of nine brown-legged native soldiers lounging in the gate-house. Beside this part of the road there were some hundreds of small monuments like double cubes from two to three feet high, and I was told that in past days anyone of Chitor who had been to Benares built one of these.

In front of the Ram Pol, the seventh and last gateway, there is a wonderful old stone building with carved pillars and a long beam-like piece of stone, now used as a bench to sit upon, carved from end to end with alternate balusters and figures. The carving round the base of this gateway is very remarkable, being in three tiers together, not higher than three feet, with human figures in the upper course, horses in the middle one and elephants below.

Beyond this gate are the ruins of old Chitor. Blue-glazed tiles still gleam from broken walls of palaces and time takes leisurely its slow revenge. There are two towers in Chitor—one, the Tower of Fame and the other the Tower of Victory. The first is close to an old Jain temple, and is itself of Jaina architecture, built probably about the time when Saxon pirates looked on the Roman ruins of Londinium.

In a niche over the very tiny doorway and on each of the other three sides at the same level, stands a perfectly nude figure which I suppose to be that of the deified saint or Tirthakarai to which the tower was dedicated. Throughout its seven storeys the tower is covered with elaborate sculpture and horizontal mouldings. The door was locked with a brass lock, and it took some hunting to find the keeper of the key.

When I bowed down and crept at last within, the dusk was filled with a great whirring sound of many things. I clambered up to the open storey at the top, and as I climbed grew more used to the subdued light and could distinguish in the carving dancing-girls with strings of jewels, strange stags among trees and lines of geese, while a myriad long-eared bats squealed about my head. There was no lightning-conductor on the Tower of Fame.

The Tower of Victory, glowing a golden yellow in the declining sun, was obviously more used to visitors, and has an easier and a cleaner stairway. It is a fifteenth century monument built to commemorate a victory over Mahmud, King of Malwa, and has nine storeys covered with carved decoration. Within this also there are many sculptures of the Hindoo mythology—Brahma, Vishnu and Siva and their various incarnations. On the top storey but one there are eight carved marble columns very old and yellow, in an inner rank, and on the outer projecting portion of the storey other marble columns. By a wooden ladder I ascended from here to the top storey which is roofed with a dome restored last century, and now protected by a lightning-rod. There were no marble pillars on this upper storey which is octagonal in shape with four open sides and four closed by stone screens. Inside, against the latter, four stone slabs about two feet square are let in to a stone framework, and two of these are old and covered with inscription.

As I was driven away, all the edges of the tower glowed like burnished copper in the sunset light.

The twin cradles of the Jaina sect were the States of Mewar and Marwar; and while the former is still independent, the latter forms with Ajmere an isolated British district in the middle of Rajputana. I had now seen at Chitor one of the most famous Jain monuments in the Tower of Fame, and was next to journey to Mount Abu to see there the celebrated Jain temples which are not much later in date.

Mount Abu is a detached hill about fifteen miles on the south-west of the Aravalli Range. From Chitor I, therefore, went northwards to Ajmere, the city which Akhbar had so frequently visited on his pilgrimages to the shrine of its saintly anchorite. This saint was of the same Persian family as the Sheik Salim Chisti whose tomb I had seen at Fatehpur Sikri. His burial-place is known as the Dargah, whither I drove from Ajmere Railway Station.

There were steps up and steps down, and then a gateway painted bright blue with gold Persian lettering upon it and doors covered with repoussé metal. In the large courtyard within, the most noticeable object is the larger of two metal cauldrons—an iron pot of gigantic size—set in stepped stone, over a furnace. This is for cooking the rice and other food, offered for charitable distribution by wealthy pilgrims. In the same courtyard there are also tall metal candelabra with niches all the way up for small oil votive lamps. The great area covered by the Dargah includes mosques and other tombs, as well as that of the saint which last is entered through a series of silver doors.

The traveller in India soon grows accustomed to the wearing of garlands; but at Ajmere not only was I adorned at the tomb of Akhbar's saintly councillor, with long strings of roses and marigolds, but when I came to remount the tonga which had been left at the entrance to the Dargah, I found that it also had been decorated and now carried on each side a tree of pink and yellow paper flowers.

At Ajmere, a really beautiful treasure of architecture is a magnificent carved screen of sandstone arches and five rows of columns behind them, the remains of an otherwise ruined mosque called the Arhai-din-ka-jompra built from the materials of a former Jain temple about the end of the eleventh century. A lake which was made about the same date as the Arhai-din-ka-jompra has an embankment used as a public promenade on which there are white marble pavilions. When I reached the edge of this lake, through the beautiful trees of public gardens, the sun was nearly setting and suffused everything with the inevitable enchantment of its golden light.

But there are ugly sights as well as beautiful ones at Ajmere, and one of the worst pieces of gaudy modern barbarism is that called the Moolchu Temple, with painted images of elephants and painted corrugated iron and common plush and gilding seen through glass screens. It must not be supposed, however, that there is no good modern native building, and not far away I saw one of the best examples in the handsome Mayo College, a splendid pile of white marble built for the education of young Rajputs of high birth.

From Ajmere I travelled South again down the other side of the Aravalli Range on the way to Abu Road. In the background the Chinwan Mountains could be faintly seen beyond nearer hills, and masses of blue-grey rock split and cracked with dark fissures. The landscape was spotted with wriggling snatches of shadow from stunted trees with dried grey leaves.

Where any earth was visible it was yellow, and where it was covered by any kind of vegetation that was yellow too. Cotton plants here and there showed maroon-coloured heads, but the only really bright colour in the general white glare was the brilliant scarlet of the dak tree blossoms which glowed like red embers. Late in the afternoon I reached Abu Road and drove thence by tonga to Mount Abu. It was a terrible journey through choking dust. I could not get at my sand-glasses, and against a scourging wind kept my eyes shut as much as possible, only opening them now and then to peep at the black-faced monkeys that stared from roadside rocks. It was like the ordeal of some fairy story where the hero has to climb an enchanted mountain with sinister and malevolent powers fighting against his ascent. Dead trees gnarled and twisted shook with fantastic menace, and countless boulders seemed to cry out like the black stones to which previous wayfarers had been transformed by the mountain demon.

It was evening and quite dark when the tonga finally stopped at the equivalent of a livery stable, and I learned that the last part of the way was expected to be done by rickshaw. In the darkness, and being weary enough besides, I offered no resistance, and at length attained food and shelter at the dak bungalow of Mount Abu.

I had come to see the Dilwarra Temples, and the next morning after I had obtained the necessary permit I walked by an easy path to these curious buildings. There was no dust-storm now but clear fresh air and plenty of greenery.

I entered an outer court and seeking for some one who should open the gate of the temples came upon a man curled up on a bench in such a way that he seemed to show all the possible creases of his fat little body. He was an effeminate-looking creature and not, I imagine, a priest—are not Jain priests always clad in white?—dressed in two pieces of silk, one of an orange colour round his chest and the other of crimson partly covering his legs. He had short black hair and wore three large pearls on a thin ring through one of his ears.

When this decorative object at last arose he consulted with another who was rubbing down sandalwood on a stone to mix it with saffron powder for painting marks or spots on the temple images. Together they admitted me and I was shown round these famous and typical examples of Jain architecture. There were the cross-legged seated stone figure of the saint at the back of the image cell, the pyramidal or domed roof, and the pillared portico. Every part, and especially the curious struts of the pillars and the interior of the roof, was covered with elaborate carving, and the whole stood within a large yard surrounded by colonnades having a series of separate image cells against the wall. All these seated marble figures were alike, and all had fishy-looking eyes of glass or crystal with black centres.

In a separate building there was an equestrian statue of Vimala Shah, who built one of these temples. The horse was clumsy and droll-looking, with a broad nose, and had a small marble elephant on each side of him.

I only saw one priest inside the temple, and he was furnished with the traditional bib of the Jainas, the white cloth over mouth and nostrils. The attendant told me this was worn in order that the priest's breath might not contaminate the image of the saint which he called God, whereas the accepted purpose is to prevent the possible destruction by the priest of even minute forms of life which would otherwise be drawn in with his breath. Absolute respect for life in all its forms is one of the chief tenets of the Jaina sect which is very much akin to Buddhism, and may have somewhat preceded it in date.

CHAPTER XXII

SIR PRATAP SINGH

"His Highness has sent a carriage for you." This was a two-horsed, two-wheeled vehicle in which I was speedily whirled away from the railway station of Idar Road, four hours' journey from Ahmadabad, along a very rough road. The Highness in question was Sir Pratap Singh, now the Maharajah of the little State of Idar.

The town of Idar itself was eighteen miles away, but close at hand beyond yellow ruined walls I could see the city of Ahmednagar at the palace of which Sir Pratap was in residence. Presently, leaving the road, we rumbled and bumped and lurched over a tract of sand covered with coarse, low bushes to the State guest-house which looked like a very ordinary dak bungalow. It was built on a square plan with doors in such positions as ensured a through draught. A large lizard scampered over the wire of the outer gate as I walked in over the matting of the verandah. Outer gates were placed on all four sides to permit the four pairs of inner double doors to be left wide open.

"I shall inform the Resident of your honour's arrival and he will arrange for your honour to pay his respects to His Highness at four o'clock." This fluent English proceeded from the man who had "met" me at the railway station.

I walked into the central room of the house which had eight double doors opening into it. All the walls and the ceilings were washed over with very pale blue. Great bees were booming and buzzing in and out over the bedsteads of which there was a large variety from the native charpoy to an iron double four-poster with brass ornaments and painted with flower garlands. In addition to the beds the furniture consisted of square wooden cane-seated chairs of ugly pattern covered with brown varnish—what is commonly known as a "nursery" table—with turned and varnished legs and no cloth, and part of a dressing-table by way of writing desk in one corner with pen, ink and paper.

In front of the bungalow, planted in the sand but quite out of the perpendicular, two square-sectioned blue wooden posts supported crookedly set lamp glasses in the blinding glare of noon sunlight.

There was no punkah in spite of the intense heat, but I counted no less than nineteen large iron rings in the ceiling. If these were not intended for punkahs perhaps they were to dissuade intending suicides by the difficulty of choosing which one to hang by!

The man who had driven me had disappeared with a promise that tiffin would come immediately, and while I was noticing the above-mentioned details I sat on one of the cane-seated chairs and Tambusami waited with an eye on the outer sand. A long time seemed to have gone by with no sound breaking the intense hush except the noise of the bees when Tambusami said: "One basket coming I see: one man coming I see," and from a blue palace beyond the tawny sandstone walls over the sand and out of the heat at last came—breakfast.

The one man carried a series of pans, fitted into one another like a tall cylinder in a frame, as well as the basket, and was accompanied by several little black Sambos carrying chatties of water on their heads. And now there were placed on the table a tea-cup with a hare-lip and the motto "Remember me," some marmalade in another tea-cup with blue cornflowers on it, and in gold the words "Think of me," and a third cup with the same motto containing some butter which looked like thin melted white lard, but when the contents of the cylinder of pans were put before me I forgot to notice what they were in my eagerness to consume them.

When four o'clock came and no one had called for me I started out alone with umbrella spread leaving Tambusami to watch our baggage at the bungalow. The heat was intense as I ploughed through the sand and scrub towards the arch in the broken wall which extended for a long distance on either side. It must at one time have been magnificent, being built of very large blocks of stone cut and squared with towers at intervals, and the gateway, with its deep but simple Gothic arch, was an imposing structure with handsome square pillars in the corners having brackets as in Jain work. As I passed through this archway I saw about forty yards ahead of me a line of houses, several storeys high, the lower part of which had evidently been built of stones from the dismantled wall. They were roofed with the half-tube tiles lipped over and under exactly like those of houses in the Pyrenees, and as I entered a street I was reminded of an old home of the former Dukes of Montmorency near Carcassonne by the carved woodwork of a house front.

Asking my way—by what must have seemed to native ears uncouth sounds and weird signs—I gradually reached what I supposed was the palace, and approaching a kind of guard-room with a number of soldiers lounging about, I asked to be directed to the Vakil. Another building was pointed out to me a little below where I was standing and thither I next turned my steps. It was a curious structure without any pretence at design, an iron spiral outside staircase in one portion and a long verandah in another upon a raised platform. I passed a few rose-bushes and walked up on to the verandah and found a long series of doors, and between them on wall and sideboards, rifles, polo-sticks, horse-trappings, bits, shields, revolvers, field-glasses, and one much dented cricket bat.

I knocked at one door after another pausing at each in hope of some response, and at the fifth door this was forthcoming and I found myself quite suddenly in the presence of His Highness the Maharajah Dhiraj Major-General Sir Pratap Singh.

Beyond the door was a vast apartment which seemed in semi-darkness as I entered from the outer glare. A young native gentleman in riding breeches and a khaki shirt came towards me and asked if I was the gentleman who had arrived that morning. It appeared there had been a misunderstanding about sending over for me, and I was at once led up to a *charpoy* with a white quilt on it upon which was reclining a strong-looking little man with a grizzled bullet head, kindly brown eyes and a grey moustache. He wore just a white cotton shirt and a thin pair of riding-breeches and had his well-shaped feet bare.

Rising into a sitting posture, Sir Pratap—for it was he—shook hands, and as soon as a chair had been brought for me we were chatting comfortably. It seemed that he had had fever badly two days before through the sudden and untimely heat and was only just recovering. Another native gentleman sitting at some distance was Sir Pratap's doctor.

Close by stood a man swinging a large fan punkah rhythmically with both hands, and outside the three window openings nearest to us bheesties (water-carriers) kept constantly pouring water upon the grass tatties or blinds.

His Highness spoke English well and was quick to understand and we talked for more than an hour on many subjects. He said he had fought plague successfully at Ahmednagar in what he believed was the only practicable way—namely by building two small cities of detached houses at some distance away and compensating the poorer people for turning out of their old dwellings. In this way he had made a clean sweep of the dirtier part of the town.

Sir Pratap expressed a great affection for our royal family and reverence for the memory of Queen Victoria, whose portrait he showed me with pride within two little folding doors of a shrine of elaborately-worked metal about two feet high and one and a half feet deep.

Spare and wiry in figure, simple and unaffected in dress, quick and alert in manner, there seemed little that was Oriental in this man, and in spite of the tatties and the fan very little suggestion of luxury in his surroundings. He said he had travelled a great deal but liked his own part of India better than any other place in the world.

"One difficult question for India," he said, "is the increasing consumption of cows' flesh and the consequent recent large increase in the slaughter of cattle. I do not believe it is good for our people in this hot climate to take to the eating of flesh. It is quite a different thing in Europe where the colder climate makes it practically a necessity. Here the price is already three times what it was a few years ago, which alone shows the diminution of cattle, and their continued slaughter for an agricultural people must produce harm. In any case we lose great numbers of cattle in our famine times which are more frequent of late, and even this year, though we shall not lose human lives through the famine, numbers of cattle must starve. Also I do not think our grain should be sent out of the country. This is no doubt good for the traders, but they are few and the continued export of grain is disastrous for the agricultural population."

Two trays of tea were brought in, one for each of us, and we poured out for each other, His Highness taking saccharine tabloids instead of sugar, and the motto "forget-me-not" upon my tea-cup suggested near relations to my breakfast furniture.

"The chief trouble of all in India," continued Sir Pratap, "is that the Mussulman will not be friends with the Hindoo. The Mussulman says the Hindoo is a bad man, and the Hindoo says the Mussulman is a bad man, and these, together with people in your English Parliament who call out and make a great noise, are all bad for India."

It was about five years since Sir Pratap moved to Ahmednagar from Idar, eighteen miles away, and his house is practically in a jungle as he delights it to be. Both carriages and motorcars he dislikes as enervating things, and roads he is not fond of, preferring his Arabs and Walers and a life in rough country half spent in the saddle.

I was introduced to His Highness's son, Dolat Singh, and also to his grandson, Himat Singh, a healthy-looking lad in shirt and riding-breeches, with a pearl in each ear, and the next day was granted a sitting by Sir Pratap for a painting, when he appeared in military uniform, with top boots and a grand array of stars and medals and a turban with a beautiful aigrette. He sat very patiently, sought in every way to make my task as easy as possible, and behaved throughout with a charming courtesy.

CHAPTER XXIII

THE MOHARAM FESTIVAL[1]

A little Mohammedan boy was sitting cross-legged upon a worn-out old quilt or rezai, the hair-stuffing of which peeped out all over it through irregular holes. The covering was partly red and partly blue. On his knees was a wooden board with a handle piece projecting at one end. This board called a "Takti," shaped like an old English horn-book, had been washed over with mud-water so that it was nearly white and former writings were covered up. In his right hand the boy held a reed pen called a "Colam" with which he made strange characters upon the board. An earthen pot held the ink for his pen. Just in front of him was a little hinge book-rest called a "Ral" on which was a "Kitab" or book of short pieces.

Beside this boy were others also writing upon "Taktis." None were more than twelve years old and most were about eight. Some wore turbans and some little round plush caps, while one had a cap of fine linen with a broidered edge; he wore a quilted jacket of yellow.

In a sing-song voice they read the words they had written. By the door was a heap of brushwood and two little mice peeped at the boys from under it.

The Maulwe sat in the middle of one side of the class upon the floor like the boys. He was very old and had a beautiful yellow beard. Some beards seem to grow yellow instead of white with age. Some of the boys could look down into the water-stream that ran along in the brick gutter. They were quite a yard above the road, but the passers-by came close to them, and once twelve camels passed with three baby camels, woolly things with long, long legs.

The sun was so dazzling that everything outside seemed to shiver and shake, but under the cool roof the boys could see quite well. The roof was partly tiled and partly thatched, and the row of brick columns supporting it at the outer edge was covered with white-washed plaster—at least it was once white, but just where Ghafur, one of the boys, leaned his back against it (when he was not bobbing his back up and down as he read) it was nearly black. How difficult it is for anything to keep white all over! It is easy to keep some patches clean, especially when they are in places we don't use. Ghafur began to eat sugar-cane when the Maulwe was not looking.

If you looked between Go Kal Chung (a boy with a dark crimson turban) and Abdul with the green coat, right across beyond the road, through a dip in the wall on the other side to the far distance—although in the dust and the sunlight all dis-

[1] Reprinted by permission from *The Fortnightly Review.*

tant things seemed nearly the same colour as the sky—you could just make out on the other side of the River Jumna the great white dome of the Taj Mahal.

I liked it best by moonlight.

In India, moonlight seems so much brighter than in England. Walking at night about the gardens I could still see the colours of the flowers; only the white roses seemed to whisper wakeful and restless, and the red ones to be silent.

The long path of water from the main entrance gateway to the pavement below the platform of the Taj is divided half-way by a circular tank and by this there is a marble seat. The soaring spirit of the vertical lines of the minarets was echoed everywhere; in the little fountains at short intervals all the way, and in the cypress trees along the garden beds parallel to the water-course. Far in the distance against the marble wall the glimmering light of a lantern moved waveringly; I could dimly distinguish the figures of some who had just been within to the tomb chamber. Then a spark, a little spurt of brighter light, gleamed out from far up the building.

The moonlight was slowly creeping round like a tide, and ever as it advanced some other of the innumerable gems set in the delicate pallor of that vast facade for some brief moment, gleamed and died again.

The next day when I passed the little school I found it closed and the reason was that Moharam had begun.

The Moharam Festival extends over many days and at Agra I saw it celebrated elaborately. Its origin was in a fight over the question of succession some time after the death of Mohammed. Two Imams, named Hassan and Hussein, direct descendants of the prophet, died in battle. The place where they were killed was called Kerbela, which means the place of sorrow. Now everything connected with that fighting is remembered and, as far as possible, reproduced or re-enacted at the time of Moharam.

For long beforehand the preparations had been going on. Old swords and maces had been brought out and brightened. At the street corners I had seen men furbishing old weapons, long gauntlet-hilted swords, as well as others making new wooden ones for fencing, covered with red or purple cloth.

The Imams, Hassan and Hussein, died on the night of the tenth day of the month of Moharam, and it is on that day that the innumerable tasias are carried in procession to the Kerbela where the Janazas, the two little biers contained within the gorgeous pagoda-like structure of the tasia, are buried in the earth.

Now when these Imams, Hassan and Hussein were fighting against Eazied, all the sources of water were closed and they suffered terribly from thirst. For this reason drink at this time, sherbet, a mixture of milk, sugar and water, or water alone, is obtainable everywhere. All along the streets at short intervals, on wooden stands the size and shape of an Elizabethan bedstead with grandly-decorated canopy, are rows of large red jars from which, in most cases, an attendant ladles the contents to smaller vessels for whoever will to drink.

Men of any means pride themselves not only on the lavish decoration of their "Tasia," but in furnishing one of these stands for free refreshment and keeping it supplied during the festival days. Here and there also I saw a man sitting in a chair, with two large pipes in front of him at which all comers were free to smoke. He kept tending the coal-bowls of the pipes.

For days the air was full of the noise of drums and cymbals, and I would see camels laden with families of children as well as crowded carts coming into the city from outlying places.

On the ninth day the crowds in the streets were very dense, but among them were kept numbers of little circular spaces in which were performed fantasias of various kinds. In one, men would be seen fencing with wooden staves and in another, to the accompaniment of drums and cymbals, a man would dance, wildly brandishing with quick thrusts and whirling, back and forth, up and down, a long quivering sword with stiff gauntlet hilt well above the wrist. Sometimes he would be quite an old greybeard. Round and round he would lead and dance, the flashing steel never, by some miracle, touching the ring of onlookers though passing within an inch of their faces. Serjeant Troy's performance in the wood with Bathsheba would have looked tame to this. Until utterly exhausted the man kept up leap and dart and bound and brandish and then as at last he sank, another out of the eager waiting crowd took up the relinquished sword and the dance continued. Sometimes the people round gave a great yell of encouragement and waved their arms. The poor vultures, much disturbed by the unwonted crowd and the great noise, flew overhead while kites, seemingly less flurried, sat upon the trees.

The most grotesque circle I saw held a fantasia of six big drums. These were really heavy and very cumbrous. The drummers danced wildly together, crossing and changing places and beating all the while, keeping on till exhaustion claimed them and then slipping out of the drum straps for others to take their places.

In costume, it is proper to wear green for Moharam and about a third of the crowd do actually have green turbans.

Comes along a grotesque tiger carried on a man's head on a wooden framework. Comes a "Saddah," a curious box-like erection shaped like a Punch-and-Judy show with the front of it all bunches of green muslin.

The streets were dense with people, but upon the roofs also men and women crowded; and towards sunset in their green, crimson, purple, amber or scarlet robes they looked in the distance like uncut jewels yielding for some mystic occasion the full intensity of their colour without shine or flash.

Another kind of display was a fight with short cloth-covered wooden sticks held in the right hand, while in the left was kept twirling a longer rod with ball ends.

Men carried children on their shoulders, and two little jesters—youngsters with whitened faces and tall pointed caps and dresses covered with jingling bells—dodged under legs and squeezed their way along.

At night, as if there were not quite enough mystery in the moonlight, the air was thick with dust from the trampling feet. I have said nothing of the "Buraks" which were as wonderful chimeras, half mythic creatures on which it is supposed the commander rode, beings with human faces and strong fore-limbs, half like peacocks with great spreading tails. Many of them were borne among the crowd on frames or platforms carried shoulder high.

Here was a space kept for the Barati dancer. In a green vest and a white loin-cloth he danced with a small skull-cap on his head. He carried whirling in his hand the "Barati," a long rod with balls of fire flaring at each end. At one side of the space kept for this dancer, three men held up a frame on which hung specimens of many of the ancient arms, "Buttas" of various kinds, and "Danarh" too, and "Patapazis"—small shields.

Men pushed the circle outward to widen it for a yet wilder dance. "*Genari Hadri!*" "*Genari Hadri!*" the crowd yelled for encouragement. A man went round pouring fresh oil on the torches called "Kuppi" and my eyes streamed with the smoke and dust. The fretwork of the projecting upper parts of the houses looked white in this light. Two large "Tasias" passed and many drummers. Then a posse of police, with their tall red hat-like turbans, pushed through the crowd with long sticks.

Out of the great round earthen coolers into the small brown pots, attendants at the "Sabils" or drinking-stands, kept on ladling. Under one, two children lay fast asleep, their dark heads as close together as the golden ones of Goblin Market, while a little girl in green kept watch over them.

These "Sabil" stands are given, some of them, by *filles de joie,* who are often lavish in charity.

A man was selling coloured plaster figures—he had a great basket of them—two pi for a big one. Paper lanterns called "Kandils" of many shapes, two feet high, hung from the houses. You must understand thousands of people were walking through and through the old city that night, and the people of the houses vied with one another to show each something more bizarre than the rest.

Some men carried trophies of swords and green streamers arranged in fan-shape on the top of a ten-foot bamboo pole. This is called "Zulfikar," and at intervals the bearer stopped, raised the pole and balanced it on his chin. "*Genari Hadri!*" shouted the crowd again, and the "Zulfikar" man marched on with his set of drummers in front of him. Then came men singing Marsias, *i.e.,* verses about the death of Hassan and Hussein—poems of regret: and men of the Shia sect did beat their breasts.

When the enemy cut off the Imams' hands they put them on the spikes of banners and here, above streamer cloths, I saw flat pieces of silvered tin cut in the shape of hands.

Many private houses threw open that night the courtyard and one of the rooms for the crowd to pass through as it did in constant pressing stream. In some of these one sat on a mimbar reading the Marsias, in others the "Tasia" was arranged for show in half of the room corded off or, when it was a very large one, in the courtyard. Bells of the jesters jingled among the crowd. In iron ladles coloured fires were being burnt in front of a colossal burak with gleaming eyes.

The "Tasias" were of infinite variety. One I saw was made entirely of cotton, with animal and architectural subjects painted all over it. In one house were twenty hand banners in one row. I followed streets narrower than that traditional narrowest of old Tours on the Loire. In some houses were grand "Torahs"—pictures, the drawing of which consisted entirely of cleverly-interwoven Arabic characters in such shapes as a camel or the British crown. There were clusters of floating oil lights in crystal glasses on gilded standing candelabras.

In one street a gigantic and most elaborate lantern had within it a revolving cylinder of cut-out figures making shadow pictures to move on its surface. Near this by another alley I was carried with the flow of people into a house where the crowd was more dense than ever. There was a rail across the room and behind that a second rail. Gold embroideries hung along the back, and in the centre stood the "Tasia" in this instance made in the shape of some buildings at Mecca. Vessels for spreading rose-water stood within the railing and a long row of lamps, and in the middle of the front face of the "Tasia" was a miniature stage about two feet square; behind this, curtains dropped and rose again and various scenes, rather on the principle of old-fashioned "trick" valentines, followed one another slowly. The trouble here was that no one wanted to move, and the press was stifling.

At last came the day of the great procession, February 12, of our reckoning. The streets were thronged in the early morning as they had been all night and the previous day and the night and day before that.

I drove past the great mosque, the Jama Masjid; the white zigzags on its dome shone brightly against the red Agra sandstone which now, in the morning light, looked as if it had a kind of bloom upon it. That was on the left—on my right hand I could see the crenelated walls of the fort, colourless against the sun now streaming across them.

Parties of people, gay in new green cloths and turbans, were on their way to take their places in friends' houses for the day. Hand-carts, with seven or more great copper vessels, were being pushed from stand to stand, refilling the great water-jars. All traffic was stopped for the day through the greater part of the city, and I soon had to leave my gharry and continue on foot my way to a house in the Kashmiri Bazaar where a place was being kept for me at a window. At three different places I passed groups of acrobats arranged high in air like a sort of human set piece of six or seven sets of limbs. It looked curious in this country to see them wearing a kind of "tights." In one case all the legs were yellow, in another purple, and in a third black.

Bands of Marsia singers were perambulating the streets. At length I found my window, or rather balcony, and from it for hour after hour I had an excellent view of all that passed. The procession of "Tasias," which did in fact take seven hours to go by, seemed as if it would never end. Stoppages were frequent, and sometimes there would be a wait of ten minutes or even a quarter of an hour. Of every material imaginable, the common denominator was a square base with two carrier poles making four handles and a series of stages diminishing vertically except at the very top where, in some instances, there was a kind of horizontal windmill or other device for movement. Some were of tin, some were gilded, some were silver; some, used year after year, were of intrinsically valuable materials; others, and these the majority, were only built for use on the one occasion, however lavishly and gaily decorated. Several were of green grass, the "Tasia" having been covered with wet cloth smothered in seed like trophies in a cottage garden exhibition, only upon a much larger scale. There were "Tasias" of quite elaborate architecture, covered entirely with flower blossoms. Some sought distinction in exaggerated height, rearing thirteen or twenty stages high in air above the topmost roofs—and these, as may be imagined, were carried with difficulty, the base poles projecting a long way so that many arms could help and cords from the top being used in some cases to steady the toppling pile. There were "Tasias" of coloured paper and "Tasias" of coloured cloths, and with each marched the people to whom it belonged, with drums and stands of old weapons. Buraks of all sizes varied the strange scene, and "Zulfikars" with their "Alams" or tall stands of arms delighted the onlookers by feats of balance during the many stoppages.

Under each "Tasia" and "Burak" was carried a supply of brushwood. For some while I had wondered what the purpose of this could be, but during one of the halts it was made plain. When the drumskins slackened a little, fire was made of some of the brushwood and the drum held over the flames until the skin became quite taut again.

The irregular line of the roofs as well as the balconies of every floor were studded with spectators up and down the street. Only where there were purdah ladies, blinds and curtains hid them from view.

The next morning I was out, just at dawn, stepping across the bodies of sleeping servants along my veranda. I had heard of a curious custom of the Shia sect of Mohammedans and was anxious to see it carried out. Whereas the Sunnis and indeed nearly all the Mohammedans of Agra, would march in a second procession to the Kerbela beyond the city and there bury in the ground the twin biers from within the "Tasias," the Shias would go down to the Jumna banks and bury theirs by the river.

Close to the pontoon bridge I found the Shias very seriously and reverently carrying out their ceremony. They appeared to take the whole matter gravely. Their "Tasias" were not large or very showy, but the burying was conducted like a solemn ritual. At this time of year the river was of course low, and the Shia gentlemen had dug a long trench close to the edge of the water. Out of each "Tasia" the two little biers garlanded with marigolds were lifted carefully under a white covering cloth, laid in the water at the bottom of the trench, and covered in with earth. Then the "Tasia" itself was broken up, the pieces thrown in and covered with more earth as the trench was refilled.

The procession of the previous day had simply been a great march round in order that all "Tasias" might be paraded through all streets of the town. Upon this day, the conclusion of the festival, they were to go to the Kerbela for the biers to be buried there. "*Hai Hassan ham na huai!*" "Oh Hassan!" I heard cried out, "I am very sorry I could not help you at the time of battle."

The Moharam Festival at Agra.

It was a wild fantastic scene that I beheld when finally after a good deal of persistence I reached the little mosque in the Kerbela, from which some dozen feet above the ground level I was privileged to watch. The whole air was filled with the deafening noise of a thousand drums. Slowly the vast series of "Tasias" advanced into the enclosure, moving them to right or left to carry out the burying where their owners chose or had some right of ground. And there were two among them, taller even than any I had seen on the previous day—so lofty that it was a wonder they could be carried at all without toppling over—bowing and bending now to one side, now to another and then quivering erect for a moment while at the top of one, a peacock turned round and round and round, and at the top of the other a wheel kept revolving. How the children shouted! Many of the grown people were like children those days and shouted too, and the whole air was colour and dust and noise.

Thus ended for that year one of the greatest religious festivals still observed in the British Empire, a festival which I was privileged to see celebrated with all its ancient pomp and circumstance.

CHAPTER XXIV

RAKHYKASH[2]

The river flowing swiftly was a glorious vivid blue, clear as crystal and dancing with gleeful hurry. There was almost a greater contrast between the water of the Ganges here at Hurdwar and at Howrah than between that of the Thames at Billingsgate and Bablock Hythe.

The Hari Ghat lies in a short sidepiece of the river, with a railed iron bridge about two feet wide crossing its neck. From this narrow bridge I looked back at the ghat with its shrines and temples, and the rocky sides of the hills above which here come down steeply. In the water itself were hundreds and hundreds of big large-scaled fish which are cherished and fed regularly. They swirled about the posts of the little bridge in a dense crowd,—dark brownish-green creatures about two feet long, some with red gills showing.

On the steps of the ghat itself no one is permitted to wear shoes, and leaving mine, I walked with stocking feet to visit the "Charan," or sacred footprints, and the Gangadwara Temple. By this a priestess played a flute, squatting upon a tiny platform. She was dressed in bright colours and spangled clothes with a strange conical hat on her head. There was a priestess similarly dressed on another wooden platform at the top of the other end of the steps. There were sacred cows, of which I had already noticed several in the street, bearing a strange deformity in an extra limb hanging loosely from the hump. In some cases this extra limb ended in a hoof, and in some cases in a second pair of horns and in one I saw both together. I wondered whether these excrescences had really been grafted on. There were various holy people about the road leading to the ghat—"Sadhus" and "Nagas" with naked bodies whitened with ashes.

A friendly Brahmin took me into the inner sanctum of the temple at At Khamba Mundi near the ghat and there, under a mauve silk coverlet, decorated with gold thread-work, rested the *Granth,* the sacred book of the Sikhs. It was rather like a body upon a wooden bed. Above, hung a canopy with a deep border of gold and silver fringe. The place was covered inside and out with paintings of the stories of the gods. In the inner courtyard over the part of the building where the book is kept, there was a tall pole bearing a once white flag and a leafless bush. On the other three sides of the courtyard the buildings were all rest-houses for pilgrims.

Now, the kindly Brahmin had a glass eye which was very far from clean and had no resemblance to its bloodshot fellow. It seemed to have been rather large for

[2] Reprinted by permission from *The Fortnightly Review.*

its socket, to have been fixed in years ago and never since disturbed. He showed me the Temple of Sarwarnath where there are statues of elephants within the surrounding courtyard. The bull Nandi was conspicuous on the high stone platform of the temple, and beside the main entrance was a tall iron pole about forty feet high ending in a large green bronze trident called the "Tarshoon," often represented in little in the hand of Siva.

Hurdwar seems to exist upon its importance as a place of pilgrimage, and to have little else of interest about it. The Brahmin, whose terrible eye was more insistent than that of the ancient mariner, told me above all places I ought to visit Rakhykash, twelve miles farther up the river and of very great holiness. It was nearly one o'clock, but it appeared just possible to get there and back that day. I had engaged for the day a vehicle called a tumtum, a kind of two-wheeled cart, and in spite of the protests from the driver that the roads would be impassable we hurried back to the bungalow for my ulster and started on a particularly rough drive.

Passing the Hari Ghat, the road, paved roughly with large round stones, led under a two-storeyed brick archway out of Hurdwar. Below flowed the swift blue river glistening in the sun, and above rose the rocky slope of the hillside. These rock slopes are the end of a line of hills striking at a sharp angle to the river. Leaving them, the way was soon along uneven country—level on the whole, but rough and tumble in detail. The road alternated between collections of boulders and stretches of sand and at intervals streams, some narrow and some wide, crossed it on their way from the hill slopes to join the wider river. Ten times we had to ford considerable rivulets apart from minor water-courses. Only once there was a bridge, wooden and primitive.

Here and there towards the first part of the journey were a few acres of cultivated ground mostly given to paddy, and in one place there was a plantation of fruit trees now snowy with blossom. Most of the way, however, was through a rough tract of jungle with large trees in places and miles of tall rough grass sometimes ten and even twenty feet high. We passed bullock-carts bringing heavy loads of broken wood, and once I saw an ox lie down on the sand under the yoke it found too hard to bear. We passed two men carrying between them in a cloth a huge python which they took out to show me—a creature twice the length of a man.

All the while, far beyond the forest on the other side of the river, mountains were in sight, pale and ethereal in the heat of the afternoon. I passed many ant-hills—ridged grey peaks of mud under which snakes often lie. At one moment a flight of green parrots would rise from near trees and cross the road screaming—at another I would see a crowd of monkeys golden in the sunlight swinging in the slender upper branches. There were cork trees with masses of tiny pink blossoms, and one kind of tree, as large as an English oak, known as the "flame of the forest," was covered with big five-petalled scarlet flowers.

It was getting ominously late and the shadows lengthened every minute. At last the tumtum driver declared that he *could* not drive over the rocky way to the village. I left him by some great trees on the roadside, and to lead me to the holy places I waylaid a boy whom I drove before me hurrying in a race with the sun—my servant following at his usual decorous pace. I think it was another mile before passing quite a number of large solid brick and stone Darmsalas (or pilgrims' rest-houses) and a small bazaar, I came out on a wide stretch of rounded boulders along the side of the river. The hills now rose from quite near the farther bank and the scene was very beautiful indeed. The water rushed along, rippling over shallows and racing through narrower channels bluer than ever.

There were no temples of any architectural pretensions, and it became evident to me that the importance of Rakhykash did not lie in its buildings at all, but in the worshipping places of the Sikhs. Along and above the shore, I came at intervals to paled enclosures within which a large and devout crowd of people sat listening to a priest who was seated beneath a thatched gable-shaped cover on wooden upright posts. The largest of these was at the head of a path made of smooth white boulders which stretched a furlong from the water's edge. At the opening to the loose tall fence were many shoes. Leaving mine with the rest, I stood for a moment at the entrance, looking inquiring permission to one of the priests. The men were grouped round the front and sides of the thatched cover, and receiving welcome I entered and sat among them on a reed mat like the rest. At one side were a crowd of women farther away than the men, all in white robes which covered their heads like white hoods lovely in the soft warm glow of the setting sun.

The thatched shelter is called the *Kuteah*. The Padre or chief priest sat just in front of the thatched opening and round him Gristis or minor priests, one of whom was speaking. When he had finished, the women all rose and went out in long single file. The sun had just set. Beyond were the mountains and infinite space. The sound of the river came faintly over the great expanse of stones.

Most of the turbaned priests were in woollen robes or togas of a colour between saffron and salmon pink. The thatched hut of long grass was, I should have said, facing the river so that the high priest looked towards it. The pilgrims and other people were in white or other colours and a few in black blankets. Just in front of the priests were four musicians, with grey clothes and white turbans, the ones nearest me with two tom-toms and the farther one with a kind of viol. They were now singing to their music words of the *Granth*. The viol player was blind and made grimaces as he sang; all had black beards. One Gristi, who had in front of him the holy book itself folded in a cloth on a book-rest, presently stopped the singers and sent a man to say they were all pleased to see me among them. He told me that they do not make temples but worship only the words of the *Granth*, and that the musicians were singing some of these words. These men all looked clean and healthy. Most of their faces were refined—some of them noble.

Slowly the light faded and when I came away the last thing I saw of that place was the splendid landscape—the river flowing under solemn hills and stars coming out. I do not suppose I shall ever see nearer to the source of the Ganges.

Darkness had fallen before I again found the tumtum. The driver was sitting with some other men who were preparing food at a fire under the trees. An elephant was supping on a heap of green branches which had been thrown down for him close by.

When we started to come back we had no lamp but borrowed a lantern a little later from a camp outside Rakhykash under promise of return by coolie next day.

The long journey back was nearly as much walk as drive. After an hour and a half the light of a fire showed above the road and we stopped to rest the horse. A man came down the rocks and said there was a holy lady there who gave tea to all travellers and had sent word she would be pleased if the sahib would stop and take refreshment. Now it was late and the night was very dark, but it would be good to rest the horse rather longer, and I went up rough steps in the rock to a level place some ten feet above the road which was here passing a piece of low hill.

On the ground were mats, but I was shown a place on a slab of stone. We were under a thatched roof without sides, and in front of me was a wood fire with one large forked branch smouldering, and every now and then this blazed up brightly as the fire was stirred. There were a few people sitting along each side, and immediately behind the fire, facing me, was a woman sitting very upright with crossed legs. She was naked to the waist, with a dark cloth round her lower limbs, and her face and body were entirely whitened with white ash. She had very long hair which fell in thick brown coils about her shoulders, but being pushed back from the forehead left her face quite uncovered. The flames cast as they danced a great shadow of the woman on a cloth hanging at the back to keep out the wind.

I learned after many questions that this woman had lost both father and mother when she was twelve years of age, and had thenceforward given her life to make refreshment for pilgrims and travellers; that she was now fifty-five years old, and that for the last five years she had stayed here: that the place was called Dudupani, and that her own name was Duthani Hookamnajee.

Of fakirs, anchorites and other holy people she was the first I had seen in India who seemed to me beautiful, and indeed had a strange loveliness. Not only did she look much less old than the age she told me, but her face had that subtle curve immediately below the cheek bones that draws like a strain of music, and which I have seen only in two women and in La Joconda, and one marble head shown as a piece by Praxiteles at the Burlington Fine Arts Club a few years ago.

Her large ecstatic eyes, her tall forehead, her long, straight nose, her delicate lips and chin were alike lovely, and the wan pallor added by the white ash made the favourite Eastern comparison to the beauty of the moon less unreal than with any princess it was ever applied to; she was not emaciated, and her body had that moderate fullness which best shows the perfection of each natural curve. Her eyes as I have said were large and dull, but although wide as if their gaze came from the depths of some far away uncharted sea, they had also in them recognition and arrest—and empire.

Oh! Flaubert with your talk of the mummy of Cleopatra—would you not rather have seen the strange beauty of this living death than any coffined husk of once warm flesh?

But when she spoke in the hush of this strange night, the sweetness of her soft low tones was almost passionately unendurable. Music not of the Venusberg but eloquent of the appealing purity of a being locked in chains of ice, doomed slowly to die, renouncing the world in which it has been placed, judging its Maker in a fatal mad conceit.

Slowly she kept moving her little hands, warming them at the fire. In a brass cup hot tea was brought to me made not with water but with fresh milk from the cow. The other people were passing round fresh pipes, with glowing coals in their flower-shaped cups. In the fire three or four irons were standing upright, and three of them had trident heads like the tarshoon at Sarwan Nath. Was this woman herself impaled on a real trident of which the irons were but outward signs?

"You have done better to see me than to see all priests," she said. I asked which of the gods she liked best, and she answered, "There is only one God." Later she said, "I shall speak of you with the God every night wherever you may be."

She put her hand down into a large brass bowl at her side and took out fruits which were passed to me on a brass dish. I ate an orange slowly and asked her if there was anything she would like sent to her from Europe. She said she wanted nothing. "I give tea—I give all—only my name I keep," and her name is Duthani Hookamnajee.

CHAPTER XXV

POLITICAL

Consequences do not appeal as a subject of interest to the typical British mind until they have arrived. But when, as was the case in our acquisition of India, a heedlessness of consequences is accompanied by ignorance of the future development of his own government into a democratic tyranny, the extension of free institutions by a conqueror to a subject race becomes fraught with aggravated dangers. These are now upon us and we have to steer between a panic withdrawal of liberties and an equally rash programme in their too rapid extension.

The more we can help India to become a nation, the more we can knit her together by conscious bonds of common needs and aspirations the better it will be for her and the better, therefore, for ourselves now that we can no longer tolerate with equanimity an exploitation of a subject race solely for our own commercial advantage.

That East is East and West is West, and never the twain shall meet, is one of the worst superstitions prevalent among British people. Let those who so glibly reiterate what I believe to be a falsehood pernicious in its tendency to preserve a bigoted exclusiveness, compare India not with the West of to-day but with ancient and mediæval Europe.

The anchorite in a cage at some street corner, mendicant friars and pilgrims with their bowls, flagellants and the innumerable sects that seek to honour God by scorning his gifts, altars made red with the blood of sacrifice, the tight-rope walker and the ballad man, religious pageantry and the pomp of kings, the calm aloofness of sequestered lives, the careless luxury of courts, the squalid existence of a servile peasantry, the sordid rookeries of each reeking town, unchecked disease and callous cruelty, the taciturn denial of every new discovery, and brooding superstition over all—the counterpart of nearly every phase of life, so often considered as typically Oriental—surely existed in past ages between Rome and Bristol.

It needs no conscious pharisaism for men of both authority and learning to contrast the ideals of modern industry unfavourably with those of renunciation and quietism and to call the one new and the other old; but this is only another way of saying that authority and learning are not always denied even to sentimentalists though they be without hope and see the world with but a single eye.

Oh, wondrous dreamings of a golden age that never was under the light of the sun! Were the people of India under Akhbar or Asoka better in any one respect than they are to-day? The wanderings of ascetic Sadhus and Yogis have probably worked towards the cementing of the country, and their spirit of detachment has at the same time helped to withdraw attention from the yoke of foreign rule.

It has been shown in the history of modern India that at a time of mutiny and under the excitement of anger at inhuman butchery, one of our bravest and (in his own profession of soldiering) most capable of men may have his ideas of civilization so far distorted as to plead for a return to methods of the most extreme savagery in the treatment of prisoners; but it has not been shown that any Englishman of recognized capability to-day has such a distorted view that he looks upon India as a permanent goose to be kept sufficiently nourished to lay golden eggs for the benefit of his own country. To whatever party he may belong, every Englishman in England, who studies Indian affairs and the relation of India to the rest of our Empire, feels that our rule should be so conducted as to prepare India for ultimate self-government and a place in the future councils of a British confederation among the other units of the Empire.

The growth of a national spirit in India under our self-appointed guardianship, while giving us just pride in the nobility of our achievement, may yield us the yet nobler crown of humility when we behold in its maturity the developed genius of our foster-children.

Mr Theodore Morison, writing on *Imperial Rule in India,* sought authority for his proposed suppression of all newspapers but a subsidized government organ in "the policy which has done so much for the progress of Mexico," and remarked, "It is apparently necessary for English politicians to behold a country given up to anarchy before they can realize that popular institutions make for the disruption of a nation which is not yet compact and unified."

The recent happenings in his chosen instance incline me to say that even Mr Morison himself would now, doubtless, admit that such despotic methods only produce an apparent and temporary calm and are certain sooner or later to break down, together with the government that enforced them.

The influence of the Press is only beginning to help the creation of a national spirit. Newspapers are naturally more likely to fan the red embers of latent animosities than to attack the infinitely more difficult and less lucrative task of sound patriotic afforestation to make a permanent fuel supply to those fires of national aspiration, which as yet have little more hold than a handful of crackling thorns.

It is as erroneous to assume that local press opposition to any particular measure of government is the sign of an united national feeling as to pretend that an united national feeling can only be created by agitation against the British rule.

The fact that there is not yet a national sympathy in India strong enough to overrule the enmity of religions or the rivalry of races, is the best of all arguments for cherishing its growth by every means in our power. National feeling must first be associated with territorial boundaries and many many will be the years to come ere the Mohammedan will lie down with the Hindoo and a little Parsee shall lead them to the sound of Sikh flutes and Christian tabors!

Mr Theodore Morison contends that all men east of Suez think themselves the slaves and chattels of the man God has set above them for their king,[3] but in whatever way they regard their relation to their rulers we, at least, may no longer regard them as slaves and chattels; rather must we think of them as wards for whom we have become responsible through the actions of our grandfathers—wards whom we have not only recognized as family relations but have trained in our own business and given just so much knowledge of our methods as to make them capable of being invaluable to our rivals though not as yet in any way competent to exercise independent authority.

There must come a time when the people of every habitable part of the world will have tried the system of government by majority of elected representatives. Even in the case of a nation like China, which has at present no desire among its proportionally small class of educated minds for such a form of rule, the popular longing for enfranchisement will arise, and sooner or later a representative form of government will be established. The obviously possible oppression and tyranny of democratic rule are dangers which no people as a whole will learn except by their own experience. The stirring spirit of life that brings man self-reliance will make him claim his share in the ordering of his own country sooner or later but in any case sooner than he has been able to learn that a measure is liberal or tyrannous, not according to the type of government that imposes it but according to the degree of liberty it secures to, or takes away from, the individuals it affects.

How many Englishmen who have ever given a thought to India have imagined themselves for a moment as natives of that land? Try to put yourself in the place of any native-born Indian and consider fairly what your thought would be about politics or government. If you were a ryot, an uneducated villager, you would know nothing of such matters. For you, all life and its affairs would be in the hands of the gods and the money-lender, and endeavours to assuage their wrath or cruelty, to induce their patronage or favour, would exhaust whatever surplus energy remained from daily rounds of toil.

But put yourself for a moment in the place of the young Mohammedan who has just left his university and is trying to obtain a berth in the post-office, or of a Hindoo medical assistant in the hospital of a country town, or of a large native landowner who has just left college and succeeded to an estate in Bengal, or of a native pleader in the courts, or of a native assistant magistrate—would you then be quite indifferent to questions of government and politics? You would feel conscious that you were being ruled by strangers whose superiority, in whatever respects you deemed them superior, was the most galling thing about them—far more so than their habitual disclination to have more touch with you than was necessary to the efficient discharge of their official duties. Among the very few you ever met, after leaving college, one Englishman might seem to you lovable; but would that reconcile you to the fact that his race was ruling yours, dividing its territories in the teeth of the protest of their powerless inhabitants, and, as you

[3] "East of Suez ... there lies upon the eyes and foreheads of all men a law which is not found in the European Decalogue; and this law runs: 'Thou shalt honour and worship the man whom God shall set above thee for thy king; if he cherish thee thou shalt love him; and if he plunder and oppress thee thou shalt still love him, for thou art his slave and his chattel.'" *Imperial Rule in India* (Page 43). Theodore Morison.

gathered from your reading, denying you rights of self-government which his own people years ago had risen in arms to obtain?

But in order to give India the chance of future autonomy and independence, we must distinguish between the extreme claims of isolated and non-representative enthusiasts and the reasonable progressive changes warranted by a gradual advance of liberal education and increase of religious tolerance: we must distinguish between the exuberance of inexperienced youths and the irritation of dissatisfied place-hunters on the one hand and the mature opinions on the other hand of enlightened Indians who have proved their power of wise judgment by years of serious responsibility in positions of trust and authority. And first and last, we must never forget, in our continued efforts to make a nation out of a tangle of many states and peoples, the tremendous power we have gradually gained to influence the general liberty and progress of the world, and that no part of that power can ever be yielded up save as the shameful shifting of a burden it is our noblest privilege to bear.

THE END.

INDEX

A

Abu Road *156*
Afghan *122, 123, 133, 142*
Afghanistan *126, 144, 146*
Afridi *124, 126, 128, 129, 130*
Aghoris *109*
Agra *100, 103, 104, 106, 133, 136, 163, 166, 167, 168*
Ahmadabad *158*
Ahmednagar *158, 160, 161*
Aindaw Pagoda *45*
Ajmere *155, 156*
Akal Bunga *117, 118, 119*
Akali *141, 142, 143*
Akhbar *99, 100, 101, 102, 104, 105, 106, 134, 135, 154, 155, 156, 175*
Alexander *52, 135, 141*
Aligar College *121*
Ali Masjid *126, 127, 128, 129, 130, 131*
Allard *133*
Amber *35, 47, 61, 78, 149, 164*
Amias *103*
Amir *128, 146*
Amir Khusran *109*
Amir of Afghanistan *104, 121*
Amir of Lucknow *103*
Amritsar *116, 118, 120*
Anundabagh *87, 88*
Aravalli Range *155, 156*
Areca *11, 60, 72*
Arhai-din-ka-jompra *156*
Armoury *58, 133, 134*
Arrakan Pagoda *46, 47*
Asoka *111, 175*
Assam *60*
Aurungzebe *83, 88*
Austin of Bordeaux *107*
Australia *62, 96, 108*

Ava *41*
Avitabile *121, 133*

B

Baba Attal *118*
Babar *124, 136*
Baluchistan *144, 145*
Bamboo *12, 13, 16, 17, 23, 24, 26, 27, 30, 33, 35, 43, 44, 55, 57, 79, 80, 88, 97, 107, 123, 129, 165*
Banyan tree *16*
Baradari *133*
Bay of Bengal *1*
Bazaars *63*
Beadon Square *70, 71, 73*
Bean Sing *86*
Bear *31, 33, 102, 171, 178*
Bee-eaters *16*
Begari Canal *145*
Benares *82, 83, 84, 85, 86, 87, 89, 91, 148, 154*
Bengal Government Offices *64, 65*
Bengali *70, 73, 74, 89*
Bernard Free Library *41*
Betel *11, 45, 65, 72*
Bhakkur Island *144*
Bhamo *24, 26, 29, 30, 31, 47*
Bhaskarananda Saraswati *87*
Bhils *61*
Black Mosque *107, 111*
Bodawpaya *41*
Bokhara *121, 124*
Bolan Pass *144, 145*
Bombay *13, 49, 73, 120, 138*
Bostan Junction *146, 147*
Botanical Gardens *76*
Bo-tree *83*
Brahma *73, 88, 117, 155*
Brahmin *5, 170, 171*
Buddha *7, 10, 12, 31, 36, 37, 39, 46, 47, 70, 99, 116, 125, 135*
Buddhist *9, 10, 11, 47, 84, 85, 125, 135*
Budge Bridge *63*
Burmah Oil Works *6*
Buxar *82*

C

Cactus *35, 36, 43, 51, 85, 86, 149, 151*

Calcutta *49, 60, 63, 64, 65, 66, 67, 68, 70, 75, 76, 81, 85, 96, 97, 135*
Camels *82, 91, 120, 126, 129, 130, 131, 138, 146, 162, 164*
Cauvery *57*
Cawnpore *88, 96, 97, 98*
Central Hindoo College *87*
Ceylon *13, 44, 51, 60, 61, 75, 84, 89, 146*
Chait Singh *89*
Chakrayantra *85*
Chaman *146, 147*
Chappa Rift *148*
Chili *3, 49*
China *17, 21, 39, 113, 121, 177*
Chinese *1, 5, 26, 30, 31, 44, 45, 79, 80, 84, 100*
Chitor *153, 154, 155*
Chitorgarh *153, 154*
Chitral *124*
Chittagonians *14*
Choultry *52*
Chowringhee *63, 65*
Cobra *69, 86*
Coffee *3, 24, 61, 113*
Colombo *51*
Coonoor *60, 61*
Corrugated iron *16, 23, 95, 156*
Cotton *51, 67, 92, 93, 122, 141, 156, 160, 166*
Cowrie money *93*
Cow Temple *84*
Crocodiles *150*
Crows *46, 69, 71, 100*

D

Dabir of Lucknow *103*
Dacoit *17, 27, 30*
Dagh of Delhi *103*
Dak tree *113, 156*
Dal *3, 49*
Dalhousie Square *65*
Dancer *5, 115, 141, 165*
Dancing *12, 21, 27, 50, 79, 90, 93, 95, 99, 147, 155, 170*
Dara Shikoh *106*
Dargah *101, 155, 156*
Darjeeling *77, 78, 79, 80*
Deccan *96, 103*
Dehra Dun *113, 115*
Delhi *74, 89, 106, 107, 108, 109, 111, 112, 132, 133, 142*
Dharbanga *65*

Dhuleep Singh *133*
Dilawar Khan *121, 123*
Dilwarra Temples *157*
Diwan-i-Am *100, 107, 108*
Diwan-i-Khas *99, 100, 108*
Drama *13, 27, 50, 72, 90*
Dravidian *51, 57*
Droog *62*
Duchess of Connaught *148*
Dufferin Bridge *85, 89*
Durga Temple *87*
Durian *10*

E

Eagle *16, 70*
Eastern Bengal State Railway *63*
Eastern Yomans *16*
Edward the Seventh *104*
Egrets *46*
Elephant Book *58*
Elephants *13, 16, 57, 58, 85, 115, 130, 132, 143, 151, 154, 156, 171*
Eng tree *16*
Etawah *95*
Eucalyptus *60, 62, 113*

F

Fakirs *88, 89, 173*
Famine *94, 160*
Fatehpur-Sikri *100, 102*
Ferryshaw Siding *24*
Flamingoes *151*
Flotilla Company *24, 26, 35*
Footprints *37, 90, 170*
Fort Dufferin *iv, 47, 48*
Fort William *63, 82*
France *5, 117, 119*
French legion *133*

G

Ganesh *55, 70, 83, 84, 154*
Gangeli Khan *123*
Garden Reach *63*
Gardens *32, 47, 75, 87, 94, 95, 130, 134, 136, 141, 146, 147, 149, 150, 151, 156, 163*
Gautama *12, 37, 46*
General Nicholson *106*

General Prendergast *49*
Ghats *85, 89*
Ghonds *61*
Ghoom *77, 78*
Glass *v, 9, 10, 12, 24, 35, 39, 44, 45, 46, 94, 103, 119, 140, 147, 156, 157, 170*
Gobindaji *150*
Gokteik *17, 18*
Golden Monastery *46*
Golden Temple *82, 83, 84, 89, 116*
Gopura *57*
Gor Khatri *121, 122*
Gourkhas *48*
Granth *117, 141, 170, 172*
Grapes *99, 122, 146*
Guru *116, 118, 119, 141*

H

Hamadryad *16*
Hanuman *70, 89, 154*
Hari Mandar *117*
Harnai Route *147*
Hastings *5, 121*
Hawks *16*
Himalayas *77, 113, 115, 144*
Hindoo *1, 3, 5, 6, 8, 19, 22, 24, 35, 37, 51, 58, 59, 60, 67, 70, 82, 83, 84, 86, 87, 89, 90, 97, 98, 99, 101, 109, 117, 121, 124, 128, 133, 135, 136, 141, 146, 150, 155, 161, 176, 177*
Hirok *146*
Hodson *109*
Hooghly *63, 67, 75*
Howrah *63, 67, 170*
Hpoongi *22*
Hsipaw *18, 22, 23, 30*
Hti *7, 22, 45*
Hulling *14*
Humayun *109, 135*
Hurdwar *170, 171*
Husainabad Imambara *94*
Hyderabad *96, 103*

I

Idar *158, 161*
Imambara *94*
Indus *144, 145*
Industrialism *97*

Iron Foundry *68*
Iron Pillar *110, 111*
Irrawaddy *24, 32, 34, 35, 36*
Italians *108*
Izzat *61*

J

Jain *85, 86, 109, 110, 154, 155, 156, 157, 159*
Jaipur *149, 150, 151*
Jama Masjid *94, 108, 111, 166*
James and Mary *63*
Jamroud *121, 126, 128*
Java *75*
Jehanara *109*
Jehangir *102, 121, 133, 136*
Juggernaut *68, 70, 87*
Jumna *95, 107, 108, 167*
Jumna River *107*
Jute *63, 67, 82*

K

Kabul *123, 124, 128*
Kachins *22, 24, 30*
Kali *55, 68, 69, 70*
Kalighat *68*
Kampani Bagan *75*
Kanishka *125*
Kanutkwin *17*
Karapanasami *55, 56*
Kashmir *106, 120, 134*
Katha *24, 25, 26*
Khaskas grass *94*
Khawbgah *99, 101*
Kheddah *13*
Khyber Pass *121, 126, 127, 129*
King Kyansittha *39*
King Naurata *39, 42*
King Thebaw *26, 47, 48, 49*
Kirowdi *100*
Kisshoor *3*
Kites *46, 100, 164*
Kojak Pass *146*
Kokand *124*
Kols *61*
Kubla Khan *36*

Kuchi Khel *128, 131*
Kurseong *77*
Kutab Minar *107, 109, 110*
Kuthodaw *47*
Kyankine *18*
Kyansittha *39*
Kyd's Monument *75*

L

Lacquer *21, 26, 36, 43*
Lady Canning's Seat *62*
Lahore *107, 123, 132, 133, 134, 135, 138, 144*
Lalamusa *120*
Landi Kotal *128, 131*
Landour *113, 114, 115*
Lansdowne Bridge *144, 147*
Lashio *18*
Lebong *79*
Leogryphs *7, 35*
Leopard *17, 80*
Llama *79*
Lord Curzon *107, 117, 125*
Lotus *39, 46, 47, 49, 100, 107*
Loungoes *14*
Lucknow *91, 92, 93, 94, 95*
Lugyis *41*

M

Madras *1, 3, 5, 58, 60, 66*
Madura *51, 52, 57*
Magwe *42*
Maharajah *85, 88, 134, 140, 150, 152, 158, 159*
Maharajah of Benares *87, 89*
Maharajah of Gwalior *86*
Maharajah of Vizianagram *87*
Maharana of Udaipur *153*
Mahrattas *67, 73, 133*
Maidan *63, 65, 75*
Maimyo *2, 17*
Major Hector Munro *82*
Malabar Coast *66*
Malay Archipelago *75*
Mandalay *iv, 35, 36, 42, 43, 44, 47, 49, 50*
Mangi *148*
Mango *100, 137*

Mantapam *52, 55, 57*
Marionettes *50*
Marochetti *97*
Marquis of Hastings *65*
Marwa *79*
Marwar *155*
Maung Nyo *22*
Mausoleum *88, 103, 104, 136*
Mausoleum of Humayun *108*
Mayo College *156*
Mayo School of Industrial Art *135*
Mecca *1, 94, 124, 151, 166*
Meerut *106, 111*
Merthil Swami *87, 88*
Mettapalaiyam *60, 61*
Mewar *151, 153, 155*
Minachi *51*
Minah *100*
Mohammed *103, 131, 163*
Mohammedan *3, 4, 5, 68, 83, 84, 86, 87, 90, 91, 93, 94, 97, 99, 104, 105, 111, 121, 136, 146, 162, 176, 177*
Moharam Festival *vii, 103, 162, 163, 168*
Mongolian *3, 4, 21, 61*
Monkeys *86, 87, 156, 171*
Monsieur D'Avera *26*
Moplas *66*
Mora *26*
Mosi Temple *85*
Mount Abu *155, 156, 157*
Mount Everest *78*
Mount Tartara *121*
Mowgwa *100*
Mr Cooper *41*
Mrs Besant *87*
Mukolo *43*
Munshi tree *69*
Museums *63*
Music *12, 27, 55, 58, 73, 89, 145, 172, 173, 174*
Mussoorie *113, 114, 115*
Mutiny *82, 91, 92, 94, 95, 106, 111, 176*
Muttra *150*
Myrabolams *96*

N

Nabang *18*
Nabha *138, 140, 141, 142, 143*

Nagas *61, 170*
Naggra *100*
Nagpur *86*
Nana Sahib *98*
Nandi *57, 83, 171*
Natindaw *42*
Nats *35, 40, 41, 42*
Natsin *42*
Nautch *5*
Nawab of Oudh *82*
Neem tree *98*
Nepaul *75, 86*
Nizam *103, 109*
Nour Jehan *102, 103, 121, 136, 137*
Nyaungoo *35, 36, 41, 42*
Nynung *16*

O

Observatories *85*
Onslow Ford *65*
Ootacamund *60*
Opium *89, 142, 151*
Otto of roses *94*
Oudh *91, 96, 98*

P

Pagan *36, 37, 38, 39, 40, 41, 42*
Pagodas *24, 36, 42, 47*
Parrots *55, 100, 135, 141, 151, 171*
Parsee *70, 176*
Peacock hawk *16*
Peacocks *16, 84, 107, 149, 151, 165*
Peacock Throne *107*
Peepul tree *88, 98, 149*
Pegu *5, 16, 39*
Peshawar *120, 121, 123, 125, 126, 128, 130, 135, 136*
Phulkian States *138, 140*
Plague *7, 18, 149, 160*
Plantain *23, 49*
Pomegranates *99, 122, 150*
Poogi *18, 19*
Poozoondoung *13, 14, 24*
Popa *41, 42*
Potter *86*
Prayer-wheels *79*

Private Dunlay *95*
Punjabis *2, 34, 47, 113*
Pwe *10, 12, 13, 26, 27, 28, 30, 50*
Python *86, 171*

Q

Queen's College *82*
Queen Sepaya *49*
Queen's Golden Monastery *46, 47*
Queen Victoria *21, 94, 141, 144, 160*
Quetta *146, 147*

R

Radha *70*
Rajah Chait Singh *89*
Rajah of Amethi *87*
Rajah of Nabha *138, 139, 140*
Rajpur *114, 115*
Rakhykash *vii, 170, 171, 172, 173*
Rama *89, 154*
Rangoon *1, 2, 3, 5, 9, 10, 14, 16, 27, 31, 41, 46, 49, 63, 125*
Ranjeet Singh *133, 134, 136, 140, 141, 142*
Ravi River *134, 136*
Rhinoceros *75*
Rice *1, 3, 14, 16, 17, 46, 49, 117, 122, 155*
Rishi *58*
River Ghamberi *154*
River Jumna *163*
Rose *9, 10, 12, 21, 27, 36, 61, 72, 78, 81, 86, 88, 89, 90, 115, 117, 119, 121, 137, 143, 146, 151, 152, 159, 166, 171, 172*
Royal Lakes *9*
Runjeet River *79*
Runnymede *60*
Ruri *144, 145*

S

Sadhus *170, 175*
Sal *96, 113*
Salay *41*
Salim Chisti *101, 102, 155*
Samrat Yantra *85*
Sandalwood *22, 46, 67, 90, 157*
Santals *61*
Sarnath *84, 85*
Sarwarnath *171*

Sawbwa *19, 20, 21, 22*
Sawbwa of Hsipaw *16, 18*
Sawche *18, 19, 21, 22*
Scythian *61*
Sedaw *17*
Segaw *26*
Sesamum *10, 122*
Seychelles *75*
Shaddra *136*
Shahijikidheri *125*
Shah Jehan *106, 109, 137*
Shannon *97*
Shan States *16, 17, 18, 20, 21*
Shias *167*
Shikarpur *144*
Shwe Dagon *5, 6, 7, 9, 46*
Shwemetyna *42*
Siam *16, 39, 75*
Sibi Junction *146*
Sikandra *95, 99, 104*
Sikhs *47, 117, 141, 142, 170, 172*
Sikkim *79, 80*
Sikra *57*
Siliguri *77, 81*
Silk *5, 10, 21, 31, 49, 72, 79, 117, 119, 121, 140, 141, 142, 157, 170*
Sind Desert *144*
Sinkan *31*
Sir David Ochterlony *106*
Sir Henry Lawrence *95*
Siriam *5*
Sir Pratap Singh *158, 159*
Sir Swinton Jacobs *151*
Sita *89, 149*
Siva *51, 55, 57, 58, 68, 69, 70, 83, 84, 86, 98, 153, 154, 155, 171*
Siwaliks *115*
Snipe *16*
Sookua *77*
Soutakar *3*
South Indian Railway *51*
Srirangam *56, 57*
St Mary's Church *58*
St Paul's Cathedral *66*
Sugar-cane *82, 122, 162*
Sukkur *144, 145*
Sundareswara Temple *51*

T

Tagaung *42*
Taj Mahal *163*
Tamarind *3, 35, 93, 126*
Tanjore *52, 57, 58*
Tappakulam *52, 55*
Tea *10, 26, 61, 75, 77, 79, 126, 159, 160, 173, 174*
Teak *7, 13, 24, 36, 46, 77*
Thaton *39, 42*
Theodore Morison *176, 177*
Thibetans *78, 80*
Thurligyaung *42*
Tiger *17, 18, 78, 164*
Tikka gharry *7, 10, 13*
Tindaria *77*
Tippoo Sultan *62*
Tirah hills *131*
Tobacco *11, 34, 82, 122*
Todas *61*
Tongu *19*
Tower Bridge *5*
Tree-climbing perch *16*
Tree-ferns *62, 77, 80*
Trichinopoly *1, 52, 53, 54, 57*
Tsar of Russia *104*
Turtles *46*
Tuticorin *51, 146*

U

Udaipur *151, 152, 153*
Ulabaria *67*

V

Vaishnavas *69, 70*
Vallam *52*
Ventura *133*
Verloocooli *3*
Vimana *51*
Vishnu *57, 69, 70, 83, 86, 90, 111, 155*
Vultures *42, 91, 100, 164*

W

Warren Hastings *82, 89*
Water-snake *9*

Wazirabad *120*
Waziristan *134*
Western Yomans *16*
Wheat *122, 128*
Wild cotton *36*

Y

Yak *80*

Z

Zakka Khels *123*
Zam Zammah *134*
Zenana *72, 73, 150*
Zoological Gardens *75*

Printed by Libri Plureos GmbH in Hamburg,
Germany